HISTORY, LITERATURE, AND MUSIC IN
SCOTLAND, 700–1560

History, Literature, and Music in Scotland, 700–1560

Edited by R. Andrew McDonald

UNIVERSITY OF TORONTO PRESS
Toronto Buffalo London

© University of Toronto Press Incorporated 2002
Toronto Buffalo London
Printed in Canada

ISBN 0-8020-3601-5

Printed on acid-free paper

National Library of Canada Cataloguing in Publication Data

Main entry under title :

History, literature, and music in Scotland, 700–1560

Includes bibliographical references
ISBN 0-8020-3601-5

1. Scotland – History – To 1603. 2. Scotland – Civilisation.
I. McDonald, Russell Andrew, 1965–

DA783.52.H58 2002   · 941.1   C2001-902354-5

University of Toronto Press acknowledges the financial assistance to its
publishing program of the Canada Council for the Arts and the Ontario
Arts Council.

University of Toronto Press acknowledges the financial support for its
publishing activities of the Government of Canada through the Book
Publishing Industry Development Program (BPIDP).

KING ALFRED'S COLLEGE
WINCHESTER

941
MCD   0227194X

For my former instructors at Trent University
And especially
In Memoriam
John T. Gilchrist

Contents

Foreword

Scottish historiography currently flourishes as never before in Scotland's two-thousand-year history. The past thirty years or so have witnessed a renaissance in history-writing not seen since the heady days of the Scottish Enlightenment. This volume provides ample testimony that the revival has not been confined to the shores of Auld Scotia.

It is truly a pleasure to welcome this stimulating and timely collection of essays on Scottish medieval history contributed predominantly by Canadians. As might be expected from a collection originating in Canada, all of the contributions have an international dimension. In describing and analysing aspects of their European prehistory, the younger Canadian scholars here represented display a refreshing willingness to probe new areas of the Scottish experience while remaining properly cognizant of the wider historical comparisons. Scotland, famously, is a small country with a rich history, and a great awareness of the larger world.

The themes explored herein are as fascinating as they are multifarious. Ale-drinking Scots and Picts between the eighth and eleventh centuries, their historical gaze fixed upon a broad historical horizon, were demonstrably as interested in their neighbours as they were in themselves. Saint Magnus of Orkney lived at a time when his earldom, often dismissed as geographically remote, was in fact at the crossroads of a world extending from Byzantium to Greenland – and beyond to North America – and from Spitzbergen to North Africa. Twelfth-century Scottish monarchs with anglicizing tendencies did not have everything their own way, living as they did with the constant threat, and often the reality, of civil war.

By the fifteenth century, Blind Hary's hugely influential poem, *Wallace*, articulated a powerful sense of Scottish national identity. That the Scots were not wholly preoccupied with such matters is suggested by Hary's contemporary, the extraordinary poet William Dunbar, who presented his astonishing vision of hell, perhaps the first but certainly not the last in the Scottish experience. The shrill sounds and painful tensions of everyday life are brought vividly alive in a highly original analysis of defamation and gender, which would later lie at the root of witchcraft accusation. Gender is also central to the sympathetic investigation of Margaret, Queen of Scots, with a view to her overdue rehabilitation in the context of late medieval misogyny. Culture, like gender, has until recently been somewhat ignored by Scottish medievalists with the laudable exception of literary historians. The volume concludes with a clarion call for the integrated study of music, a plea which, with reference to integration, is completely apposite for Scottish medieval historiography in general.

The editor, publisher, and all concerned are to be congratulated on their enterprise and initiative. It is noteworthy that the histories of Canada and Scotland briefly intersected in the early Middle Ages. According to the *Vinland Sagas*, a Scots couple, Haki and Hekja, accompanied Thorfinn Karlsefni's Viking expedition to Labrador and Newfoundland. They could run faster than the deer, and it was they who found grapes and wheat in this new and promising land. The contents of this book are just as tasty and in some ways just as surprising. Enjoy!

Edward J. Cowan
Professor of Scottish History
University of Glasgow

Acknowledgments

A volume of this nature incurs many debts of gratitude. First and foremost, I am grateful to all of the contributors, not only for their efficiency in preparing and submitting their chapters, but also for their patience in responding to editorial queries. Special thanks are due to Ted Cowan, Professor of Scottish History at the University of Glasgow, for writing the Foreword; to Constance Demb and Sheila Campbell, for organizing the one-day symposium on medieval Scotland at the University of Toronto which gave rise to this volume; to Elizabeth Ewan, for reading a draft of the introductory essay and offering many helpful suggestions; to my colleagues George Brunsden, Jan Curtis, and David Mullan at the University College of Cape Breton, for their assistance and advice on a variety of issues, whether factual, contextual, or editorial; and to Barry Gabriel, for producing the maps. I would also like to express my gratitude to Kristen Pederson and the staff at University of Toronto Press for the professionalism and enthusiasm with which they have guided this book through the various stages of publication. The dedication acknowledges a debt of a different kind.

Finally, I would be negligent if I did not mention the continual support and encouragement I have received from my wife, Jacqueline, my editor of first and last resort, who has seen this project through from its inception to its conclusion, and who offered many helpful suggestions along the way.

Generous subsidies from UCCB and from the Scottish Studies Foundation toward the publication of this work are gratefully acknowledged.

Timeline

This timeline is selective and is meant to illustrate events mentioned in the text. It is not intended to provide a comprehensive guide to Scottish history.

c. 500	Kingdom of Dál Riata established on west coast of Scotland
c. 563	Saint Columba establishes monastery at Iona in Hebrides
597	Death of Saint Columba
c. 690	Adomnán of Iona writes *Life of St Columba*
794	First recorded Viking raids in Hebrides
c. 843	Kenneth I, king of Scots of Dál Riata, gains the kingship of the Picts
c. 849	'Scottish Chronicle' begun at Dunkeld
mid-9th century	*Prophecy of Berchán* begun
late 9th century	Norse earldom of Orkney established
995 or 996	Conversion of Earl Sigurd the Stout of Orkney to Christianity
1056	Death of Flann of Monasterboice
1116 or 1117	Death of Magnus Erlendsson (Saint Magnus) on Egilsay
1124–53	Reign of David I; intensification of European influences in Scotland
1130	Insurrection against King David I led by Malcolm MacHeth and Angus of Moray; battle of Stracathro and death of Angus
c. 1136	Work begins on stone minster at Kirkwall, Orkney, dedicated to Saint Magnus

1160–1	King Malcolm campaigns in Galloway and brings Fergus, lord of Galloway, to heel
1164	Invasion of Scottish mainland led by Somerled, king of Argyll and the Isles; battle of Renfrew and death of Somerled
1187	Insurrection led by Donald MacWilliam; battle of Mam Garvia and defeat of Donald by Roland, lord of Galloway
c. 1188	Gerald of Wales (Giraldus Cambrensis) writes his *Topographia Hibernica*
c. 1200	*Orkneyinga Saga* composed
1211–12	Insurrection led by Guthred MacWilliam and his defeat
1215	Farquhar MacTaggart suppresses MacWilliam uprising and is knighted
1230	Suppression of the last MacWilliam uprising and death of an infant MacWilliam
1266	Treaty of Perth cedes Western Isles to Scotland from Norway
1296	Edward I's first invasion of Scotland
1297	Battle of Stirling Bridge; Scots, led by William Wallace and Andrew Moray, defeat English
1298	Battle of Falkirk; Scots defeated
1305	Capture and execution of William Wallace
1306	Robert Bruce claims kingship of Scots
1307	Death of Edward I of England
1314	Battle of Bannockburn; Scots defeat English
1329	Death of Robert I
c. 1375	Barbour writes *The Bruce*
c. 1380	John of Fordun writes *Chronica Gentis Scotorum*
c. 1470s	Blind Hary composes *The Wallace*
c. 1460– c. 1520	William Dunbar
1488–1513	Reign of James IV
1503	Marriage of Margaret Tudor to James IV of Scotland
1513	Death of James IV at battle of Flodden
1513–28	Minority of James V
1560	Reformation Parliament

Scottish Monarchs, c. 500–1542

The list is not intended to be comprehensive before 1005. Some dates and even the sequence of some of the early kings remain contentious.

c. 500	Fergus Mor mac Erc
c. 842–58	Kenneth I
858–62	Donald I
862–77	Constantine I
877–8	Aed
878–89	Eochaid with Giric
889–900	Donald II
900–43	Constantine II
943–54	Malcolm I
954–62	Indulf
962–6	Dubh
966–71	Culen
971–95	Kenneth II
995–7	Constantine III
c. 997–1005	Kenneth III
1005–34	Malcolm II
1034–40	Duncan I
1040–57	Macbeth
1057–8	Lulach
1058–93	Malcolm III 'Canmore'
1093–7	Donald III Bán
1094	Duncan II
1097–1107	Edgar

1107–24	Alexander I
1124–53	David I
1153–65	Malcolm IV
1165–1214	William I
1214–49	Alexander II
1249–86	Alexander III
1286–90	Margaret, 'the Maid of Norway'
1290–2	First Interregnum
1292–6	John Balliol
1296–1306	Second Interregnum
1306–29	Robert I
1329–71	David II
1371–90	Robert II
1390–1406	Robert III
1406–37	James I
1437–60	James II
1460–88	James III
1488–1513	James IV
1513–42	James V

Abbreviations

APS	*Acts of the Parliaments of Scotland.* Ed. T. Thomson and C. Innes. 11 vols. Edinburgh, 1814–75.
CGS	Johannes de Fordun. *Chronica Gentis Scotorum.* Ed. W.F. Skene. Trans. F.J.H. Skene. 2 vols. Historians of Scotland Series. Edinburgh, 1871–2.
EETS	Early English Text Society.
ES	*Early Sources of Scottish History* A.D. *500 to 1286.* Ed. A.O. Anderson. 2 vols. Edinburgh, 1922; repr. Stamford, 1990.
ITS	Irish Text Society.
JMH	*Journal of Medieval History.*
OS	*Orkneyinga Saga: The History of the Earls of Orkney.* Trans. H. Pálsson and P. Edwards. Harmondsworth, 1978.
RS	Rolls Series.
SAEC	*Scottish Annals from English Chroniclers* A.D. *500 to 1286.* Ed. A.O. Anderson. London, 1908.
Scotichronicon	*Scotichronicon by Walter Bower in Latin and English.* Gen. ed. D.E.R. Watt. 9 vols. Aberdeen/Edinburgh, 1987–98.
SHR	*Scottish Historical Review.*
SHS	Scottish History Society.
SLJ	*Scottish Literary Journal.*
SRS	Scottish Record Society.
SS	*Scottish Studies.*

SSL	*Studies in Scottish Literature.*
STS	Scottish Text Society.
TGSI	*Transactions of the Gaelic Society of Inverness.*
ZCP	*Zeitschrift für celtische Philologie.*

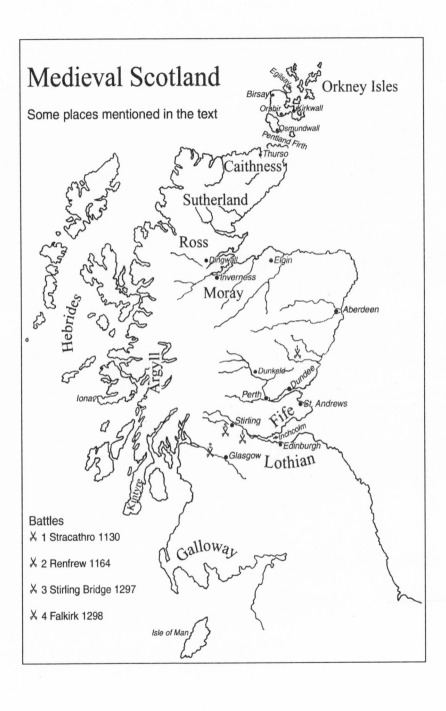

Medieval Scotland

Some places mentioned in the text

Orkney Isles

Eglisay
Birsay
Orphir Kirkwall
Osmundwall
Pentland Firth
Thurso
Caithness
Sutherland
Ross
Dingwall Elgin
Inverness
Moray
Aberdeen
Hebrides
Argyll
Dunkeld Dundee
Perth St. Andrews
Iona Stirling Fife
Inchcolm
Glasgow Edinburgh
Lothian
Kintyre
Galloway
Isle of Man

Battles

⚔ 1 Stracathro 1130

⚔ 2 Renfrew 1164

⚔ 3 Stirling Bridge 1297

⚔ 4 Falkirk 1298

HISTORY, LITERATURE, AND MUSIC IN SCOTLAND, 700–1560

Introduction:
Medieval Scotland and the
New Millennium

R. ANDREW McDONALD

At the close of the twentieth century, medieval Scotland fascinates us as never before – a fascination that extends to the interested layperson as well as the academic specialist. Medieval Scottish themes have been glamorized by Hollywood, romanticized in popular novels, simulated in computer games, and, of course, have spawned an array of books, articles, and conference sessions. Indeed, as Professor E.J. Cowan remarked in his Inaugural Lecture as Chair of Scottish History and Literature at the University of Glasgow in 1995, 'the potential interest in Scottish Studies has never been greater.'[1]

If, however, it is easy to identify the trend, it is more difficult to account for this waxing interest in things both medieval and Scottish. Certainly the twentieth century, and especially its closing decades, has seen a tremendous resurgence of interest in the Middle Ages in general,[2] while Celtic culture has also become much more popular – so much so that it is tempting to speak of a fin de siècle 'Celtic Renaissance.' No doubt this potent combination of things medieval and Celtic has contributed to the renewed interest in medieval Scotland, but it is also possible to identify other factors at work. Mel Gibson's portrayal of the Scottish hero William Wallace, in his Oscar-winning 1995 epic film *Braveheart*, was received in Scotland with a response that 'veered between the seriously farcical ... and the potentially tragic,'[3] so that it is hardly surprising that most serious historians sensibly avoid references to it. Nevertheless, historical warts notwithstanding, *Braveheart* does seem to have whetted the appetite of the movie-going public in North America for further tastes of less romanticized history: one of the most frequently asked questions in my classes is 'How historical is

Braveheart?[4] At a deeper level, however, it is clear that the medieval past resonates deeply in contemporary Scottish politics; in fact, there can be little doubt that recent developments in Scottish politics (culminating in the election of a Scottish parliament, for the first time in nearly three centuries, in May of 1999) have stimulated a greater interest in that country's past, and especially its medieval past.[5] The return of the famous Stone of Scone – the block of sandstone on which Scottish kings were supposed to have been inaugurated until the 1290s – to Scotland from Westminster in 1996, after seven centuries of captivity (it was carted off to England by the conquering Edward I in 1296), serves to highlight the links between the late thirteenth and the late twentieth centuries.[6] Similarly, the famous Declaration of Arbroath of 1320 (actually a letter sent in the name of thirty-nine Scottish barons to Pope John XXII) has increasingly come to mean 'something practical to politically engaged Scots,'[7] and maintains a relevance beyond its historical significance. How appropriate it is, then, that questions of national identity are being vigorously pursued by historians, that the Declaration of Arbroath has assumed a place in Scottish political rhetoric and thought in the 1990s, and that 'freedom' should have been a major theme in Mel Gibson's late twentieth-century movie dealing with the late thirteenth and early fourteenth centuries.[8] As has been recently noted, 'age-old events can have a practical resonance across the centuries, and this gives us a focus on the broader question: "does medieval Scottish history really matter?"'[9] The answer that the late twentieth century has provided is a resounding 'yes.'[10]

Not surprisingly, the output of both popular and scholarly material has kept pace with this rising tide of interest. Building upon foundations that were laid by Victorian scholars and antiquarians such as Hume Brown, Cosmo Innes, Andrew Lang, E.W. Robertson, W.F. Skene, and Patrick Tytler, to name but a few, medieval Scottish studies came of age in the 1960s. That decade saw not only the publication of the first edition of what would become one of the standard one-volume histories of ancient, medieval, and early modern Scotland,[11] but also G.W.S. Barrow's seminal study, *Robert Bruce and the Community of the Realm of Scotland* (1965; now in its fourth edition). This work, described by another prominent Scottish medievalist, A.A.M. Duncan, as 'the first modern book on medieval Scottish history,'[12] showed the extent to which Scottish history had both come of age and attained academic respectability. By the seventies and eighties, multi-volume histories of Scotland brought Scottish history into the academic mainstream. First out of the gate was the *Edinburgh History of Scotland*, published in four volumes between 1965 and 1975, and described by one reviewer as a 'basic scholarly guide to the history of the Scottish nation.'[13] It was anchored by A.A.M. Duncan's *Scotland: The Making of the Kingdom* (1975), while Ranald Nicholson contributed volume two, *Scotland: The Later Middle Ages* (1974), which carried the story into the middle of the sixteenth century. Reviews of these two volumes indicate just how innovative each was, and how great were the gaps in scholarship that they began to bridge.[14] By the early eighties, another multi-volume series, the *New History of Scotland*, had appeared. No fewer than three volumes covered the Middle Ages, while the early modern era was covered in a fourth.[15] The series, which was generally well received by reviewers, did more than just present contemporary thought on each of the periods covered: some volumes, especially the first, offered provocative new interpretations of Scottish history that stimulated vigorous debate.[16]

Even as the final volumes of the *New History* appeared in 1984, however, there were already signs that the trickle of general works on medieval Scotland was giving way to a torrent of new scholarship, as more specialized works on the subject began to appear. The years between 1980 and 1985 witnessed the publication of further seminal studies by G.W.S. Barrow,[17] and two ground-breaking volumes by Keith Stringer.[18] Barbara Crawford's important and influential book, *Scandinavian Scotland*, appeared in 1987, and the publication of Norman MacDougall's *James IV* in 1989 inaugurated a nine-volume series (still ongoing), *The Stewart Dynasty in Scotland*, which has revolutionized our views on royal power and Crown-nobility relations in the later Middle Ages. Nothing, however, symbolizes the growth and development of writing on Scotland's medieval past quite so much as the Festschrift commemorating the retirement of G.W.S. Barrow from the Sir William Fraser Chair of Scottish History and Palaeography at the University of Edinburgh in 1992. Although concerned with themes that were central to Barrow's own work, the volume, which included contributions by some of the foremost historians of medieval Scotland, nonetheless tackled everything from the early kings of

Strathclyde to crafts in thirteenth-century Aberdeen.[19] Thus, when Alexander Grant examined the achievements of medieval Scottish historiography in 1994, it was not without good cause that he remarked, 'Over the last twenty or thirty years immense progress has been made in our understanding of virtually every aspect of medieval Scotland.'[20] Little wonder, then, that Scottish historical writing is now widely regarded as having undergone a period of revitalization since the 1970s that has been appropriately described as a renaissance – a trend that is all the more remarkable for the relatively small community of scholars engaged in research in the field.[21]

Indeed, it could be argued that the nineties have seen Scottish historical studies reach a critical mass. One good indication of this is the degree of introspection that has crept into the discipline: not only are Scottish historians cognizant of the past and present state of the discipline, but they are also increasingly concerned with mapping out new directions for future study and research. In 1993, for instance, a symposium held at the University of Strathclyde to launch the Research Centre in Scottish History addressed the question Whither Scottish History? 'The occasion,' remarks Tom Devine, 'was a unique one, because it was the first time in recent years that medieval, early modern and modern specialists have come together to discuss and debate the condition of Scottish historical studies.'[22] That conference brought together scholars concerned with all periods of Scottish history, but there is every indication that medieval Scottish studies has also reached a critical mass of its own. An indication of this unquestionably comes with the publication in 2000 of *Freedom and Authority: Scotland c.1050–c.1650*, a Festschrift for one of the noted record scholars in the field, Grant G. Simpson. Part one of the volume is entitled 'Historians and the Uses of History' and includes essays dealing with the state of medieval Scottish studies in the year 2000, as well as Brotherstone and Ditchburn's '1320 and A'That: The Declaration of Arbroath and the Remaking of Scottish History,' which aims to make sense of the place of the famous Declaration in the late twentieth-century Scottish political arena.[23]

Introspection aside, there are other ways to gauge the vitality of Scottish studies. On the one hand, as the foregoing discussion has illustrated in a very limited fashion, there has been a substantial increase in the quantity of works produced, dealing with all periods.

A good guide to the proliferation of writing on Scottish history is the large index compiled to supplement the two-hundredth issue of the *Scottish Historical Review* (the major organ for the dissemination of scholarship in the field) in the fall of 1996. It shows a steady increase in the quantity of historical writing dealing with Scotland in general, but the years since 1996 have been so productive that even this guide must be supplemented by the book review pages of more recent issues of this and other journals.[24] On the other hand, and as the Festschrifts for Barrow and Simpson so nicely illustrate, it is not just a matter of a steady increase in the quantity of material being published – there is also a much wider range of material being produced, riding successive waves of enthusiasm for different types of inquiry which are invigorating the study of history generally, and supplementing more traditional approaches and topics with a wealth of new themes, issues, topics, and methodologies.[25] As one recent reviewer summed it up: 'put at its simplest, Scottish historical studies have become increasingly pluralistic and multifarious.'[26]

Exactly how pluralistic and multifarious Scottish historical writing has become can be demonstrated by surveying the diversity of material published in the nineties. Many of these studies have been concerned with what might be considered 'traditional' subjects, such as the Wars of Independence,[27] the nobility,[28] kings and kingship,[29] as well as the Church, saints, and monasticism,[30] although it is important to note that all of these topics have been informed by new methodologies and paradigms, and many have advanced considerably from the state of historical scholarship even thirty years ago. At the same time, however, there has also been an intensification of interest in Celtic Scotland,[31] the highlands, islands, borders, and peripheral regions of the Scottish kingdom,[32] Scottish identity,[33] and towns and town life.[34] Other subjects, hitherto largely neglected, including the Scottish economy,[35] women,[36] historical writing,[37] law,[38] literacy and charter-use,[39] power centres,[40] late medieval and Renaissance culture,[41] and popular culture in general,[42] have also garnered substantial scholarly attention and promise to open up whole new fields of inquiry. Not only the quantity, then, but also the diversity of scholarship dealing with medieval Scotland produced in the nineties is impressive; as Norman MacDougall put it in 1994, 'our diversity of views on the nature of Scotland's history is a source of strength, not of weakness.'[43] But this is not to say that historical studies of medieval Scotland have

exhausted themselves – far from it, in fact. Many facets still remain
to be further elucidated, and Scottish medieval scholarship can be
expected to continue to move in new and exciting directions in the
twenty-first century.

One notable feature of medieval Scottish historiography is the
manner in which the broadening scope of British history, liberated
from the Stubbsian, Anglocentric, constitutional mode,[44] has influenced scholars of medieval Scotland. As new paradigms and methodologies have been introduced to the study of Britain, they have, in
turn, prompted serious re-examination of a number of themes in
Scottish history, including the relationship between the core and
periphery of the medieval kingdom and the connections of Scotland
with Ireland, Europe, and the wider world, to name but a few.[45] Of
even greater interest, however, is the way in which aspects of these
re-examinations are now beginning to feed back into the broader
loop of British historical studies: for example, R.R. Davies's recent
study, *The First English Empire: Power and Identities in the British
Isles, 1093–1343* (2000), is well informed by the many publications
of Scottish medievalists in the preceding ten years or so. It would
appear, then, that less than a decade after Tom Devine remarked
that Scottish historical studies had yet to make a mark on international scholarship, they are beginning to do just that.[46]

Neither Scottish archaeology nor literary and textual studies
have been outpaced by these developments in historical writing.
Indeed, Scottish archaeology, like historical writing, has undergone
something of a renaissance in the past two decades, a development
that is nicely illustrated by B.T. Batsford's *Historic Scotland* series,
which now encompasses some dozen or so titles interpreting both
historical eras and specific sites, ranging from ancient Orkney and
Shetland to the fortresses of the 'Forty-Five'; one of those titles is
the masterful survey *Medieval Scotland* (1995), by Peter Yeoman,
which sums up the current state of medieval Scottish archaeology
and includes important chapters on towns, town life, castles, and
rural settlement.[47] Such a wide-ranging series can only be built, of
course, upon more specialized scholarship deriving from the excavation and interpretation of specific sites, and the last twenty years
have seen plenty of this, too, including important work at Finlaggan on the island of Islay (the seat of the lords of the Isles),
Whithorn (second only to Iona among early medieval holy places),
Edinburgh castle, and the medieval burghs of Perth and Aberdeen,

to name but a few sites that have been scrutinized by Scottish archaeologists in recent years.[48] In addition to excavations at important sites, there has also been a movement toward the re-examination and reinterpretation of well-known artefacts, monuments, and works of art, such as the famous St Andrews sarcophagus (a Pictish masterpiece described as 'one of the most intriguing early medieval sculptures in Europe') or the early medieval sculpted stones at Govan Old Parish Church in Glasgow. While these studies have yielded a wealth of new interpretations, at the same time contributing broadly to our understanding of the dynamics of medieval Scottish society,[49] the perspective of the archaeologists has also enhanced our knowledge of the processes contributing to the formation of the medieval Scottish kingdom.[50] Also, the nineties have not been without their share of stunning new discoveries. One of the most significant of these occurred with the exposure and subsequent excavation of a Viking boat burial on Sanday, Orkney, in 1991, which has 'made a significant contribution to the corpus of pagan Norse burials, not just for Orkney but also for the whole of Scandinavian Scotland.'[51]

Equally exciting and important for the student of medieval Scotland is the proliferation of new editions and translations of texts and documents. Scottish studies enjoy a solid tradition of publishing texts and documents that stretches back to the antiquarian clubs of the nineteenth century.[52] The inception of the *Regesta Regum Scottorum* series in the sixties, along with M.O. Anderson's *Kings and Kingship in Early Scotland* (1973), set a whole new standard for such endeavours, and the nineties have by no means fallen short of the bar.[53] It is certainly significant that the year 1990 witnessed the first reprinting of A.O. Anderson's classic *Early Sources of Scottish History A.D. 500–1286* since its original publication in 1922. The reprinting of this 'indispensable tool for the study of Scottish medieval history'[54] both symbolized the revitalization of Scottish medieval studies since the seventies and foreshadowed some of the accomplishments of the nineties in the realm of textual studies. Charter scholarship, for instance, has continued to flourish, with editions of the charters of David I (1124–53) by G.W.S. Barrow, as well as careful studies of the acts of the lords of Galloway to 1234 by Keith Stringer and the records of Archibald, fourth earl of Douglas (d. 1424), by Alexander Grant.[55] In a more literary vein, new collections and translations of some of Scotland's earliest poetry were undertaken,[56] as was a new edition of Adomnán's *Life of St Columba*.[57] There also appeared a masterful fresh translation of John Barbour's epic fourteenth-century poem *The Bruce* by A.A.M. Duncan; according to one authority, 'this excellent, accessible and affordable edition will undoubtedly become the standard text well into the 21st century.'[58] In any ordinary decade, this in itself might have been a singularly phenomenal achievement. Unquestionably, however, the most significant development of the nineties was the completion of a new bilingual edition (Latin and English) of that 'Scottish national treasure,'[59] namely, Walter Bower's fifteenth-century *Scotichronicon*, undertaken in eight volumes of text and translation and one volume of commentary in a mere eleven years between 1987 and 1998![60] Up until the inception of this project, Bower's text was accessible primarily through a printed edition published in Edinburgh in 1759; even this, however, was in Latin, and no complete translation had ever been attempted before. This amazing feat has been rightfully regarded as a 'landmark in Scottish historical scholarship,'[61] and it seems to have stimulated a whole new movement within Scottish medieval studies for the critical re-examination of the texts upon which our knowledge of the past is based.[62]

The year 2000 marked the appearance of a new, one-volume, synthetic history of medieval Scotland – the first since Dickinson's landmark work of 1961.[63] Janus-like, this volume gazes back across the tremendous outpouring of scholarship of the past twenty-five years (particularly that of the nineties) and at the same time looks ahead, too. With further synthetic histories and whole new series on medieval Scotland expected, and with the knowledge of what solid foundations now lie beneath, the future looks bright indeed for medieval Scottish scholarship.

The present volume had its genesis in a one-day symposium on medieval Scotland held at the University of Toronto in the spring of 1998. That symposium tapped into the surging tide of interest in medieval Scotland, and papers on history, literature, archaeology, and music provided participants, not with a broad overview of Scottish history or chronology, but rather, more uniquely, with insights into narrow slices of medieval Scottish society. In keeping with the multi-disciplinary spirit of the symposium, this volume presents a series of eight essays from different disciplines dealing with various aspects of medieval Scotland. Two of the papers originally presented at the symposium are included here, in much revised form, while six other essays have been specially commissioned for this collection and appear in print for the first time. Although the book is not intended to serve as a comprehensive introduction to its subject, it can be read with profit by anyone with an interest in the field, and it is offered as a multi-disciplinary contribution to the study of medieval Scottish civilization.

Thematically, the essays presented here deal with a wide variety of topics and approaches to the past. Thus, there are papers on historical writing, literature, history, identity, gender issues, and music, representing both traditional and innovative approaches from established scholars with international reputations as well as more junior scholars who are only beginning to make their mark. Each essay makes a contribution to its own particular field, presenting a cross-section, as it were, of the present state of knowledge in its area, while at the same time pointing toward new directions in research, interpretation, and methodology; several papers are broad in scope and conception, while others are more narrow in focus and intent. Chronologically, the papers range from the seventh to the sixteenth centuries, although the coverage is uneven: seven of the eight essays concentrate on the period after the eleventh century, and fully four of these deal with the fifteenth and sixteenth centuries, a period variously regarded as 'late medieval' or 'early modern' but one which is considered medieval for the purposes of this book.[64]

With current developments in British and Scottish politics, not to mention with Scottish history departments flourishing and Scottish publishers producing ever larger catalogues of Scottish material, it is easy to imagine that the resurgence of interest in Scottish studies is confined to the shores of Auld Scotia. In fact, Scottish studies are becoming an increasingly global concern, occupying scholars not only in Scotland and Britain but also in North America, Europe, and Australia. It is therefore perhaps fitting – if entirely unplanned and accidental – that scholars who live and work in North America have contributed all of the papers in this volume. This is the first such volume of which I am aware, and the fact that it has proven possible to solicit eight essays on medieval Scottish subjects from North American scholars is surely yet another good

indication that Scottish studies have reached a critical mass, not
just within Scotland itself but within a global context.

As we have seen, one of the most fruitful fields of inquiry in medieval Scottish studies since the eighties has been the critical re-
examination of the sources upon which our understanding of the
past is based. One of the foremost scholars in this field is Benjamin
Hudson, who has published new translations of the *Prophecy of
Berchán* as well as the so-called Scottish Chronicle, and whose
detailed studies of these problematic sources have served as jump-
ing-off points for important explorations of the pan-Gaelic world of
Ireland and Scotland in the early Middle Ages.[65] In the opening
essay, Professor Hudson draws attention to the fact that Scottish
historians tend to use English, Irish, and other 'foreign' sources, and
he sets out to rectify this situation by examining, in sweeping fashion, the early medieval writings of the Scots for events in both their
own lands and the lands of their neighbours: this is the 'Scottish
Gaze' of the title of his paper. Hudson demonstrates that a uniquely
Scottish viewpoint can be recovered and elucidated in these early
texts, and he demonstrates how the Scottish point of view changed
over the centuries, from a western orientation in the early Middle
Ages to a broader perspective by the early High Middle Ages. The
paper also demonstrates that Gaelic Scotland enjoyed close links
with both the lands to the west – Ireland – and to the south – Strathclyde, England, and the Continent. Thus, Hudson reminds us that
medieval Scotland was far from isolated in either cultural or political terms; this theme remains pervasive throughout the subsequent
essays.

Just as Hudson's paper addresses a void in traditional scholarship
dealing with historical literature among the early Scots, so the next
paper turns its gaze toward another long-neglected subject. George
Brunsden's contribution, 'Earls and Saints: Early Christianity in
Norse Orkney and the Legend of Magnus Erlendsson,' which moves
into the late eleventh and early twelfth centuries to consider the
life and legend of Saint Magnus of Orkney (d. 1117), examines Magnus as a contender for power in the fiercely competitive world of
the Norse Orkney earldom, and then explores his conversion to
Christianity, his martyrdom, and the rise of a cult dedicated to him.
In undertaking this study, Brunsden not only sheds light on the
Orkney earldom at a crucial but incompletely understood juncture

in its history, but also shows its place in the development of the Western Christian community – thus locating this remote principality within important trends in recent medieval scholarship dealing with conversion and Western Christendom.[66] Basing his examination upon a critical and comparative study of the Scandinavian saga tradition, Brunsden further develops one of the themes of the preceding paper by re-evaluating another set of primary source materials. Finally, just as Hudson highlights the place of Scotland within the broader Gaelic and northern European world, Brunsden's paper takes up this theme by emphasizing the dual connection of Viking Scotland to not only the broader Scandinavian world that stretched from Greenland to Norway but also to Western Christendom as a whole.

Scottish historical writing of the past twenty-five years or so has been particularly concerned with the processes whereby the four or five disparate peoples – including Scandinavians – living in northern Britain were welded into a unified and coherent medieval kingdom ruled by a powerful dynasty of Scottish kings – the so-called Canmore dynasty after Malcolm III 'Canmore' (1058–93), who is generally regarded as its founder. Indeed, the centrality of this theme to medieval Scottish historiography is evidenced by the titles of volumes such as *Scotland: The Making of the Kingdom* or *Kingship and Unity: Scotland 1000–1306*. But just how unified and coherent was the Scottish kingdom in the twelfth and thirteenth centuries? Some historians have remained uneasy and expressed reservations about the apparent early unity and harmony of the kingdom,[67] and the recent trend in Scottish medieval scholarship toward detailed examination of the peripheral regions of the kingdom such as Galloway, Argyll, and the far north has shed important new light on the questions of both unity and the relations between the core and periphery of the medieval kingdom.[68] My own essay, '"Soldiers Most Unfortunate": Gaelic and Scoto-Norse Opponents of the Canmore Dynasty, c. 1100–c. 1230,' offers a reassessment of instances of resistance to the Scottish kings of the twelfth and thirteenth centuries, and attempts to analyse not only who the opponents of the Scottish kings were, but what motivated them. I suggest that there was a considerable degree of cooperation among the leaders of resistance to the Scottish kings, that their incursions posed more of a threat than is usually realized, and, arguing that history is ultimately written by the winners, I show that consideration of the losers is also important if we are to fully understand the political development of the medieval Scottish kingdom. This paper represents an attempt to approach the history of medieval Scotland not only from the perspective of the losers, but also from a perspective detached from that of the Canmore dynasty situated at the heart of the medieval kingdom.

The development of a Scottish national identity was under way during the twelfth century,[69] but is generally agreed to have accelerated during the Wars of Independence of the late thirteenth and fourteenth centuries – which wars quickly turned into, among other things, a 'War of Historiography.'[70] Richard J. Moll's essay carries us forward from the twelfth century to the fifteenth – a time of intense literary activity – to consider Blind Hary's poem *The Wallace*, described as 'the most remarkable of all early stories in Scots.'[71] Although it was composed in the 1470s, this action-packed, anti-English poem takes as its theme the life of the Scottish hero and patriot William Wallace, who was executed by the English some 170 years earlier in 1305.[72] Setting his examination firmly within the context of current discourse on medieval nationalism,[73] Moll explores Hary's work for clues about the development of national identity in Scotland and discovers a more complex picture than might at first seem apparent. Moll's main thesis is that Hary recognized the political and cultural disunity in Scottish society, and that he crafted the figure of Wallace in order to promote unity in the face of the English threat. One way that he did this was to redefine subtly the concept of common blood: in *The Wallace*, blood is defined by support for the cause of Scottish independence, not simply by ethnicity or birthplace. Moll also suggests that Hary's story of Wallace echoes internal strife in the 1470s, particularly in relation to the struggle between James III and the duke of Albany. Finally, in terms of methodology, this essay represents an excellent example of the breaking down of barriers between literature and history to better examine nationalism in a critical manner.

One of Blind Hary's younger contemporaries was William Dunbar (c. 1460–c. 1520). Like Hary, he may have begun to write in the reign of James III (1460–88) but is generally associated with the court of James IV (1488–1513), which provided him with both an audience and subject matter; with a reputation as one of 'the Makars,' his place in Scottish literature is assured.[74] The next essay, 'Carnival at Court and Dunbar in the Underworld,' by Mary Robbins, considers Dunbar's bizarre yet compelling poem 'Off Februar the fyiftene nycht,' a dream vision describing the dance of the deadly sins and a tournament, which take place in hell on Fasterns Eve (Shrove Tuesday). The dance of the deadly sins and the tournament have in the past often been considered as separate pieces, but here Robbins treats them as two halves of one poem with a serious, didactic intent, in which the didacticism is disguised but not obliterated by the humour of its carnivalesque entertainment. Robbins is thus able to show how the poem can be interpreted as a warning to the court of King James IV; as she concludes, 'at the heart of these demonic events is Dunbar's indictment of human frailty and perhaps his caution about its ultimate effect upon the social framework of Scotland.' The theme of the carnivalesque or 'topsy turvy' inherent in the poem also enables Robbins to apply the important work of Mikhail Bakhtin, something that has been done only occasionally for Middle Scots poems in general and for Dunbar in particular.[75] By working Dunbar into the Bakhtinian tradition, Robbins not only casts new light on the poem 'Off Februar the fyiftene nycht,' but also draws Scottish literary studies into a well-established English and Continental tradition. This same effect is also accomplished by utilizing extensive comparisons with other medieval views of the underworld, which enables Robbins to point out precisely how Dunbar's vision of hell compares to that of other medieval writers.

One of the most productive trends in medieval scholarship over the past twenty or so years has been the study of women of all social orders and occupations in the medieval world. Women in Britain and Ireland have not been left behind, and it is fitting, then, that the next two essays concentrate on very different aspects of gender in late medieval Scotland. Elizabeth Ewan's paper, '"Many Injurious Words": Defamation and Gender in Late Medieval Scotland,' which was awarded the Royal Historical Society's prestigious David Berry Prize in Scottish History for 1999, offers an innovative discussion of the late medieval tradition of insult, the entertaining nature of which should in no way mask its mastery of the sources and its importance as an original contribution to the subject. Her essay examines many different aspects of the boisterous tradition of insult (or 'flyting'),[76] including chastity, resentment toward authority, gender differences in insulting, and punishment. Through careful evaluation of court records from almost every burgh in Scotland, Ewan constructs a compelling portrait of Scottish popular culture, urban life, and gender relations in the sixteenth century. Moreover, by drawing upon a wealth of recent material on her subject from the broader British and European contexts, Professor Ewan once again reminds us that late medieval Scotland shared much with its neighbours.

Margaret McIntyre's essay, 'Tudor Family Politics in Early Six-teenth-Century Scotland,' transports us from flytings in the streets of Edinburgh to the very centre of power in early sixteenth-century Scotland: the royal court. This examination of Margaret Tudor, sis-ter of King Henry VIII of England (1509–47), wife of King James IV of Scotland, and mother of King James V (1513–42), is firmly rooted in recent discussions of queenship and queenly power in late medieval Europe and Britain,[77] but examines a new area: sibling relations. In this reassessment of one of Scotland's lesser-known queens, McIn-tyre explores the complex and sometimes conflicting configura-tions of power within which Margaret Tudor moved, and under-lines the difficulties faced by a woman whose attempts to reconcile the demands of her natal and marital families were met with vary-ing degrees of success. Through an examination of various official documents, McIntyre pinpoints the complex issues of gender, fam-ily, and authority in early sixteenth-century Scotland, and argues that Margaret's access to formal power was contingent upon the successful integration of her dual identities as mother of the Scot-tish king and sister of the English king. The essay also shows how Margaret's sexual reputation was closely tied to her ability to main-tain authority. Although Scottish historians writing through the ages have generally been unkind to Margaret, this essay calls such interpretations into question, and concludes that Margaret Tudor was able to transcend and challenge sixteenth-century notions of gender.

Despite its major importance, medieval Scottish music has been largely relegated to rather obscure specialist journals. In the final article in this collection, '*Commeationis et affinitatis gratia*: Medi-eval Musical Relations between Scotland and Ireland,' Andrea Budgey sets out to explore exactly what we know about Scottish medieval music and its relationship to Irish music. Utilizing the tantalizing remarks of the late twelfth- and early thirteenth-century scholar Gerald of Wales (d. 1223) on Celtic musical traditions as a window onto these problems, Budgey asks questions such as 'Can we trust Gerald's descriptions?' 'What instruments were used in medieval Scotland and Ireland?' and 'What religious music was employed?' Having laid the foundations by addressing these basic issues, Budgey then develops the theme of cultural interactions not only between Ireland and Scotland ('a powerful and cohesive musical culture') but also Scotland and Europe, while her concluding remarks, dealing with questions of assimilation and acculturation between European and Celtic influences in the eleventh to thirteenth centuries, highlight the contributions and significance of musicology to the broader field of Scottish studies as a whole. Indeed, this essay provides an excellent example of how the growth of Scottish studies over the last thirty years has brought new perspectives to the past as well as an integrated approach that incorporates historical, literary, and musicological methodologies and perspectives.

Although each essay develops its argument without reference to other papers in the collection, certain broader themes do nevertheless emerge which serve to link the contributions, making the sum of the whole much greater than its constituent parts. The most obvious of these unifying strands is the light that each paper sheds upon the various raw materials from which the past is recreated, thus providing not only an overview of the sources available for investigation but also a critical study of how different kinds of sources can be used to illuminate different facets of the past, including political history, historical writing, gender, society, identity, and music.[78] Benjamin Hudson, for instance, in considering the 'Scottish gaze,' utilizes a wide variety of material, ranging from saints' Lives to 'prophecies,' chronicles, and poems. George Brunsden, in his assessment of Saint Magnus of Orkney, is forced to confront the saga literature, always a difficult and contentious body of material through which to navigate, while I myself reassess a variety of chronicles and annals, English and Scottish in provenance, for evidence not only about the margins of the twelfth-century kingdom but also about how these regions were viewed by the history-writing elites at the centre of that kingdom. Elizabeth Ewan brings her expertise to bear on burgh records and legal documents in search of evidence on gender and defamation, while Margaret McIntyre re-examines official documents, including royal correspondence, in her reassessment of Margaret Tudor's public and private roles. Both Richard J. Moll and Mary Robbins turn to medieval Scottish verse for their evidence, reminding us that literature can also provide valuable insights into the culture, society, and attitudes of the past – and Andrea Budgey's unique exploration of music in medieval Scotland and Ireland also, of necessity, draws upon a wide variety of intriguing source materials, ranging from musical manuscripts to stone carvings. Thus, taken as a whole, the essays collected here illustrate not only the diversity of materials available to the investigator, but also the equally impressive diversity of approaches which may be applied to them. Indeed, one of the more valuable contributions of the essays contained in this volume may well be that they respond directly to the criticism that 'Scottish historians need to be alive to the new themes, issues, topics and questions which are invigorating historical scholarship outside Scotland.'[79]

Apart from the raw materials of the past themselves and their use by historians, other themes also emerge from these essays. Most of the papers touch, in one way or another, on the question of the medieval Scots and the wider world, whether historical writing, politics, nationalism, the afterlife, gender, or music is under consideration. Not surprisingly, connections with Ireland figure prominently, as evinced in the essays by Hudson and Budgey, and, to a lesser extent, in my own essay; but both Robbins and Moll are able to place their respective discussions of the afterlife and nationalism within a broader European context, while Brunsden's paper reminds us of the strong Scandinavian imprint upon parts of what is now Scotland and its place in the Northern world. The ability of the contributors to relate events in Scotland to the wider world puts further lie to the already defunct notion that medieval Scotland was somehow backwards, isolated, or out of touch with the rest of the British Isles and the European Continent.

Finally, two other important sub-themes also demand recognition. The first of these is gender. The essays by Ewan and McIntyre, both firmly rooted in recent scholarship in their respective areas, serve as potent reminders not only of how much work has been undertaken in recent years on questions of gender in medieval studies, and medieval Scotland, in particular, but also of how far there is yet to go. Ewan's ground-breaking essay reveals just how much evidence remains to be gleaned from burghal and legal documents about women's lives, while McIntyre's reassessment of Margaret Tudor demonstrates how Scottish queens and queenship have traditionally been ignored in favour of Scottish kings and kingship, and how sadly lacking are so many previous attempts to understand female figures of power in late medieval and early modern Scotland.

The second remaining theme of note is that of entertainment and culture. At first glance, this may seem solely the preserve of Andrea Budgey's revealing look at music in medieval Scotland and Ireland. But when we consider that both Robbins's essay on Dunbar and Moll's paper on Blind Hary's *Wallace* deal with medieval literature, which was itself a form of entertainment, windows begin to open on the wider world of late medieval culture and entertainment. Indeed, as Robbins points out, one of the major difficulties in dealing with Dunbar's poem 'Off Februar the fyiftene nycht' is knowing where to draw the line between its role as entertainment and its function as satire.

There can be little argument that the study of medieval Scotland is firmly established on the academic and popular scenes. Yet surely one of the most exciting aspects of the fin de siècle revival of Scottish studies is not just the mere fact of its occurrence, but the rich and vibrant texture that it has taken on in a remarkably short period of time. This is largely the result of the application of numerous different theoretical frameworks and methodologies to Scottish studies by scholars working worldwide in a broad range of disciplines. In one regard, then, the essays in this volume capture something of the diversity and depth of work currently under way on medieval Scottish society. Yet, at the same time, it is to be hoped that the papers presented here will serve as a stimulus and a point of departure for further research, discussion, and debate. For, as the inquiries into medieval Scotland during the past decades have shown, the recreation of the past is an ongoing process, and 'it remains to be seen what the twenty-first [century] will make of this remarkable phenomenon, now worldwide, which craves the attention of scholarly interest rather than the arrogance of academic dismissal.'[80]

Notes

1 E.J. Cowan, *Scottish History and Scottish Folk*, Inaugural Lecture, Chair of Scottish History and Literature, University of Glasgow, 1995 (Glasgow, 1998), 27.

2 See the stimulating remarks in C. Frayling's *Strange Landscape: A Journey through the Middle Ages* (London, 1995), chapter 1.

3 See T. Brotherstone and D. Ditchburn, '1320 and A'That: The Declara-

tion of Arbroath and the Remaking of Scottish History,' in *Freedom and Authority: Scotland c.1050–c.1650: Historical and Historiographical Essays Presented to Grant G. Simpson*, ed. T. Brotherstone and D. Ditchburn (East Linton, 2000), 26–7.

4 For a good answer, see the review of the movie (along with *Rob Roy*, starring Liam Neeson) by E.L. Ewan in *American Historical Review* 100/1 (Oct. 1995), 1219–21.

5 It is interesting to note that the British archaeologist Simon James has argued that the 'invention' of the Atlantic Celts owed much to the political situation in the British Isles in the early eighteenth century; see S. James, *The Atlantic Celts: Ancient People or Modern Invention?* (London and Madison, WI, 1999), especially chapter 3.

6 On the stone, see G.W.S. Barrow, 'Some Observations on the Coronation Stone of Scotland,' *SHR* 76 (1997), 115–21; on inaugurations, see J. Bannerman, 'The King's Poet and the Inauguration of Alexander III,' *SHR* 68 (1989), 120–49.

7 Brotherstone and Ditchburn, '1320 and A'That,' in *Freedom and Authority: Scotland c.1050–c.1650*, 13. Much has been written on the Declaration. In addition to the very useful remarks in the article by Brotherstone and Ditchburn, see also A.A.M. Duncan, *The Nation of Scots and the Declaration of Arbroath* (London, 1970); G.G. Simpson, 'The Declaration of Arbroath Revitalised,' *SHR* 56 (1977), 11–33; and E.J. Cowan, 'Identity, Freedom and the Declaration of Arbroath,' in *Image and Identity: The Making and Re-making of Scotland through the Ages*, ed. D. Broun, R.J. Finlay, and M. Lynch (Edinburgh, 1998), 38–68.

8 See M.D. Sharp, 'Remaking Medieval Heroism: Nationalism and Sexuality in *Braveheart*,' *Florilegium* 15 (1998), 251–67.

9 Brotherstone and Ditchburn, '1320 and A'That,' in *Freedom and Authority: Scotland c.1050–c.1650*, 10.

10 See *Why Scottish History Matters*, ed. R. Mitchison (Saltire Society, Edinburgh, 1991), in which eight leading historians attempt to answer this question.

11 W.C. Dickinson, *Scotland from the Earliest Times to 1603* (London, 1961). In 1977 the third edition of this work was substantially revised and edited by A.A.M. Duncan.

12 Duncan, *Nation of Scots and the Declaration of Arbroath*, 38; see also Duncan's review essay, 'The Community of the Realm of Scotland and Robert Bruce,' *SHR* 45 (1966), 184–201.

13 H.R. Loyn, review of *Scotland: The Making of the Kingdom*, by A.A.M. Duncan, *SHR* 55 (1976), 195–7; quotation at 195.

14 See note 13 above, as well as I.B. Cowan's review of R. Nicholson, *Scotland: The Later Middle Ages*, in *SHR* 56 (1977), 189–91.

15 A.P. Smyth, *Warlords and Holy Men: Scotland* A.D. *80–1000* (London, 1984); G.W.S. Barrow, *Kingship and Unity: Scotland 1000–1306* (London, 1981); A. Grant, *Independence and Nationhood: Scotland 1306–1469* (London, 1984); J. Wormald, *Court, Kirk and Community: Scotland 1470–1625* (London, 1981).

16 See, for instance, reviews of Smyth by A. MacQuarrie in *SHR* 64 (1985), 178–81, and by W.D.H. Sellar, 'Warlords, Holy Men and Matrilineal Succession,' *Innes Review* 36 (1986), 29–43. Sellar remarks that Smyth's book 'should do much to advance the study of a period that has attracted too little scholarly attention, even if not all of Dr. Smyth's theories will emerge unscathed' (41). And the debate continues: see A. Woolf, 'Pictish Matriliny Reconsidered,' *Innes Review* 49 (1998), 147–67.

17 *The Anglo-Norman Era in Scottish History* (Oxford, 1980).

18 *Earl David of Huntingdon: A Study in Anglo-Scottish History* (Edinburgh, 1985); *Essays on the Nobility of Medieval Scotland* (Edinburgh, 1985). The latter is an edited collection of papers.

19 *Medieval Scotland: Crown, Lordship and Community. Essays Presented to G.W.S. Barrow*, ed. A. Grant and K.J. Stringer (Edinburgh, 1993).

20 A. Grant, 'To the Medieval Foundations,' *SHR* 73 [Special Issue: Whither Scottish History? Proceedings of the 1993 Strathclyde Conference] (1994), 4–24; quotation at 4.

21 T.M. Devine, 'Whither Scottish History? Preface,' *SHR* 73 (1994), 1–3 at 1; on the community of scholars, see R.D. Oram, 'Gold into Lead? The State of Early Medieval Scottish History,' in *Freedom and Authority: Scotland c.1050–c.1650*, 42.

22 Devine, 'Whither Scottish History? Preface,' 1.

23 Full reference in note 3 above.

24 *SHR* 75 Supplement (1996); note also the remarks of J. Stevenson in 'Writing Scotland's History in the Twentieth Century: Thoughts from across the Border,' *SHR* 76 (1997), 103–14.

25 See, *inter alia*, L.O. Fradenburg, *City, Marriage, Tournament: Arts of Rule in Late Medieval Scotland* (Madison, 1991), which draws on a wide range of methodologies and sources in its discussion of sovereignty in late medieval Scotland.

26 Stevenson, 'Writing Scotland's History in the Twentieth Century,' 106.

27 A. Fisher, *Killing Ground: The Scottish Wars of Independence 1296–*

1346 (Stroud, forthcoming); F. Watson, *Under the Hammer: Edward I and Scotland 1286–1307* (East Linton, 1998); C. McNamee, *The Wars of the Bruces: Scotland, England and Ireland, 1306–1328* (East Linton, 1997); A.A.M. Duncan, 'The War of the Scots, 1306–23,' *Transactions of the Royal Historical Society* 6th ser. 2 (1992), 125–51.

28 M. Brown, *The Black Douglases* (East Linton, 1998); A. Young, *Robert the Bruce's Rivals: The Comyns, 1212–1314* (East Linton, 1997).

29 N. Aitchison, *Macbeth: Man and Myth* (Stroud, 1999); J. Cameron, *James V: The Personal Rule, 1528–1542* (East Linton, 1998); D.D.R. Owen, *William the Lion 1143–1214: Kingship and Culture* (East Linton, 1997); S. Boardman, *The Early Stewart Kings: Robert II and Robert III* (East Linton, 1996); M. Brown, *James I* (Edinburgh, 1994); C. McGladdery, *James II* (Edinburgh, 1990); *Scotland in the Reign of Alexander III 1249–1287*, ed. N. Reid (Edinburgh, 1990).

30 *Conversion and Christianity in the North Sea World*, ed. B. Crawford (St Andrews, 1998); A. MacQuarrie, *The Saints of Scotland: Essays in Scottish Church History, A.D. 450–1093* (Edinburgh, 1997); *Studies in the Cult of St Columba*, ed. C. Bourke (Dublin, 1997); M. Dilworth, *Scottish Monasteries in the Late Middle Ages* (Edinburgh, 1995); A.D.M. Barrell, *The Papacy, Scotland and Northern England, 1342–1378* (Cambridge, 1995); B.T. Hudson, 'Kings and Church in Early Scotland,' *SHR* 73 (1994), 145–70; J. MacQueen, *St. Nynia* (Edinburgh, 1990).

31 M. Newton, *Handbook of the Scottish Gaelic World* (Dublin, 2000); J. Roberts, *Lost Kingdoms: Celtic Scotland and the Middle Ages* (Edinburgh, 1997). One modern critic has remarked that 'the [nineteen] eighties and nineties ... have generated a veritable deluge of Celtic book titles not to mention the clamjamfry of nonsense that is now popularly deemed to constitute part of Celtic heritage' (E.J. Cowan, 'The Invention of Celtic Scotland,' in *Alba: Celtic Scotland in the Medieval Era*, ed. E.J. Cowan and R.A. McDonald [East Linton, 2000], 23).

32 C. Neville, *Violence, Custom and Law: The Anglo-Scottish Border Lands in the Later Middle Ages* (Edinburgh, 1998); R.A. McDonald, *The Kingdom of the Isles: Scotland's Western Seaboard c.1100–c.1336* (East Linton, 1997); *Government, Society and Religion in Northern England 1000–1700*, ed. J. Appleby and P. Dalton (Stroud, 1997), in which several essays deal with Anglo-Scottish relations; C. Phythian-Adams, *Land of the Cumbrians: A Study in British Provincial Origins A.D. 400–1120* (Aldershot, 1997); D. Brooke, *Wild Men and Holy Places: St. Ninian, Whithorn, and the Medieval Realm of Galloway* (Edinburgh, 1994); *Moray: Province and People*, ed. W.D.H. Sellar (Edinburgh, 1993);

Galloway: Land and Lordship, ed. G. Stell and R. Oram (Edinburgh, 1992).

33 D. Broun, *The Irish Identity of the Kingdom of the Scots in the Twelfth and Thirteenth Centuries* (Woodbridge, 1999); *Image and Identity: The Making and Re-making of Scotland through the Ages*, ed. Broun, Finlay, and Lynch; B. Webster, *Medieval Scotland: The Making of an Identity* (Basingstoke and London, 1997); D. Broun, 'The Origin of Scottish Identity,' in *Nations, Nationalism and Patriotism in the European Past*, ed. C. Bjørn, A. Grant, and K.J. Stringer (Copenhagen, 1994), 35–55.

34 E. Ewan, *Townlife in Fourteenth-Century Scotland* (Edinburgh, 1990); E.P.D. Torrie, *Medieval Dundee* (Dundee, 1990). There are essays on Scottish medieval towns in *Conservation and Change in Historic Towns*, ed. E.P. Dennison (York, 1999); and there are many Scottish contributions to the *Cambridge Urban History of Britain Volume 1: c.600–c.1540*, ed. D. Palliser (Cambridge, 2000).

35 N. Mayhew and E. Gemmill, *Changing Values in Medieval Scotland: A Study of Prices, Money, and Weights and Measures* (Cambridge, 1995).

36 *Gendering Scottish History: An International Approach*, ed. T. Brotherstone (Glasgow, 2000), which contains several essays on the medieval period; *Women in Scotland c.1100–c.1750*, ed. E. Ewan and M. Meikle (East Linton, 1999); E. Sutherland, *Five Euphemias: Women in Medieval Scotland 1200–1420* (New York, 1999); F. Downie, '"La voie quelle menace tenir": Annabella Stewart, Scotland, and the European Marriage Market, 1444–56,' *SHR* 78 (1999), 170–91; A.J. Wilson, *St Margaret of Scotland* (Edinburgh, 1993). A similar trend exists for Ireland: *'The Fragility of Her Sex'? Medieval Irish Women in Their European Context*, ed. C.E. Meek and M.K. Simms (Dublin, 1996).

37 In addition to the work of D. Broun cited above, note 33, see also R.J. Goldstein, *The Matter of Scotland: Historical Narrative in Medieval Scotland* (Lincoln, NE, and London, 1993), as well as the articles by D. Broun, 'The Birth of Scottish History,' *SHR* 76 (1997), 4–23, and B.T. Hudson, 'The Scottish Chronicle,' *SHR* 77 (1998), 129–61, and *idem*, 'The Language of the Scottish Chronicle and Its European Context,' *Scottish Gaelic Studies* 18 (1998), 57–73.

38 H. MacQueen, *Common Law and Feudal Law in Medieval Scotland* (Edinburgh, 1993).

39 See *Literacy in Medieval Celtic Societies*, ed. H. Pryce (Cambridge, 1998); D. Broun, *The Charters of Gaelic Scotland and Ireland in the Early and Central Middle Ages* (Cambridge, 1995). As the titles of these works suggest, this topic is one that is not restricted to Scotland, and

that has engaged scholars of the medieval world in general; see especially M.T. Clanchy, *From Memory to the Written Record: England 1066–1307*, 2nd ed. (Oxford, 1993).

40 *Scottish Power Centres from the Early Middle Ages to the Twentieth Century*, ed. S. Foster, A. Macinnes, and R. MacInnes (Glasgow, 1998).

41 *The Rose and the Thistle: Essays on the Culture of Late Medieval and Renaissance Scotland*, ed. S. Mapstone and J. Wood (East Linton, 1998); *Stewart Style 1513–1542: Essays on the Court of James v*, ed. J.H. Williams (East Linton, 1996); C. Edington, *Court and Culture in Renaissance Scotland: Sir David Lindsay of the Mount* (Amherst, 1994); *The Renaissance in Scotland: Essays Presented to John Durkan*, ed. A.A. MacDonald, M. Lynch, and I.B. Cowan (Leiden, 1994).

42 *The Ballad in Scottish History*, ed. E.J. Cowan (East Linton, 2000); see also Professor Cowan's Inaugural Lecture, cited above, note 1.

43 N. MacDougall, 'Response: At the Medieval Bedrock,' *SHR* 73 (1994), 25–9, at 29.

44 Heralded by G.W.S. Barrow, *Feudal Britain* (London, 1956), this trend began to come to fruition in the late eighties and early nineties: *The British Isles 1100–1500*, ed. R.R. Davies (Edinburgh, 1988); R.R. Davies, *Domination and Conquest: The Experience of Ireland, Scotland and Wales, 1100–1300* (Cambridge, 1990); R. Frame, *The Political Development of the British Isles 1100–1400* (Oxford, 1990); D. Crouch, *The Image of Aristocracy in Britain 1000–1300* (London, 1993); *Uniting the Kingdom: The Making of British History*, ed. A. Grant and K.J. Stringer (London and New York, 1995), which contains several essays dealing with the Middle Ages; *Britain and Ireland 900–1300*, ed. B. Smith (Cambridge, 1999).

45 The work of Seán Duffy has been particularly important in these regards; see especially 'Irishmen and Islesmen in the Kingdoms of Dublin and Man, 1072–1171,' *Ériu* 43 (1992), 93–133, and 'The Bruce Brothers and the Irish Sea World, 1306–29,' *Cambridge Medieval Celtic Studies* 21 (1991), 55–86. See also T. Thornton, 'Scotland and the Isle of Man, c.1400–1625: Noble Power and Royal Presumption in the Northern Irish Sea Province,' *SHR* 77 (1998), 1–30. The *New History of the Isle of Man, Volume III: The Medieval Period 1000–1405*, ed. S. Duffy (Liverpool, forthcoming), will certainly make a substantial contribution to the history of Man and the Irish Sea region.

46 Devine, 'Whither Scottish History? Preface,' *SHR* 73 (1994), 1. R. Bartlett, *The Making of Europe: Conquest, Colonization and Cultural Change 950–1350* (Princeton, 1993), is a seminal work that draws

material from Celtic Britain into even broader European themes and trends.

47 Another title by Yeoman, *Pilgrimage in Medieval Scotland* (London, 1999), is a fine survey of its subject that draws together literary and archaeological material.

48 D.H. Caldwell and G. Ewart, 'Finlaggan and the Lordship of the Isles: An Archaeological Approach,' *SHR* 72 (1993), 146–66; P. Hill, *Whithorn and St Ninian: The Excavation of a Monastic Town, 1984–91* (Stroud, 1997); P. Yeoman, *Excavations within Edinburgh Castle 1988–91* (Edinburgh, 1997); *Excavations in the Medieval Burgh of Perth 1979–81*, ed. P. Holdsworth (Edinburgh, 1987). Other important titles include *Scotland: Environment and Archaeology, 8000 B.C.–A.D. 1000*, ed. K.J. Edwards and I.B.M. Ralston (Chichester, 1997); *The Archaeology of Argyll*, ed. G. Ritchie (Edinburgh, 1997); I. Armit, *The Archaeology of Skye and the Western Isles* (Edinburgh, 1996); and *Scottish Archaeology: New Perspectives*, ed. W.S. Hanson and E.A. Slater (Aberdeen, 1991).

49 *The St Andrews Sarcophagus: A Pictish Masterpiece and Its International Connections*, ed. S. Foster (Dublin, 1998), quotation at 7; A. Ritchie, *Govan and Its Early Medieval Sculpture* (Stroud, 1994).

50 S. Foster, *Picts, Gaels and Scots* (London, 1996); S.T. Driscoll, 'Formalising the Mechanisms of State Power: Early Scottish Lordship from the Ninth to Thirteenth Centuries,' in *Scottish Power Centres*, cited in note 40 above; S.T. Driscoll, 'The Archaeology of State Formation in Scotland,' in *Scottish Archaeology: New Perspectives*, cited in note 48 above.

51 O. Owen and M. Dalland, *Scar: A Viking Age Boat Burial on Sanday, Orkney* (East Linton, 2000). The quotation is from J. Graham-Campbell and C. Batey, *Vikings in Scotland: An Archaeological Survey* (Edinburgh, 1998), 138 – another important work in its own right.

52 For some comments on this tradition, see M. Ash, '"A fine, genial, hearty band": David Laing, Daniel Wilson and Scottish Archaeology,' in *The Scottish Antiquarian Tradition: Essays to Mark the Bicentenary of the Society of Antiquaries of Scotland and Its Museum, 1780–1980*, ed. A.S. Bell (Edinburgh, 1981), 86–113, at 89–90.

53 For some remarks on the significance of the *Regesta* series as well as a critique of the trends in scholarship that it initiated, see Oram, 'Gold into Lead?' in *Freedom and Authority: Scotland c.1050–c.1650*, 34–6.

54 Dustjacket of the 1990 reprint.

55 *The Charters of David I*, ed. G.W.S. Barrow (Woodbridge, 1999); K.J. Stringer, 'Acts of Lordship: The Records of the Lords of Galloway to 1234,' and A. Grant, 'Acts of Lordship: The Records of Archibald, Fourth Earl of Douglas,' both in *Freedom and Authority: Scotland c.1050–c.1650*, 203–34, 234–75. See also G.W.S. Barrow, 'The Scots Charter,' in *Scotland and Its Neighbours in the Middle Ages* (London, 1992). It is to be hoped that Cynthia Neville's 'Charter-writing and the Exercise of Lordship in Celtic Scotland,' which was presented at the North American Conference of British Studies in October 2000, will soon appear in print.

56 *The Triumph Tree: Scotland's Earliest Poetry A.D. 550–1350*, ed. and trans. T.O. Clancy (Edinburgh, 1998); *Iona: The Earliest Poetry of a Celtic Monastery*, ed. and trans. T.O. Clancy and G. Markus (Edinburgh, 1995).

57 Adomnán of Iona, *Life of St Columba*, trans. R. Sharpe (London, 1995).

58 John Barbour, *The Bruce*, ed. and trans. A.A.M. Duncan (Edinburgh, 1997); quotation from E.J. Cowan, 'Identity, Freedom and the Declaration of Arbroath,' in *Image and Identity*, 63n4.

59 D.E.R. Watt, 'A National Treasure? The *Scotichronicon* of Walter Bower,' *SHR* 76 (1997), 44–53, at 47.

60 Walter Bower, *Scotichronicon*, general editor D.E.R. Watt, 9 vols (Aberdeen/Edinburgh, 1987–98). Readers daunted by eight volumes of text will be gratified with the 'condensed' version: Walter Bower, *A History Book for Scots: Selections from Scotichronicon*, ed. D.E.R. Watt (Edinburgh, 1998).

61 D. Broun, review of *Scotichronicon*, vol. 4, *SHR* 77 (1998), 104–5.

62 *Kings, Clerics and Chronicles in Scotland 500–1297: Essays in Honour of Marjorie Ogilvie Anderson on the Occasion of Her Ninetieth Birthday*, ed. S. Taylor (Dublin, 2000); see also S. Boardman, 'Chronicle Propaganda in Fourteenth-Century Scotland: Robert the Steward, John of Fordun, and the "Anonymous Chronicle,"' *SHR* 76 (1997), 23–43. See also the works of B.T. Hudson cited in note 37 above.

63 A.D.M. Barrell, *Medieval Scotland* (Cambridge, 2000); Webster's book, *Medieval Scotland: The Making of an Identity*, cited in note 33 above, covers much more ground than the title would suggest, and might also be considered a one-volume history.

64 This volume adopts the terminology of the *SHR*, which regards the medieval period as running to 1560.

65 See the works cited in note 37 above, as well as *The Prophecy of Ber-*

chán: Irish and Scottish High-Kings of the Early Middle Ages (Westport, CT, and London, 1996) and Kings of Celtic Scotland (Westport and London, 1994).

66 See, for example, R. Fletcher, The Conversion of Europe: From Paganism to Christianity 371–1386 A.D. (London, 1997); and P. Brown, The Rise of Western Christendom: Triumph and Diversity A.D. 200–1000, The Making of Europe (Oxford and Malden, MA, 1996).

67 Note especially the comments of D.P. Kirby in his review of A.A.M. Duncan's Scotland: The Making of the Kingdom in English Historical Review 91 (1976), 837–8: 'a preoccupation with the early unity of Scotland and its subsequent strength and (by 1286) "harmony" is perhaps misplaced' (838).

68 See, inter alia, K.J. Stringer, 'Periphery and Core in Thirteenth-Century Scotland: Alan Son of Roland, Lord of Galloway and Constable of Scotland,' in Medieval Scotland, ed. Grant and Stringer, 82–113; A. Grant, 'The Province of Ross and the Kingdom of Alba,' and R.A. McDonald, 'Rebels without a Cause? The Relations of Fergus of Galloway and Somerled of Argyll with the Scottish Kings, 1153–1164,' both in Alba: Celtic Scotland in the Medieval Era, 88–126, 166–86.

69 E.J. Cowan, 'Myth and Identity in Early Medieval Scotland,' SHR 63 (1984), 111–35.

70 R.J. Goldstein, The Matter of Scotland: Historical Narrative in Medieval Scotland (Lincoln, NE, 1993), chapters 2–3.

71 The History of Scottish Literature. Volume 1: Origins to 1660 (Mediaeval and Renaissance), ed. R.D.S. Jack, 4 vols (Aberdeen, 1988), 32.

72 Much has been published on Wallace since Mel Gibson's movie Braveheart, but the best modern study remains A. Fisher, William Wallace (Edinburgh, 1986).

73 See, for example, B. Anderson, Imagined Communities: Reflections on the Origins and Spread of Nationalism (London and New York, 1991); A. Hastings, The Construction of Nationhood (Cambridge, 1997); Medieval Europeans: Studies in Ethnic Identity and National Perspective, ed. A.P. Smyth (New York, 1998).

74 See History of Scottish Literature, ed. Jack, especially chapter 5; and P. Bawcutt, Dunbar the Makar (Oxford, 1992).

75 M. Bakhtin, Rabelais and His World, trans. H. Iswolsky (Bloomington, 1984; first pub. Moscow, 1965).

76 P. Bawcutt, 'The Art of Flyting,' SLJ 10/2 (1983), 5–24.

77 For example: Medieval Queenship, ed. J.C. Parsons (New York, 1993); Women and Sovereignty, ed. L.O. Fradenburg (Edinburgh, 1992); and

Queens and Queenship in Medieval Europe, ed. A.J. Duggan (Woodbridge, 1997).

78 A seminal study of the source materials for Scottish history is B. Webster, *Scotland from the Eleventh Century to 1603*, The Sources of History: Studies in the Uses of Historical Evidence (Ithaca, 1975).

79 Devine, 'Whither Scottish History? Preface,' 3.

80 Cowan, 'Invention of Celtic Scotland,' 23.

1

The Scottish Gaze

BENJAMIN T. HUDSON

Much has been written on Scottish history in the Middle Ages from different viewpoints. English, Irish, and Scandinavian records have all been surveyed for their remembrances, a search outwith the kingdom so intense that a landmark of Scottish historiography is titled *Scottish Annals from English Chroniclers*.[1] As revealing as those foreign views can be, equally informative is a survey of the writing of history by the Scots, not only for events in their own lands, but also those of their neighbours. For a long time there had been little attention given to, or interest in, the writing of history among the Scots prior to the Anglo-Scottish conflicts. More recently, the identification of those works either composed in the domain of the Scots king, or by a Gaelic-speaker from northern Britain, now allows for some comment on how the Scots viewed their own affairs and those of their neighbours.[2] Those writings provide a perspective of insular history from the Scots' point of view as it changed through the centuries, beginning with a western orientation in the early Middle Ages that later became a more broadly encompassing view as it extended to the east and south. As expected, in keeping with their time and place, the early Scottish records are most interested in the great princes, the local aristocracy, and the Church. The divide between history and literature was unknown, however, to these writers, and an important aspect is the literary flavour found in even unimaginative works such as king lists, where traces of oral storytelling or verse-making still can be seen.

There was a tradition of scholarly writing among the Gaelic speakers of northern Britain for centuries before the movement eastward into the lands of the Picts. Even while the Scots were con-

The Scottish Gaze

DÁL RIATA

Shetland

Orkney

Applecross

PICTLAND

Dunnottar

Hebrides

Dunkeld

Scone

Iona

St. Andrews

STRATHCLYDE

North Channel

NORTHERN
UÍ NÉILL

ULAID

NORTHUMBRIA

CONNAUGHT

Armagh

SOUTHERN
UÍ NÉILL

Monasterboice

Man

Ripon

York

Kells

Clontarf

Dublin

LEINSTER
Osraige

MUNSTER

EAST
ANGLIA

WESSEX

fined to the territory of Dál Riata, along the western seaboard, the writings produced at the monastery of Iona, or by former members of the *familia*, exhibit the larger world-view that would be one of the characteristics of later Scottish histories.[3] If the memories of its founder, Columba, or Colum Cille ('Dove of the Church,' d. 597), are accurate, then writing and scholarship were aspects of the Iona community during his lifetime in the sixth century. This is hardly unexpected. Not only was the monastery founded by an exile, but there were a variety of cultures represented there: Irish, Pictish, and British (or Welsh). Yet for a community located at the very edge of Europe, the breadth of its horizon was wide indeed. For history, into which category can be placed saintly biography (so far as medieval writers were concerned), there was a beginning at least by the seventh century in the *vita* or *Life* of Columba of Iona written by a Cummène the White, from whose work an excerpt was included in Adomnán's *vita* of the saint, warning of the perils of Dál Riatan attacks on the northern Irish dynasty of Uí Néill (O'Neills).[4] Abbot Adomnán also wrote a geographical guide to the Holy Land using information supplied, at least in part, according to his testimony, by a visitor named Arculf, who was from Gaul.[5] For a curious cleric, a survey of the places so familiar from a reading of the Bible is not surprising. There was, however, a deliberation to Adomnán's interest in the wider European world, as is evident from his work on Columba, which mentions news brought to Iona by a ship which had sailed to Dál Riata from Gaul.[6]

Sometimes the search goes even farther afield, as material collected in one place is incorporated into a composition from another area. In the second half of the eighth century, another abbot of Iona, named Sléibne (d. 767), visited the church at Ripon, where he discovered (so he thought) the date of the *adventu* of the Saxons into Britain.[7] His information was used as a source by at least one writer outside northern Britain, and it seems appropriate that the unique source of this piece of information is an aside in a copy of Nennius's *History of Britain* preserved at Chartres.[8] There might have been a greater longevity to his work than the Chartres manuscript suggests. John of Fordun, writing in the fourteenth century, gives a specific date for the arrival of the Saxons, which he places among the events of the Dál Riatan prince Eochaid, son of Fergus.[9] His information might reflect knowledge of Sléibne's historical work, either from the Chartres text or a now-missing manuscript. A world geography by a ninth-century monk named Dícuill was written on the Continent (where he was probably a teacher in the palace school of the Frankish king Louis the Pious, d. 840) in 825, but he had begun to collect his materials while residing in the isles to the north of Ireland and Britain, most likely in the Hebrides.[10] He records the Irish presence in the Faroes and Iceland in the eighth century, and Dícuill also mentions the early movement into the west of the Vikings.[11] Although the chronology of his life is uncertain, it is very possible that Dícuill's residence in the northern islands was as a monk on Iona, since he mentions his teacher, Suibne, who might have been Abbot Suibne II (d. 772).[12]

Remaining in Dál Riata, but less certainly at Iona, are some pieces which show a more local interest. Sometime in the eighth century was produced a tract now known as the *History of the Men of Britain (Senchus Fer nAlban)*.[13] This was a genealogy of the clans of Dál Riata, to which was appended a naval muster roll, giving the details of the contribution which each of the main kindreds would supply when required for an expedition. The materials were reworked later, probably in the tenth century. There was also a chronicle maintained, probably at either Iona or Applecross, that concluded in the middle of the eighth century.[14] This chronicle was responsible for the entries of Scottish interest that are so prominent in the surviving Irish annals.

By the ninth century, however, the *scriptoria* situated along the coasts of Ireland and Britain were being raided by the Vikings. This led to a relocation of many of the communities. The raids of the late eighth and early ninth centuries were devastating for Iona. Before the end of the first quarter of the ninth century, the leadership of the Columban community was divided between Ireland and Britain. Whether or not this division and movement had been planned before the Vikings, or was caused by them, leadership of the Columban houses in Ireland was transferred to Kells, while that of Britain was moved to a church in the centre of northern Britain, at Dunkeld. This followed the military success of its patrons from Dál Riata, the royal dynasty of Cenél nGabráin, as they moved eastward.[15]

Scottish Historical Writing

Those early records were written by individuals who did not consider themselves to be Scots, as the term would later be understood,

but Irish residing in Britain. They were merely geographically
remote from Ireland, but not intellectually and culturally. The conflicts and emigrations beginning in the mid-eighth century that led
to the creation of Scoto-Pictish kingdoms by the ninth century cul-
minated in the ascendancy of the dynasty of Kenneth I (Cináed mac
Alpín, d. 858) south of the Highlands in mid-century. After the
expansion of the Scots domain from the Hebrides to the North Sea,
writings from this new state began to appear, although the question
of an emerging Scottish consciousness is difficult to resolve for this
period.[16] There appears to have been the continued maintenance of
records in northern Britain, which were incorporated in Irish chronicles. This is suggested by an entry in the *Annals of Ulster* for the
year 871, describing the return of the Viking chieftains Olaf and
Ivar from their raids in Britain back to Ireland with boatloads of
captives.[17] The information is given in two languages, the first part
in Irish and the second in Latin:

> Amlaiph ⁊ Imar do thuidecht afrithisi du Ath Cliath a Albain dibh
> cetaib long et preda maxima hominum Anglorum et Britonum et Pic-
> torum deducta est secum ad Hiberniam in captiuitate
>
> [Olaf and Ivar returned to Dublin from Britain with two hundred
> ships, and a great prey of English, Welsh, and Picts were led by them to
> Ireland in bondage.]

The Latin section is worth a closer look, especially the phrase *ad
Hiberniam*. This type of prepositional phrase (*ad* with the accusa-
tive signifying destination), it has been argued, shows composition
outside Ireland.[18] The construction of the Latin part of the entry
indicates a view that looked from northern Britain to Ireland, with
its specific identification of three of the five population groups in
the north and by the need to specify where the captives were led.
An Irishman would immediately know that Dublin was in Ireland,
but not necessarily someone living outside the island.

At this time, works of obvious Scottish provenance begin to
make their appearance. Three records are particularly informative:
the 'Scottish Chronicle,' a contemporary record from the mid-ninth
to the late tenth century; a tenth-century poem on western European kings in the 'Versified Psalter' (*Saltair na Rann*); and the
history of the great lords of Ireland and Scotland known as the

Prophecy of Berchán. The first of the trio takes us back to Dunkeld, the head of the Columban houses in Britain by the mid-ninth century. This record of early Scottish affairs known as the 'Scottish Chronicle' was written in Latin, with a few Gaelic words and phrases, and it was begun at Dunkeld probably about 849; the exemplar of the extant version was taken to St Andrews in the mid-tenth century.[19] The chronicle begins during the reign of Kenneth I in Pictavia (842–58) and abruptly ends, c. 973, during the reign of Kenneth II (Cináed mac Máel Choluim, 971–95). The existing copy seems to be missing material that appeared in the original, and a particularly important lacuna is for the period from c. 866 to 874. The other two works were written in the vernacular of the Scots, that is, Middle Irish. The 'Versified Psalter' is a lengthy retelling of biblical history, and it has a particular interest for students of apocalyptic thought with its section on the signs preceding the Last Judgment.[20] Within the 'Psalter' is a poem whose verses on contemporary princes seem to have been composed sometime in the last quarter of the tenth century; chronological information in this section dates its composition to about the year 988.[21] The survey of kings begins with Kenneth II and then gives the names of powerful lords in Ireland, the kings of the English and Western Franks, the Emperor, and *comarba* or 'heir' of Saint Patrick, before ending with the king of Strathclyde, Malcolm son of Dyfnal (975–94). The last of the three texts, and one especially useful for this topic, is the *Prophecy of Berchán*, a verse history of the powerful lords among the Irish and Scots from the ninth to the eleventh century.[22] This survives more or less completely in about 206 stanzas, although the obscurity of language has made interpretation difficult.

The Scottish material might have been consulted by more people than just the Scots. In addition to speculation prompted by the curious phrasing of the entry about the return of the Vikings to Dublin in the year 871, a comparison of the Irish *Annals of Ulster* with the 'Scottish Chronicle' is worthwhile. There are indications that the secular Scottish information in the Irish record comes from the same manuscript tradition as the 'Scottish Chronicle.' With the exception of the period 866 to 874, which is discussed below, from the reign of Kenneth I to the conclusion of the chronicle c. 973, every secular Scottish event noted in the Irish record is also found, usually in more detail, in the 'Scottish Chronicle.' When comparison is made of the basic information in the *Annals of Ulster*, the

'Scottish Chronicle' has details of geography that illustrate the usefulness of a local record. For the year 875 the *Annals of Ulster*, incorporating what has been described as an 'Irish World Chronicle,' note merely a slaughter of the Picts by the Vikings. Not until we turn to the 'Scottish Chronicle' is there found the additional information that this slaughter reached as far as Atholl, that is, into the very heart of the new Scoto-Pictish kingdom. There is also material in the 'Scottish Chronicle' that is absent from the Irish annals, such as the list of St Andrews's bishops. In the occasional instance when the *Annals of Ulster* appear to be more informative, this might be due to Irish informants. For example, in 918 the Scots fought a Viking army in Northumbria. The 'Scottish Chronicle' gives only the announcement of the battle, while the *Annals of Ulster* have an unusually detailed description of the arrangement of the Viking forces. These same Vikings were, however, also active in Ireland, and they could well have been the ultimate source of information; in contrast, the Scottish dispositions pass by unremarked.

How to explain the Scottish information in the *Annals of Ulster* that is absent from the 'Scottish Chronicle'? The lacuna in the extant copy of the 'Scottish Chronicle' for the years 866 to 874 is the reason why it has no mention of the Viking attack of 870–1 or the death of Arthgal of Strathclyde at the hands of the Scots king in 872, both found in the *Annals of Ulster*. Other omissions, such as the absence of the obit for Abbot Tuathal of Dunkeld (865) and the death of Cellach of Kildare among the Picts in 865, could be explained by the manuscript tradition of the extant version of the 'Scottish Chronicle.' An ancestor of this chronicle was at St Andrews c. 966, and the missing information could have been discarded during a subsequent recopying. A copyist at St Andrews need not have been interested in the affairs of other religious houses, especially if they had claims on the affections of royal patrons.

Literary contact between Irish and Scottish *scriptoria* is shown by the drowning of the *fer léighinn* (lit. 'man of reading'; i.e., the head of the monastic school) of Kells named Macnía Ua hUctáin, together with thirty associates, during his return from Scotland to Ireland in 1034. Another possible avenue for transmission of Scottish materials into Ireland is Armagh. The author of the mid-eleventh-century version of the *Prophecy of Berchán* is not known certainly, but a likely candidate is one Dubthach *Albanach* (Dubthach the Scotsman), who was a teacher at Armagh and died in 1065.[23] Dubthach was a long-serving member of the community who had some fame in his own lifetime because of his teaching of the Old Testament. A Scottish author resident and writing in Ireland would explain why the poem survives in Irish manuscripts but not, except for some lines in Manus O'Donnell's *Life of Columba*, in manuscripts preserved in Scotland.

The influence of Scottish writings or writers need not have been solely outside Britain. Looking within the Scottish kingdom, it is clear that the composer of the *Prophecy of Berchán* used some chronicle record among his sources. The record that it most closely follows is the 'Scottish Chronicle.'[24] After the 'Scottish Chronicle' or its exemplar ended, the *Berchán* poet could have relied on personal recollection or the accounts of eyewitnesses. The specific geographical information in the *Prophecy of Berchán*, especially the list of places where kings were slain or buried, suggests that the poet had visited these sites. All of them are south of the Grampians and easily accessible to a traveller.

The Scots could be as self-obsessed as any of their neighbours, and as narrowly provincial in their outlook. For example, in its ninth-century section the 'Scottish Chronicle' is concerned primarily with affairs in the middle regions of the early Scottish kingdom, basically the area around Perthshire.[25] Even when looking beyond the kingdom, a Scottish interest often is the reason, such as its report of the raids of Kenneth II into northwestern England. Sometimes this very inward look reveals the perception of the author. The poem on the kings embedded in the 'Versified Psalter' not only begins its survey with Kenneth II, but he is described at length in words of fulsome praise, unlike, with one exception, the other monarchs. Among his successes, he is credited with the rule of half of Ireland.[26] The above-mentioned exception, which confirms, as it were, the orientation of its maker, is the king of Strathclyde, Malcolm son of Dyfnal, with whom the kingly section concludes with an equally fulsome panegyric.[27] The relatively brusque recitation of monarchs such as the English or Frankish kings reinforces the poem's orientation.

The early Scottish monarchs were closely tied to Ireland through marriage and culture, which is reflected in Scottish writings. The expansion of the Scots into the lands of the Picts extended a Gaelophone language and cultural region that now began in southwestern

Ireland and ended at the North Sea.[28] Thus the 'Scottish Chronicle'
lists the death of the Irish high-kings Máel Sechnaill I (Malachy I, d.
862), Áed *Findlíath* (Aed 'the handsome warrior') mac Néill (d. 879),
Flann *Sinna* (Flann 'of the [river] Shannon') mac Máel Shechnaill (d.
916), and Niall *Glúndub* (Niall 'black knee') mac Áeda (d. 919),
together with obits for Cormac mac Cuilennáin (the famous scholar
cum cleric *cum* king, who was slain in 908), as well as Áed's son
Donald (Domnall mac Áeda, d. 915), the king of Ailech and half-
brother of Niall *Glúndub*. With the exception of Cormac, those
princes are all from the powerful northern Irish Uí Néill confedera-
tion. The family of Kenneth I had marriage connections with them,
through his daughter Máel Muire (d. 913).[29] The strength of this
bond did fade, however, and the decay of the Uí Néill supremacy a
century later is first visible in the verses on the kings in the 'Versified Psalter.' The list includes the Irish princes Brian of Munster,
Domnall of Leinster, and Cathal of Connacht in addition to the
minor Uí Néill lord Fergal of Ailech. Astonishing is the omission of
Máel Sechnaill II of the southern Uí Néill, who not only was a
descendant of Máel Muire, but also at that time was recognized as
the Irish high-king.

The outward look was not entirely to the west, but continued to
follow the interests of the Scots. One direction was to the south.
Beginning in the tenth century, the 'Scottish Chronicle' looks at
English and Strathclyde events, including the death of Donald, king
of Strathclyde, and later the English king Æthelstan (924–39). The
increasing power of the dynasty of Wessex, in the person of Æthel-
stan and his family, led to their challenge to the supremacy of the
Scottish lords in northern Britain. By the end of the tenth century,
Scottish interest was turning in another direction, east to the Con-
tinent. This eastward orientation is reflected in the poem on the
kings in the 'Versified Psalter,' with its inclusion of the English king
Edgar, the emperor Otto, and Lothair, king of the western Franks.
Continental houses were the destination of Scottish clergy such as
Catroë, who left the Scots domain during the reign of Constantine II
(Causantín mac Áeda, d. 952) to go first to Metz and then to Waul-
sorts.[30] As pure speculation, it might be considered that there was
an economic aspect to the orientation of the Scottish records. The
flight of the future Danish king Svein 'Forkbeard' Haraldsson to the
protection of the Scots during his exile might have been following a
trade route between Denmark and Scotland.[31]

Such interest did not flow in only one direction. By the early eleventh century, Frankish writers were turning their attentions to northern Britain. The Cluniac historian Radulf Glaber described the battles between Malcolm II (Máel Coluim mac Cináeda, 1005–34) and Cnut the Great (1016–35), king of the Danes and English, the son of Svein 'Forkbeard.' He described Malcolm in glowing terms, in contrast with his reservations about Cnut.[32] Malcolm is a great warrior and truly Christian king, while Cnut engages in barbarous behaviour and has to be persuaded to live in peace with his neighbour. Radulf's informant about Malcolm might have been responsible for the brief story about Brendan the navigator, who, in this version, becomes an Englishman from East Anglia. Writing slightly later, the Norman historian William of Jumièges preserved accounts of the lord of the Hebrides, named Lagman, who aided Duke Robert II in his fight against Count Otto of Chartres; William claims that one of Lagman's brothers-in-arms was the future Saint Olaf of Norway.[33]

The *Prophecy of Berchán* is especially illuminating when investigating the Scots historical view. The poem's verses fall into three sections: Irish, hagiographical, and Scots. The original 'prophecy' was a poem on the coming of the Vikings to Ireland that was composed in the mid-ninth century by a Scots émigré named Berchán mac Muiredaich, who was a dynast of the northern Scots clan of Cenél Loairn (kindred of Loarn). The poem was popular, and, as part of the pseudonym tradition found among the Gaels, an eleventh-century Scottish continuator was inspired to append to it a lengthy summary of the great lords among the Irish and the Scots from the mid-ninth century to his own day. Later that same century, an Irish writer added a final brief continuation on the Scots kings. The Irish and Scots sections were linked together by stanzas on three saints prominent in both Ireland and Britain: Patrick, Brigit, and Columba.

The use of an earlier poem as the inspiration for a later reviser or continuator was not limited to the *Prophecy of Berchán*. There is the example of the verse history known as 'The Phantom's Frenzy' (*Baile in Scáil*). This poem is contemporary with the eleventh-century section of the *Prophecy of Berchán*, and it was composed by the *comarba* (hereditary abbot) of Armagh named Dub-dá-Leithe (d. 1064). 'The Phantom's Frenzy' is a pseudo-prophecy of the supreme kings of Ireland from prehistory to the eleventh century, who are identified by a sobriquet (illuminated by glossed proper names).[34] The model for it is an earlier poem called 'Conn's Vision' (*Baile Chuind*) composed in the seventh century.[35] There is a distant possibility that either the *Prophecy of Berchán* or the 'Phantom's Frenzy' inspired the production of the other, for at Armagh an exact contemporary of Dub-dá-Leithe was Dubthach 'the Scotsman,' who has been put forward as a candidate for the authorship of the eleventh-century stratum of the prophecy.

The piecemeal method of composition found for the *Prophecy of Berchán* was not rare, and composite poems are found in Irish and Scottish contexts. For example, a so-called prophecy attributed to Bécc mac Dé was originally composed in the eleventh century, and then brought up-to-date with additional verses in the twelfth century.[36] A verse from this poem is later found embedded among stanzas from the *Prophecy of Berchán*, illustrating the longevity and mobility of isolated quatrains.[37] The addition of a verse or verses to a poem is also visible in the metrical list of Scots kings from the legendary past to Malcolm III (Máel Coluim mac Donnchada, d. 1093) known as the 'Scottish Poem' (*Duan Albanach*) or, from its initial words, *A éolcha Alban uile* (O you learned ones of all Alba).[38] The poem was composed in Scotland, probably for the court of Malcolm III. The original verses ended with a *dúnad* (conclusion) that was a witty play on the opening words, closing with the statement that the only one who knew the duration of the currently reigning monarch (Malcolm III) was *an t-Éolach as éolach* (the Learned One who is learned [i.e., God]). The *dúnad* was required in Gaelic poetry, and this type is called *saigid* (attainment); it repeats the opening word(s) and was thought to be the best form. At some point the 'Scottish Poem' was taken to Ireland, where were added two explanatory statements, one in a prose preface and the other in a verse placed after the last stanza of the original poem. This postscript verse was supplied with its own *dúnad*, which has led earlier scholars to the erroneous conclusion that the poem was composed in Ireland. So both the 'Scottish Poem' and the *Prophecy of Berchán* provide illustrations of, for the former, multiple conclusions indicating the later addition of explanatory information and, for the latter, stray verses that became attached to the poem. This type of enlargement continued in Scottish writings, even as Scots Gaelic began to assume some distinctions from Irish Gaelic. For example, in the sixteenth-century Scots Gaelic manuscript known as the *Book of the Dean of Lismore*, a ballad concerning the band of

Irish warrior heroes called the Fian at Eas Ruaidh (Assaroe, co. Donegal) has five stanzas not found in earlier copies, and one of those stanzas is found only in Scottish copies.[39] Those verses add nothing to the plot and they have been described as elaborative, which shows the development of the poem during the period in which the *Book of the Dean of Lismore* was being written.[40]

Some of the difficulties in writing history during the eleventh century are visible in the *Prophecy of Berchán*. The earlier Irish section exhibits some confusion in the arrangement of its information that lessens as events become closer to the lifetime of the writer. For example, not only do the verses about the ninth-century Munster prince Fedelmid mac Crimtháinn (Felim son of Crimthann) incorrectly follow the verses for the early tenth-century Uí Néill prince Niall *Glúndub*, but the verses for Niall's grandson Domnall ua Néill (Donald grandson of Niall) come before those for his predecessors Ruaidrí ua Canannáin (Rory grandson of Canannan) and Congalach mac Máel Mithig (Congalach son of Máel Mithig).[41] Only by the end of the tenth century does the chronology match the prince in the Irish section. Unlike the Scottish verses, there is an obscurity to the Irish material in *The Prophecy of Berchán* that seems to be deliberate and reflects the fact that the poet was not well informed, as he was for the Scottish material.

This problem of chronological confusion was not limited to the *Berchán* poet. Other insular writers looking backwards over several centuries faced similar, if not identical, difficulties. An example is provided by the 'Scottish Poem' (*Duan Albanach*), which for the ninth century and earlier includes in its list of the lords of Dál Riata several individuals who probably were not, such as Conall son of Tadc, who was slain in 807 in Kintyre, and omits others who were ruling, such as Fergus son of Eochaid, who died in 781 and is described as king of Dál Riata in the contemporary chronicle embedded in the *Annals of Ulster*. Similarly, Irish texts could confuse Scottish events, such as the 'synchronisms' of kings in Ireland and Scotland often attributed to Flann of Monasterboice.[42] Once again, there is confusion in the eighth- and ninth-century sections, very similar to that in the 'Scottish Poem.' Even for Irish events, works written in Ireland such as 'The Victorious Career of Cellachan of Cashel' (*Caithréim Cellacháin Caisil*) illustrate how badly a twelfth-century writer could confuse tenth-century events.[43] The author often appears to be plucking names from pedigrees to provide individual characters for his saga, regardless of their actual generation.

A useful comparison can be made with the *Prophecy of Berchán's* information for two princes: the Irish high-king Áed *Findlíath* (862–79) and his contemporary and brother-in-law the Scots monarch Constantine I (Causantín mac Cináeda, 862–76), the son of Kenneth I. The verses on Áed correctly identify his dynasty of Ailech but give the erroneous information that his mother died in childbirth. She did not die then (she died in 861), and survived long enough to see her grandchildren grow to adulthood. Beside this slight error, the poem provides an interesting view of important Irish events, as, for example, the battle of Killineer, fought in 868. The *Prophecy of Berchán* claims that Áed fought against the Leinstermen near the Boyne. The Uí Néill–dominated *Annals of Ulster* present this more as a family feud, between Áed and his nephew Flann mac Conaing of Brega, who merely had some Leinster and Viking allies. In short, the *Prophecy of Berchán* is suggesting that there was more of a threat to Áed's kingship than the Irish record implies.

The somewhat vague information for Áed can be contrasted with that for Constantine. He is described as the herdsman of the cattle of the Picts (a poetic way of saying that he collected his taxes in the form of cattle), his death is placed precisely at Inverdovat in Fife, and four major battles are listed for his reign. Three battles were against the Vikings, all of which are noted in the annals, and the fourth battle was fought against King Arthgal of Strathclyde at a place named Cathluares, which we know from the *Life of Kentigern* by Jocelin of Furness to be the former name of Glasgow. The defeat for Arthgal revealed in the *Prophecy of Berchán* explains the notice in the *Annals of Ulster* that he was slain *a consilio* (by the advice) of Constantine.[44]

The Scottish View of Irish History

Notwithstanding some confusion on details, when turning to Irish history it is possible to estimate how useful the Scottish gaze can be. In Ireland, as everywhere else, there was a tendency on the part of medieval writers to refashion historical materials in order to reflect contemporary concerns. There had long been an attempt by the Irish clergy to promote the idea of a king of all Ireland, for which they could have found evidence in older traditions. Various

kings of the prehistorical period were claimed to have ruled the
entire island, and occasionally their rule was extended to Britain as
well.[45] In the records of the seventh and eighth centuries there is
evidence of how the clergy were considering the theory of a
supreme ruler in Ireland. Various princes are styled 'king of Ireland,'
and a single monarchy is implied by writers such as Adomnán in
his *Life of Columba* and by the anonymous eighth-century author
of the historical prophecy 'Conn's Frenzy,' the model for the later
'Phantom's Frenzy.'

The process of revisionism among the Irish was visible by the
ninth century, when details of earlier history were being arranged to
reflect dynastic interests. Máel Muru of Otháin (d. 887) compiled a
list of the great lords up to the time of his contemporary, the high-
king Fland *Sinna*, that presents the Uí Néill as supreme in Ireland.[46]
There are also indications that during the ninth century, 'Conn's
Frenzy' was reworked in the interests of specific princely families
of the Uí Néill. The process was completed with the appearance of
the 'Phantom's Frenzy,' in which the information was revised once
again, by Dub-dá-Leithe, so that the Uí Néill princes appear almost
exclusively as the Irish overlords during the historical period.[47]

On the subject of political supremacy in Ireland, the Scottish historical writings often find themselves in agreement with modern
scholarship rather than with medieval Irish records. In the mid-
ninth century there are what might be described as the beginnings
of a national overlordship in the person of Máel Sechnaill I mac
Máel Ruanaid (Malachy I). He is the first of the great princes in Berchán's verses, where he is described as the 'speckled,' while in the
'Scottish Chronicle' he is styled 'king of the Irish.'[48] He used the
turmoil caused by the ravages of the Vikings to take hostages from
the other provinces, and in the conservative *Annals of Ulster*, Máel
Sechnaill is awarded the title of 'king of all Ireland.' The truth of
this is shown in his reordering of the political landscape of Ireland
at the council of Rahugh (co. Meath) in 859, when the sub-province
of Osraige was removed from the southern sphere of influence and
attached to Máel Sechnaill's orb, the northern part of Ireland. At the
same time, implications of primacy became attached to the ceremonial site of Tara, and already in 840 the Munster prince Fedelmid
mac Crimtháinn camped there in pursuit of his claims to be recognized as high-king.

The title of supremacy in Ireland seems to have been a nebulous thing during the later ninth and tenth centuries, and the usefulness of an outsider's viewpoint is illustrated by the 'Scottish Chronicle.' This record does not begin the reign of Máel Sechnaill's successor Áed *Findlíath* until about 864, two years after Máel Sechnaill's death, revealing that Aed had to devote some time to gathering support for his claims of supremacy. This confirms the contemporary information in the *Annals of Ulster*, and demonstrates the error of later Irish histories of the eleventh century that begin Áed's recognition as supreme lord of Ireland immediately upon Máel Sechnaill's death.

In many respects who is considered the Irish high-king at any particular time depends on who was doing the writing. While the *Prophecy of Berchán* and the Munster texts claim that Fedelmid of Munster, identified as 'the great ram' in *Berchán*, was a high-king of Ireland before his death in 847, the records maintained in the north, such as the *Annals of Ulster*, do not. Even among the northern princes there seems to have been some controversy about supremacy. The Cenél Conaill dynast Ruaidrí Ua Canannáin is included among the kings of Ireland in the *Prophecy of Berchán* and in the Munster tract *Cocad Gáedel re Gallaib*, but not in the later king lists of Flann of Monasterboice (see below) or those found in the *Book of Leinster*.[49]

Revisionism was not limited to one dynasty, and by the eleventh century a southern reworking of history was being made in the interests of the Uí Briain (O'Briens) of Dál Cais, the dynasty of Brian mac Cennétig, who was high-king from 1002 to 1014. Their rise to supremacy in the province of Munster was followed by a successful effort to usurp the Uí Néill lords as high-kings in the eleventh century. The Uí Briain writers used verse to give dignity and authenticity to prose pieces, such as the 'War of the Irish against the Vikings' (*Cocad Gáedel re Gallaib*). That was ostensively a history of the Viking wars in Ireland, which was compiled from older tracts and elaborated/reworked in the late eleventh century as a history of Brian mac Cennétig or Brian *bórumha* ('Brian of the cattle tribute'), who became successively king of Munster and high-king of Ireland. There is particular interest here for students of Scots literature, because the earliest manuscript verses for the *Prophecy of Berchán* are found in the *Book of Leinster*'s version of the 'War of the Irish against the Vikings,' describing the arrival of the Vikings in Ireland.

Possibly the most influential of the eleventh-century verse historians was the head of the monastic school of the church of Monasterboice, who is known as Flann *Mainistrech* (Flann of Monasterboice, d. 1056), a contemporary of both Dub-dá-Leithe and Dubthach of Armagh. Flann composed poems on kings of individual Irish dynasties and titular high-kings, and he has been credited with the authorship of synchronisms of the powerful princes among the Irish and Scots, an ancient form of establishing some chronological order. Today his best-known works are the seven poems he wrote on the Uí Néill dynasties of Cenél nEógain, Clann Cholmáin, and Síl nÁeda Sláine, which have information that is also found in the *Prophecy of Berchán*.[50] During the Middle Ages, possibly the most influential of his writings was the poem 'The Kings of (Many-)sided Tara' (*Ríg Themra tóebaige*), written between 1014 and 1022, which gives a list of the high-kings of Ireland.[51] In those verses the overlordship of Ireland is credited almost entirely to the Uí Néill princes, with only the occasional 'intruder' from outside the dynasty. The second king in the recitation is Ailill Molt mac Nath Í of Uí Fiachrach of Connacht, at the edges of the historical period, and the penultimate monarch is from Flann's lifetime, Brian mac Cennétig of Dál Cais of Munster. This is a reflection of the tendency to 'tidy up' history on the part of eleventh-century Irish historians. Flann was not alone, as Dub-dá-Leithe of Armagh shows, but his success can be measured by how he was imitated by the synthesizing historians later in the century and afterwards. His list would be expanded by Gilla Cóemáin mac Gilla Samthainne in his poem 'Here Is the Completion' (*Attá sund forba*.)[52] By the end of the century, this had become accepted historical memory, and it would be enshrined in the reworking of Irish history called *The Book of Invasions of Ireland* (*Lebor Gabála Érenn*), which was written in the mid-twelfth century.[53]

Thus the different selection of Irish kings given by the *Prophecy of Berchán* in comparison with those given by Flann and Dub-dá-Leithe has benefits for the historian. First, the *Prophecy of Berchán* does not have the dynastic myopia found in works by individuals who were the champions of a particular dynasty such as the Uí Néill, like Flann Mainistrech, whose monastery of Monasterboice (co. Louth) was within the lands of the southern Uí Néill dynasty of Síl nÁedo Sláine (descendants of Aed Slane), or Dub-dá-Leithe, whose church at Armagh either had within its precincts, or very nearby, a residence for the great lords of the northern Uí Néill dynasty of Cenél nEógain (kindred of Eogan). This prompts the question, is the *Prophecy of Berchán* based on unique information? For the Irish kings, the similarities in the material common to the works of the *Berchán* poet, Dub-dá-Leithe, and Flann suggest that they shared a source of information. Mac Neill suggested that Flann was following a chronicle cognate with the *Annals of Ulster*, and evidence of this can also be seen in the *Prophecy of Berchán*.[54] The *Berchán* poet also used materials with a southern orientation, which explains why Fedelmid and Cormac are included in the verses with details that are elsewhere found only in the Munster records. For example, only the *Prophecy of Berchán* and the *Annals of Inisfallen* insist that a Leinster princess was abducted by Fedelmid. After the death of Máel Sechnaill II in 1022, the *Prophecy of Berchán's* information bears little resemblance to any extant record, which suggests that personal knowledge supplied the information. In short, the *Berchán* poet does not seem to have had access to any substantially different information on Irish affairs than his contemporaries. So the *Prophecy of Berchán* gives some idea of how a similar body of information was being emphasized by Irish writers who had differing loyalties and, at the same time, how that history was viewed by those outside the control of the powerful Irish dynasties.

When other medieval historians from outside Ireland looked at Irish history, they echoed the *Prophecy of Berchán*. For example, while Fedelmid of Munster is omitted from the extant Irish king lists, he is included as one of the principal Irish high-kings by the twelfth-century historian Gerald of Wales in his *History and Topography of Ireland*, who uses his reign as a chronological marker.[55] There is also negative support, in a statement found in the king list in the *Book of Invasions*, that Fedelmid was not included in the list because he was not found in the northern records.[56] Cerball of Osraige is another ignored individual, and no record other than the *Prophecy of Berchán* includes him among the great princes of his day. But he had an international reputation not shared by his Uí Néill counterparts. His obit is included in the earliest version of the Welsh chronicle known as *Annales Cambriae*, and he is mentioned in a number of Scandinavian sagas as the premier Irish monarch of the ninth century.[57] Cerball's fame was also enduring, and the eleventh-century compilation of annals known as the *Fragmentary*

Annals, which contains an Osraige-oriented document, has a section on his career that can best be described as Cerball's saga.[58]

As has been suggested for the 'Scottish Chronicle,' this is not to deny that there was a self-serving motivation for the *Prophecy of Berchán,* in which many of the great lords who are mentioned, from Máel Sechnaill I to Máel Sechnaill II, had some connection with the Scots. Niall *Glúndub,* his grandson Domnall úa Néill (Donald the grandson of Niall), his great-grandson Máel Sechnaill II, and their cousin Congalach mac Máel Mithig were all descendants of the Scottish king Kenneth I, while the ninth-century monarchs Áed *Findlíath* and Fland *Sinna* were his sons-in-law. The ninth-century Vikings Olaf and Ivar had raided the Scots (as discussed earlier), while a Scottish mormaer named Domnall mac Eimhin had fought for Brian mac Cennétig at the battle of Clontarf. This leaves only Fedelmid mac Crimthainn, Cormac mac Cuilennáin, Ruaidrí Ua Canannáin, and Cerball mac Dúnlaigne among the Irish princes found in the *Prophecy of Berchán* with no known connection with the Scots. Rather than speculate idly, it could be suggested simply that they were better known than the surviving records would lead one to think, as has already been demonstrated for Fedelmid, Cerball, and Cormac.

The *Prophecy of Berchán,* then, provides material for speculation about patterns of Scottish interest that become visible when compared with other works of a Scottish provenance. The deaths of Máel Sechnaill I, Áed *Findlíath,* Óláfr, Cormac mac Cuilennáin, Fland *Sinna,* and Niall *Glúndub* are all given in the 'Scottish Chronicle'; there also might be a reference to Ruaidri Ua Canannáin's family in an obscure entry.[59] In the survey of contemporary rulers given in the kingly poem in the 'Versified Psalter' (*Saltair na Rann*) there is found Brian mac Cennétig, but not Mael Sechnaill II.

The struggle for supremacy among the great princes was a complex affair in Ireland, but the *Berchán* poet joins with Flann Mainistrech and Dub-dá-Leithe to present a model of the Irish political scheme in which powerful overlords completely dominated their subordinate princes and were recognized as high-kings. Unlike his Irish contemporaries, however, the *Berchán* poet is less inhibited and biased in his selection. Nonetheless, these writers see the high-kings as standing apart from other men, who are identified either by location – the Leinstermen – or simply as a group such as the Vikings. Scottish and Irish historical works both indicate that by the eleventh century the age of the small independent Gaelic king-doms had given way to the amalgamation of power in the hands of a few great dynasties who played out their contests on a larger stage.

The Historical Gaze

When turning to the history of the Scots as presented in the contemporary Scottish works, a slightly different view of history emerges. Fitness for the office appears to have been as important as lineage. This is a reflection of the position of the Scots as wanderers between two worlds – Gaelic and non-Gaelic – that was a relic of the bi-coastal situation of their kingdom on the western British coast in Dál Riata. Dál Riata had been a special case in the political scheme as early as the sixth century, and the importance of the 'convention' of Druim Cett in 575 was its attempt to place this geo-graphic anomaly within the structure of Irish political life. On the other side of the North Channel, in northern Britain, Dál Riata was merely one of several kingdoms competing for supremacy. In some of these kingdoms, the ruling dynasties were, as in Dál Riata, comparatively recent arrivals in Britain, such as the Angles, who established the kingdom of Northumbria. Older kingdoms were dis-appearing after conquest, such as the British kingdom of Gododdin, which was absorbed into Northumbria. Other kingdoms, such as Strathclyde, were survivals from the Roman domination of Britain that were still powerful. In this area of rapidly changing circum-stances, the status of Dál Riata would be determined by the ability of its princes.

How is this reflected in the outlook of Scottish writers from the ninth to eleventh century? One aspect is their working within a broad historical horizon, which became a trait of Scottish literature. The Scots seem to have adopted a widely encompassing view, which had been attempted on a small scale by eighth-century Irish writers, who marked it with allusion. To give one example, there is the political symbolism of ceremonial ale, an archaic indication of sovereignty among the Gaels and the Picts. An Old Irish (circa eighth-century) list of the realms in Ireland identifies them by their association with royal ales. That list is given a broader view with the addition of two kingdoms in Britain: Dál Riata and Angus, an important Pictish kingdom. In Dál Riata 'warriors performed great feats for the sake of the drinking,' while the Picts had 'ales red like wine.'[60] The *Berchán* poet uses the imagery of a ceremonial draught in connection with the reign of Constantine II, whose prosperous reign would include ale.

As illustrated earlier, this historical view that encompassed Ireland and Britain is a pronounced feature of the 'Scottish Chronicle,' the poem on the kings in the 'Versified Psalter,' and the *Prophecy of Berchán*. By the eleventh century, this broad view had come full circle back to Ireland, when some Irish writers began to adopt it, perhaps from the Scots. Toward the end of his life, Flann of Monasterboice composed a poem on world kingship called 'Make Easy for Me, O God from Heaven' (*Réidig dam a Dé do nim*), which might have been intended as a preface to his earlier Irish verses.[61] Although it is part of patristic learning, and little more than a list of the names of kings with the length of their reigns, the poem speaks volumes about the expansion of the bounds of interest on the part of Irish scholars of the early High Middle Ages.

Scottish writings also provide an indication of political theory. The Scots saw secular life dominated by kings, and the extant writings show that they were supporters of a strong monarchy/overlordship. There is no other way to read the *Prophecy of Berchán*, with its insistence on high-kings, without coming to this conclusion. The same idea of power is proposed by the poem on the kings in the 'Versified Psalter,' where Kenneth II is king of the Scots, and there is no mention of any Scottish prince such as the lord of Cenél Loairn. This tendency is visible earlier, in the ninth-century entries in the 'Scottish Chronicle.' Although the kings are not exclusively from the male line of Kenneth I, any outsiders are either connected with the family, as in the case of Eochaid ap Rhun, whose father was the king of Strathclyde and whose mother was a daughter of Kenneth, or they are brusquely dismissed, as in the case of his foster-father Giric (Giric mac Dúngail, d. c. 889).

The records argue that by the eleventh century the Scots writers were well aware of political developments elsewhere in Europe, as political theorists in England and the Empire were promoting the idea of a strong central monarchy emerging from political rivalries, whose princes were supplied by specific dynasties that had eliminated rivals, even from within their own ranks. This evolution had its supporters among the Gaels, and by the eleventh century the Scots were well on the path toward a single monarch when, from 1040 to 1054, Macbeth (Mac bethad mac Findláech, d. 1057) ruled alone, without a subordinate king under him. After the mid-eleventh century, Scottish historians essentially looked only to the ultimately victorious kindred of Cenél nGabráin and ignored all others, such as Cenél Loairn (the clan of the original Berchán and Macbeth), unless their princes also controlled Cenél nGabráin.

In his enumeration of the Scottish princes, as has been seen for the Irish lords, the *Berchán* poet is something of an original. While the Scots kings found there are mainly dynasts of Cenél nGabráin, several princes – Giric mac Dúngail and his brother Constantine – are from their northern rivals Cenél Loairn, and one prince – Eochaid ap Rhun – from Strathclyde. Two of those princes – Eochaid and Constantine – are so obscure that they are found elsewhere only in the 'Scottish Chronicle' (Eochaid) and a ninth-century king list embedded in a later compilation known as 'king-list L' (Constantine).[62] As occurred among the Irish historians, there was a 'tidying-up' of Scottish history. The recitation of the late ninth-century kings found in the *Prophecy of Berchán* or the 'Scottish Chronicle' stands in contrast with the Scottish king list produced for the court of Malcolm III, known as 'king-list B,' which omits Eochaid of Strathclyde and Giric's brother Constantine, a practice followed by subsequent lists and chroniclers, such as John of Fordun and Andrew of Wyntoun.[63]

Like their counterparts elsewhere in Europe, the Scottish writers used literature to complement history. The 'Scottish Chronicle' contains a synopsis of a now lost tale on the raid of Malcolm I (943–54) into Northumbria in 949, described as the 'raid of the white ridges.' The *Prophecy of Berchán* has a reference to the tale of the destruction of the Picts by Kenneth I, known as the 'Pitfall of Scone,' as well as a literary remembrance of the great famine of 965 in Ireland, 'when not everyone will sell, west and east, his son and daughter for food.'[64] The similarity with heroic tales is also found in the vocabulary. High status is announced in the *Prophecy of Berchán* by the use of adjectives other than 'king' (*rí*) or 'kingship' (*ríge*) to describe these princes. An example is the word *donn*, which can mean the colour 'brown,' but in these verses seems to stand regularly for its secondary meaning of 'lord,' 'chief,' or 'prince.' The *Prophecy of Berchán* also generously deploys adjectives from the poetic arsenal in describing these monarchs and their actions. Malcolm II 'leaps through battle' (*lém tre chath*), while Kenneth I 'will feed scald-crows' (*bíaidhfes baidhbh*), both terms signifying their willingness to trust to arms. The king of Fortriu, and cousin of Kenneth I, named Constantine son of Fergus (Causantín mac Fergusa, d. 820), is described as 'the red flame that will awaken war' (bidh lasair dercc dúisgfes cath).

The Berchán poet's identification of princes by the use of sobriquets was an established practice of insular writers, as shown for the Irish kings Áed Findlíath (Áed 'the handsome warrior') and Fland Sinna (Fland 'of the river Shannon'), or the king of Strathclyde named Owen 'the Bald' (Eugenius Calvus, d. 1016/18). Some of the names in the Prophecy of Berchán match those found in other sources. The 'furious/madman' (dasachtach) found among the Scottish monarchs is Donald II (Domnall mac Causantín, d. 900), who is identified as Domnall dasachtach in the synchronisms attributed to Flann Mainistrech. The king described as the adaltrach in the Irish section is the Clann Cholmáin dynast Máel Sechnaill II, who is called Máel Sechnaill adaltrach in other tracts. Sometimes the name of the king lends itself to the play on words of the poet. The mid-tenth-century king Ruaidrí Ua Canannáin is called simply ruaid, 'the red,' while his contemporary in Scotland, Dub mac Máel Choluim, is called simply dub, 'the black.' Occasionally the sobriquet appears to have been popular, but replaced. The late tenth-early eleventh-century Scottish king Kenneth III (Cináed mac Duib, d. 1005) is identified as donn, 'chief,' but in the later Scottish king lists he is known by the name of greimm, which translates as 'lordship' but also has the extended meaning 'chieftain.' Other Scottish works use such descriptions in connection with the princes, such as the 'Scottish Poem,' where the 'hero' is Constantine I, or the 'pure, wise' is Duncan I (1034–40).

There is also a conservative element in Scottish writing that is visible in language and action. The 'Scottish Chronicle,' for example, was being written as Old Irish gave way to Middle Irish, yet the Gaelic vocabulary looks back to the older forms of words.[65] The Berchán poet deliberately attempts to recreate an atmosphere that looks back to the heroic age, and the kings in the poem behave as princes from the sagas acted. The visible sign of their power is the holding of hostages or the enslavement of their enemies. The implication in the poem is that their kingdoms are small in area, and they are described in terms appropriate for the túath (people, kingdom). Any diplomacy is primitive and warlike, confined to kings travelling round their borders. These princes are warriors, and their fitness to reign is described in terms of sympathetic magic, such as plentiful food and abundant hospitality. The refrain *nos géba* (literally 'he will take her'; i.e., he will wed her), used in the *Prophecy of Berchán* to identify a new king, shows the sovereignty of the land personified as a woman, a relic of the pre-Christian idea of a king marrying the goddess of the kingdom. This is a customary refrain in literature, and the description of the inauguration of a king as *banais* (marriage) gives some indication of the pre-Christian ritual.[66]

Not all is archaism, however, and the importance of law and rights is emphasized. In the 'Scottish Chronicle' there are three references to laws, two times when laws are being proclaimed and once when the violation of divine law is given as an explanation for the overthrow of the Picts. Fascination with the law is seen in other Scottish situations. The annexation of the kingdom of Strathclyde by the Scots during the reign of Malcolm II meant that some legal differences had to be reconciled, so that the tract *Leges Brittos inter Scottos* was composed, which regularized the fines for crimes of violence between the Scots and the men of Strathclyde.[67] Malcolm's descendant, David I (1124–53), was lord of Strathclyde before his elevation to the kingship, and he is justly famous as the father of medieval Scottish legal and administrative development. Regardless of the violent terms employed by the *Berchán* poet, he is not nostalgic for a time of unrelenting warfare, which is the antithesis of the well-regulated society under just laws. Ferocity is well and good only so long as it is employed against one's foes. Donald II (889–900) is called 'the madman' because of his ravages against his people and the Church, which, it is implied, led to divine anger and to his death outside his own fortress of Dunnottar. The verses on Fland *Sinna* praise him for the peace he secured for his own people. In short, princes were being held to a standard of conduct, and the implication is that an unjust ruler does not deserve the loyalty of his subjects.

This emphasis on the conduct of the prince reflects ideas on statecraft that had been circulating among the Gaelic clergy since the ninth century.[68] They were given expression by two Irish scholars writing at Carolingian courts. Smaragdus wrote in his *Via Regis* that the king is responsible for the spiritual well-being of his people, while, a generation later, Sedulius Scottus expanded this idea and stated in his *Liber de Rectoribus Christianis* that a king was the deputy of Christ.[69] The 'Scottish Chronicle' emphasizes the role of the king as the upholder of the law when Constantine II becomes the guardian of the rights of the Church. These works of Smaragdus and Sedulius were written in an atmosphere of consolidation, as the descendants of Charlemagne (768–814) were emphasizing their recent royal past while studiously avoiding their earlier non-royal status as Mayors of the Palace. Much the same tactic was adopted by the descendants of the Dál Riatan princes as they moved eastwards into the lands of the Picts. In Irish and Scottish records, they are described as kings of Pictavia or of Alba, and the 'Scottish Chronicle' shows them beginning to behave as Sedulius and Smaragdus believed 'national' kings should act. Unlike the Carolingians, however, they had an ancient royal status, and a tenth-century set of Scottish genealogies that was partially brought up-to-date in the eleventh century continues to use the nomenclature of the primary dynasties of Dál Riata to identify the leading families of Scots living in what had been the lands of the Picts.[70] This indicates that older kindred names continued to have a currency among the powerful Scottish families. Politically the Scots were moving within the general currents of European change, but culturally there remained a conservative element that manifested itself in various aspects, such as group identification.

A full investigation of the Scottish historical gaze during the early Middle Ages and High Middle Ages must do more than consider merely a few texts. Nevertheless, even those records are useful to Irish as well as British historians. The perspective on Irish affairs given by the 'Scottish Chronicle' and the *Prophecy of Berchán* is slightly different from that of the Uí Néill–dominated records. While the Scottish works acknowledge the power and influence of the Uí Néill princes, they also present a view of the struggle for supremacy in Ireland that shows powerful princes coming from the south of the island. The validity of this perception is supported by Welsh and Anglo-Norman historical writings, in which individuals such as Cerball of Osraige and the Munster lords Cormac and Fedelmid are given a prominent position. The Scottish records also give the student of Irish history some appreciation of the extent of revision that the early history of Ireland underwent in the eleventh and twelfth centuries.

Of even greater importance is the view of Scots history found in the 'Scottish Chronicle,' the *Prophecy of Berchán*, and the 'Scottish Poem.' As was taking place across the North Channel, Scottish history was being revised in the late eleventh century and afterwards. The success of the descendants of Kenneth I in defeating their rivals prompted later writers to project the circumstances of their own day back into the past. When reading the 'Scottish Chronicle' and the *Prophecy of Berchán*, however, one discovers that there were significant stretches of time when the descendants of Kenneth I faced considerable challenges. Just as important, these works show certain preoccupations of the early Scottish kingdom, such as the importance of laws and the desire for a strong monarchy. At the same time, the past continued to intrude, and in the descriptions of individual princes writers dipped into the heroic vocabulary from the world of the early Irish sagas. The usefulness of these documents for cultural history in addition to political affairs is an area to be explored.

The writings from late medieval Scotland have been justly recognized as an important part of European literature. Of no less importance for their time are the works from the beginnings of the Scottish kingdom. The Scottish gaze not only extends across a period of Scottish history that has been thought to be obscure, but it also offers new insights into the affairs of Ireland and Britain.

Notes

1 *Scottish Annals from English Chroniclers, A.D. 500 to 1286*, ed. A.O. Anderson (London, 1908).

2 B. Hudson, 'Historical Literature of Early Scotland,' *SSL* 26 (1991), 141–55; and *idem*, 'The Conquest of the Picts in Early Scottish Literature,' *Scotia* 15 (1991), 13–25. See also T. Clancy, 'Scotland, the "Nennian" Recension of the *Historia Brittonum* and the *Lebor Bretnach*,' in *Kings, Clerics and Chronicles in Scotland 500–1297*, ed. S. Taylor (Dublin, 2000), 87–107; and D. Howlett, *Caledonian Craftsmanship* (Dublin, 2000). For a different view, see K. Hughes, *Celtic Studies in the Early Middle Ages*, ed. D. Dumville (Woodbridge, 1980), especially the chapter 'Where Are the Writings of Early Scotland?'

3 For a selection, see *Iona: The Earliest Poetry of a Celtic Monastery*, ed. T.O. Clancy and G. Markus (Edinburgh, 1995). A discussion of the monastery's literary resources is by T. O'Loughlin, 'The Library of Iona in the Late Seventh Century: The Evidence from Adomnán's *De Locis Sanctis*,' *Ériu* 45 (1994), 33–52. For an interesting problem in literary

transmission, see A.A.M. Duncan, 'Bede, Iona and the Picts,' in *The Writing of History in the Middle Ages*, ed. R.H.C. Davis and J.M. Wallace-Hadrill (Oxford, 1981), 1–42.

4 *Adomnán's Life of Columba*, ed. A.O. Anderson and M.O. Anderson (Oxford, 1991), 188–90; while the insertion of this passage by Adomnán is debated, it is clear that he did make use of Cumméne's work; see page 189n214 and page xxv. For more discussion, see the new translation by R. Sharpe: *Life of St Columba of Iona* (London, 1995), 209 (text) and 357–9 (discussion).

5 Adomnán, *De Locis Sanctis*, ed. B. Meehan, *Scriptores Latini Hiberniae*, vol. 3 (Dublin, 1983), 36.

6 *Adomnán's Life of Columba*, 54.

7 The text is edited by F. Lot, *Nennius et l'historia Brittonum: Étude critique, suivie d'une édition des diverse versions de ce texte* (Paris, 1934). For the identication of Sléibne, see A. Anscombe, 'The Identification of "Libine Abas Iae" in the Historia Brittonum,' *ZCP* 1 (1897), 274–6; and E.W.B. Nicholson, 'Filius Urbagen,' *ZCP* 3 (1901), 107.

8 Chartres Archives, MS 98. For comment, see F. Liebermann, 'Nennius,' in *Essays in Medieval History Presented to Thomas Frederick Tout*, ed. A.G. Little and F.M. Powicke (Manchester, 1925), 33; and J. Kenney, *The Sources for the Early History of Ireland: Ecclesiastical*, ed. L. Bieler (New York 1966; repr. Dublin, 1979), 153.

9 *CGS*, i, 98 [Bk. 3, ch. 12].

10 Dícuill, *Liber de Mensura Orbis Terrae*, ed. J.J. Tierney, *Scriptores Latini Hiberniae*, vol. 6 (Dublin, 1967), 12. See also M. Esposito, 'Dicuil: An Irish Monk in the Ninth Century,' *Dublin Review* 137 (1905), 327–37; and *idem*, 'An Irish Teacher at the Carolingian Court: Dicuil,' *Studies* 3 (1914), 651–76.

11 *Liber de Mensura Orbis Terrae*, ed. Tierney, 74–6.

12 Ibid., 62; see also page 12, where Tierney is hesitant to associate Dícuill with any particular insular monastery. For an argument in favour of Iona, see Kenney, *Sources for the Early History of Ireland*, 545.

13 Edited and translated, with commentary, by J. Bannerman, *Studies in the History of Dalriada* (Edinburgh, 1973).

14 K. Hughes, *Early Christian Ireland: Introduction to the Sources* (Ithaca, 1966), 122–3; and M.O. Anderson, *Kings and Kingship in Early Scotland* (Edinburgh, 1973), 9.

15 M. Herbert, *Iona, Kells and Derry* (Oxford, 1988), 68; B. Hudson, 'Kings and Church in Early Scotland,' *SHR* 73 (1994), 153.

16 See E.J. Cowan, 'Myth and Identity in Early Medieval Scotland,' *SHR* 63

(1984), 111–35; and M. Herbert, 'Sea-divided Gaels,' in *Britain and Ireland 900–1300*, ed. B. Smith (Cambridge, 1999), 87–97.

17　*The Annals of Ulster to A.D. 1131*, ed. G. Mac Niocaill and S. Mac Airt (Dublin, 1984).

18　Bannerman, *Studies in the History of Dalriada*, 11–12.

19　A diplomatic edition was included by Anderson in *Kings and Kingship in Early Scotland*, 249–53, while an edition and translation is by B. Hudson, 'The Scottish Chronicle,' *SHR* 77 (1998), 129–61. For comment, see B. Hudson, 'The Language of the Scottish Chronicle and Its European Context,' *Scottish Gaelic Studies* 18 (1998), 57–73.

20　*Saltair na Rann*, ed. W. Stokes, *Anecdota Oxoniensia*, Medieval and Modern Series I.iii (Oxford, 1883); the apocalyptic materials are discussed by St John D. Seymour, 'The Signs of Doomsday in Saltair na Rann,' *Proceedings of the Royal Irish Academy* 36 (1922), C, 154–63; and W. Heist, *The Fifteen Signs before Doomsday* (East Lansing, 1952).

21　The verses on the kings are found in *Saltair na Rann*, ed. Stokes, at page 34, lines 2341–80. For a study of those verses, see G. Mac Eoin, 'Date and Authorship of Saltair na Rann,' *ZCP* 28 (1960), 51–67.

22　B. Hudson, *The Prophecy of Berchán* (Westport, CT, and London, 1996).

23　*Prophecy of Berchán*, 120–1.

24　Hudson, 'Historical Literature,' 146.

25　Hudson, 'The Language of the Scottish Chronicle,' 71.

26　*Saltair na Rann*, lines 2349–52: 'The reign of fair Kenneth / son of Malcolm over Alba; / over Ireland besides, a half part of the land / to Kenneth son of Malcolm.'

27　*Saltair na Rann*, lines 2373–6. On the kings of Strathclyde, see A. MacQuarrie, 'The Kings of Strathclyde, c. 400–1018,' in *Medieval Scotland: Crown, Lordship and Community*, ed. A. Grant and K.J. Stringer (Edinburgh, 1993), 1–19.

28　B. Hudson, 'Gaelic Princes and Gregorian Reform,' in *Crossed Paths: Methodological Approaches to the Celtic Aspect of the European Middle Ages*, ed. B. Hudson and V. Ziegler (Lanham, 1991), 62

29　For her marriages and descendants, see B. Hudson, *Kings of Celtic Scotland* (Westport, CT, and London, 1994), 171.

30　*Acta Sanctorum quotquot toto Urbe coluntur vel a Catholicis Scriptoribus celebrantur*, 66 vols (Brussels, 1780–), Mart. I, 469–81 (for March 6th). W.F. Skene, *Chronicles of the Picts, Chronicles of the Scots and Other Early Memorials of Scottish History* (Edinburgh, 1867), 109–16, reprinted this *vita* from John Colgan, *Acta Sanctorum Veteris Scotiae seu Hiberniae* (Louvain, 1645), but the Bollandists' text is superior. An abridged translation of Catroë's *vita*, with copious notes, is in *ES*, i, 431–43. For comment, see B. de Gaiffier, 'Notes sur le Culte des SS Clement de Metz et Caddroë,' *Analecta Bollandiana* 85 (1967), 21–43; and Hudson, 'Kings and Church in Early Scotland,' 157–8

31 Hudson, *Kings of Celtic Scotland*, 101–2.

32 Rudolfus Glabrus, *Historiarum Libri Quinque / Five Books of the Histories*, ed. J. France (Oxford, 1989), 54–6.

33 William of Jumièges, *Gesta Normannorum Ducum of William of Jumièges*, ed. E. Van Houts, 2 vols (Oxford, 1995–8), i, 18–20. In the text, Lagman is identified as *rex Suerorum*, a corruption of *rex Suðriorum*; see A. Gautries, *Les noms de personnes Scandinaves en Normandie 911 à 1066* (Lund, 1954), 69, for discussion and references.

34 The text is found in two manuscripts, and parts have been edited by K. Meyer, 'Das Ende von Baile in Scáil,' *ZCP* 12 (1918), 232–8, and *idem*, 'Der Anfang von Baile in Scáil,' *ZCP* 13 (1921), 371–82; and R. Thurneysen, 'Baile in Scáil,' *ZCP* 20 (1936), 213–27. For brief discussions, see E. O'Curry, *Lectures on the Manuscript Materials of Ancient Irish History* (Dublin, 1861, repr. 1873), 387–90; and M. Dillon, *Early Irish Literature* (Chicago, 1948), 107–9. A new edition is by K. Murray, '*Baile in Scáil*: The Literary and Historical Perspective' (PhD diss., University College, Dublin, 1997), which will be published by the Irish Text Society.

35 G. Murphy, '*Baile Chuind* and the Date of Cín Dromma Snechta,' *Ériu* 16 (1952), 145–51.

36 E. Knott, 'A Poem of Prophecies,' *Ériu* 18 (1958), 55–84.

37 The attribution of this verse to Berchán is found only in M. O'Clery's transcript of the 'War of the Irish against the Vikings' (*Cogadh Gaedhel re Gaillaibh*); see *Prophecy of Berchán*, 34: 'Ní bía cell ná cathair cáidh / ní bía dúnadh ná ríghráith / fiodhglas ná magh ná maitheis / gan dul uile a n-anflaitheis' [There will not be a church nor monastery pure, there will not be a fortress nor royal palace, a greenwood nor a plain nor property, but all will degenerate into tyranny]. Compare this with stanza 37 in Knott, 'Poem of Prophecies,' 66, where the final line is defective: 'Ní bía cell ná cathair cáidh / ní bia rodún ná roráith / fidh glas nó magh gan dul as/ a n-aithintus' [There will not be a church nor a monastery pure, there will not be a great fortress nor a great rath, green wood nor plain, but will pass away and become unrecognizable].

38 K.H. Jackson, 'The Poem *A Eolach Alban Uile*,' *Celtica* 3 (1955), 149–67; and *idem*, 'Duan Albanach,' *SHR* 36 (1957), 125–37.

39 The poem *Aithnidh damh sgéal beag ar Fionn* (I know a little tale about Finn) is at pages 220–2 in the manuscript. An edition and translation is

in T. McLauchlan, *The Dean of Lismore's Book* (Edinburgh, 1862), 20–5 (English), and 14–19 (Gaelic); and *Heroic Poetry from the Book of the Dean of Lismore*, ed. N. Ross (Edinburgh, 1939), no. xxi, line 1693 ff. See also T. O'Rahilly, 'Indexes to the Book of the Dean of Lismore,' *Scottish Gaelic Studies* 4 (1934–5), 36, no. 11.

40 D. Meek, 'Development and Degeneration in Gaelic Ballad Texts,' in *The Heroic Process*, ed. B. Almquist et al. (Dun Laoghaire, 1987), 152.

41 In the case of Fedelmid, the confusion may stem from the author's effort to present the kings by region in imitation of the synchronisms attributed to Flann of Monasterboice; see *Prophecy of Berchán*, 160. For Ruaidrí, see T. Ó Canann, 'Aspects of an Early Irish Surname: Úa Canannáin,' *Studia Hibernica* 27 (1993), 114–20.

42 R. Thurneysen, 'Synchronism der irischen Könige,' *ZCP* 19 (1933), 81–99; and A. Boyle, 'The Edinburgh Synchronisms of Irish Kings,' *Celtica* 9 (1971), 169–79; who notes (p. 170) that the attribution to Flann is based largely on the appearance of this tract in a manuscript containing other pieces by him.

43 *Caithréim Cellacháin Caisil*, ed. A. Bugge (Christiania, 1905). For a discussion, see D. Ó Corráin, 'Caithréim Cellacháin Chaisil: History or Propaganda,' *Ériu* 25 (1974), 1–69.

44 Hudson, *Kings of Celtic Scotland*, 52.

45 This is seen in genealogy, where the domain of the prince Niall of the Nine Hostages is said to have included all of northern Europe; see M.A. O'Brien, *Corpus Genealogiarum Hiberniae* (Dublin 1962; repr. 1976), 122.

46 E. Mac Neill, *Celtic Ireland*, ed. D. Ó Corráin (Dublin, 1982), 39; and the additional note by Ó Corráin, pages 186–7.

47 *Prophecy of Berchán*, 97. The Uí Néill domination of the writing of history in Ireland is visible in a genealogical tract written in Leinster in the early twelfth century, which states baldly that all high-kings of Ireland were dynasts of Uí Néill with two exceptions, Báetán mac Cairill of Ulaid and Brian Boru of Munster; the former is dismissed by the comment 'he was not one of the great princes.' See O'Brien, *Corpus Genealogiarum Hiberniae*, 124.

48 F.J. Byrne, *Irish Kings and High-Kings* (London, 1973; 2nd ed., 1987), 114.

49 *Cogadh Gaedhel re Gallaibh (The War of the Gaedhil with the Gaill; or, The Invasions of Ireland by the Danes and Other Norsemen)*, ed. J.H. Todd, 2 vols, RS (London, 1867).

50 E. Mac Neill, 'Poems by Flann Mainistrech on the Dynasties of Ailech,
    Mide and Brega,' *Archivum Hibernicum* 2 (1913), 37–99.
51 *Book of Leinster, Formerly Lebar na Núachongbála*, ed. R.I. Best et al., 6
    vols (Dublin, 1954–83), iii, 509–15.
52 *Book of Leinster, Formerly Lebar na Núachongbála*, ed. Best, iii, 491–5.
53 *Lebor Gabála Érenn*, ed. R.A.S. Macalister, 5 vols, ITS (Dublin, 1938–
    56), v, 540–65.
54 Mac Neill, 'Poems by Flann Mainistrech,' 47.
55 Gerald of Wales, *History and Topography of Ireland*, trans. J. O'Meara
    (London, 1982), 118.
56 *Lebor Gabála Érenn*, v, 558.
57 *Prophecy of Berchán*, 137.
58 *Fragmentary Annals of Ireland*, ed. J. Radnor (Dublin, 1978).
59 The passage 'Domnal filius Caíríll mortuus est' [Donald son of Cairill
    died] is placed among the events of Cuilén son of Iduilf (966–71); see
    Hudson, 'Scottish Chronicle,' 160 and note 65.
60 *Scéla Cano meic Gartnáin*, ed. D.A. Binchy, Mediaeval and Modern
    Irish Series, no. xviii (Dublin, 1975), 18; Dál Riata at lines 478–9, and
    Gerginn (i.e., Angus) at lines 484–5.
61 S. Mac Airt, 'Middle-Irish Poems on World Kingship,' *Études Celtiques*
    6 (1953), 255–80; 7(1956/57), 18–45; 8(1958/59), 98–119 and 284–97.
62 The list is printed in Skene, *Chronicles of the Picts*, 296–7, and a table
    with comparison of the various lists is in Hudson, *Kings of Celtic Scot-
    land*, 167.
63 List B is found in several manuscripts of the late Middle Ages; a modern
    diplomatic edition (from Bodleian MS Laud 610, f. 87 r) is printed in
    Anderson, *Kings and Kingship*, 261–3, with variant readings. An
    abridged translation is in *ES*, i, cxxxvii–cxl; for a discussion see Hudson,
    'Historical Literature of Early Scotland,' 148.
64 The reference to the 'Pitfall of Scone' is at stanza 123 of the *Prophecy of
    Berchán*: 'the fools in the east [i.e., the Picts], they dig the earth ... a
    deadly goad-pit' (tair na buirb, tochlait talmhan ... brodlainn bodhba);
    while the famine of 965 is at stanza 53, 'Ní recfa cách thíar is tair, ar
    bíad a mac 's a ingen.'
65 Hudson, 'Language of the Scottish Chronicle,' 68–9.
66 There are numerous studies of this topic; for a particularly useful dis-
    cussion, see P. Mac Cana, 'Aspects of the Theme of King and Goddess in
    Irish Literature,' *Études Celtiques* 7 (1955/56), 76–114, 356–413; 8
    (1958/59), 59–65.
67 Printed in *APS*, i, 663–5.

68 Hudson, 'Kings and Church in Early Scotland,' 156; and K. Veitch, 'The Alliance between Church and State in Early Medieval Alba,' *Albion* 30 (1998), 193–220, especially 212–13.

69 Smaragdus, *Via Regis*, in *Patrologiae Cursus Completus: Series Latina*, compiled by J.P. Migne, 221 vols (Paris, 1844–64) [*PL*], 102, cols. 933–70 (at 933); Sedulius Scottus, *Liber de Rectoribus Christianus*, in *PL*, 103, cols. 291–332 (at 293–5).

70 Printed in Bannerman, *Studies in the History of Dalriada*, 65–6; and see also the abridged version preserved in the *Book of Leinster*, ed. Best, vi, 1471–2.

2

Earls and Saints:
Early Christianity in Norse Orkney
and the Legend of Magnus Erlendsson

GEORGE M. BRUNSDEN

For quite a long time the brothers Paul and Erlend ruled over Orkney
in harmony and goodwill, but as for their sons, while Magnus was a
quiet sort of man, Hakon and Erling grew up to be very arrogant,
though tall, strong and talented in many ways. Hakon Paulsson
wanted to be foremost among the brothers' kin ...[1]

This excerpt from *Orkneyinga Saga* foreshadows the bitter struggle
waged for sole title over the Scottish Northern Isles, a conflict ultimately resulting in the death of Earl Magnus Erlendsson. Title to the
Orkneys had been hotly contested ever since the earldom's legendary inception in the ninth century. As a man of God, Magnus was
perhaps ill-suited for survival in a hostile environment[2] longingly
romanticized by the Icelandic Sagas. Yet of all the Norse Orcadian
earls, the Holy Earl Magnus was among the best remembered, and
his legend one of the most enduring. Magnus was the focal point of
a miracle cult, his name attached to a cathedral in Kirkwall, while
prayers and hymns were recited in his honour. The strength of Magnus's cult was dependent upon time-honoured tradition, and the
nature of early Christianity within the Norse community.

Magnus Erlendsson's life (c. 1075– c. 1116) is mainly related in
three sources: *Orkneyinga Saga*, *Shorter Magnus Saga*, and *Longer
Magnus Saga*. All sagas, including these, were produced in Iceland a
century or more after events they purportedly relate, being at least
partially based upon oral tradition – features which might beg
caution before accepting their narratives as historical fact.[3] The extant version of *Orkneyinga Saga* was compiled c. 1230, being based
upon an earlier lost saga of the same name composed around the

Earls and Saints:

Some Family Relationships of Magnus Erlendsson

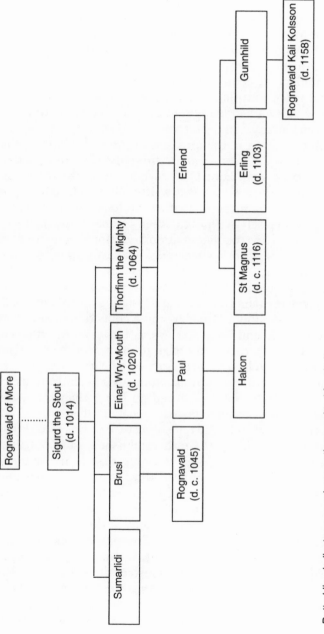

Dotted line indicates several generations omitted for clarity.

end of the twelfth century. This first *Orkneyinga* was liberally plundered, in all probability, by Snorri Sturluson when writing the history of Saint Olaf. A rendition of Olaf's saga was later incorporated by Snorri into his *Heimskringla* (c. 1220s). *Orkneyinga*'s 1230 redaction in turn borrowed from Snorri's tome, and was composed at the intellectual centre of Oddi, Iceland. Certain inhabitants of Oddi claimed a familial relationship to the Orcadian earls, and probably were aware of many traditions associated with them.

Numerous manuscript sources for *Orkneyinga* have been described, some dating to the thirteenth century.[4] However, the most intact version of *Orkneyinga* is interpolated within sagas about Olaf Tryggvason and Saint Olaf, forming constituent parts of the vellum *Flateyjarbók*, which was written by two Icelandic priests c. 1390. It is worth mentioning that the various renditions of the saga do not agree precisely with each other – recently the 'many clerical additions found in the *Flateyjarbók* version' have been noted.[5] *Orkneyinga Saga* is not a single tale, but really a composite of several smaller ones or *þættir*.[6] Among the first to tackle the saga's unity was Vigfusson,[7] who noted several separate components: a mythological introduction, an Earls' Saga, Saint Magnus's Saga, a Book of Saint Magnus's Miracles, and a collection of stories related to Earl Rognavald and Svein Asleifsson. *Orkneyinga*'s final episode, from the onset of Earl Harald's reign to the rise of the Scottish earls, c. 1214, was not judged by Vigfusson to be part of the saga, though most modern editors and translators now include it as part of *Orkneyinga*.[8] Taylor later proposed no fewer than thirty-two distinct components, though he still recognized a unified Magnus saga.[9] If correct, all this tends to suggest that prior to *Orkneyinga*'s composition, a separate, yet firmly established, Saint Magnus tradition existed. (This 'embryonic' Magnus saga is not synonymous with either the *Shorter* or *Longer Magnus Saga*, though undoubtedly the former helped inspire the latter two.)

Two additional sagas deal with the Orcadian saint. *Shorter Magnus Saga* is based upon an early copy of the revised *Orkneyinga Saga*, with various additions from traditional sources, and was probably composed around 1250. *Longer Magnus Saga*, however, was composed sometime early in the fourteenth century and was partially based upon an *Orkneyinga Saga* similar to that later preserved in *Flateyjarbók*. By its own acknowledgment, *Longer Magnus Saga* relies upon a Latin saint's life (*vita*) for at least some of its information: 'Master Robert, who hath collected and composed the Saga of the holy earl Magnus in Latin, so begins his Prologue as may here be heard.'[10] Possibly this *vita* was the inspiration for the life of Magnus as contained in both *Magnus Saga*s and *Orkneyinga Saga*. The *vita* itself may have been composed in 1136, for the saga's author states that 'Master Robert wrote this story ... of saint Magnus ... when twenty winters were passed from his martyrdom.'[11] If an accurate statement, then this *vita* was composed prior to any known versions of the sagas discussed, and therefore theoretically could have helped inspire the creator(s) of the initial Saint Magnus *þáttir*.

The level of direct textual relationship between the *vita* and the *þáttir* of Magnus is not wholly clear, however. Taylor saw varying degrees of contact with the story of Magnus as contained in *Orkneyinga Saga*.[12] Bibre conversely saw a closer relationship between Robert's text and *Longer Magnus Saga*, since the latter appeared to directly refer back to the former. Lacking this direct reacquaintance, *Orkneyinga*'s version of Magnus's *þáttir*, and *Shorter Magnus Saga*, in particular, might both be only indirectly related to the *vita*.[13] Certainly the 'feel' of *Shorter Magnus Saga* is very much akin to that of the traditional Icelandic saga, rather than medieval Latin hagiography. A better example of a work which reads like hagiography is *Longer Magnus Saga*. However, even in its case, there is incorporated material which appears to be the product of localized Icelandic oral tradition.

A question mark looms over the identity of the *vita*'s author, the mysterious Master Robert. Metcalfe thought the author was an Orcadian, but ventured no further guesses as to his identity.[14] A more 'definitive' guess is offered by Pálsson and Edwards:

> Very tentatively, it has been suggested that Robert may have been Robert Crickdale, who wrote a Latin life of Thomas à Becket *c.*1173–4. Robert was a Canon in Cirencester *c.*1130–41, and a Prior in Oxford 1141–74, and he is known to have visited Scotland. The Life of St Magnus ... bears a certain similarity to the life of Becket, Earl Hakon functioning in much the same relationship to Magnus as Henry II to Becket.[15]

Master Robert's identity aside, it seems likely that *Longer Magnus Saga*'s compiler was an Icelandic cleric. Such an individual would

possess the ability to acquire, then translate into Icelandic, a Latin
text relating a saint's life. An Icelandic cleric would also be the likeliest individual possessing a knowledge of the literary conventions
associated with both saga and *vita*. As such, one Abbot Bergr Sokka-
son, linked to the Benedictine monasteries of northern Iceland,
might well prove a likely candidate.[16]

These three sagas combine in presenting a tantalizing picture of
an individual who became Orkney's native saint after dying a mar-
tyr's death. Magnus's life, however, was one of many belonging to a
long line of Orcadian earls, whose exploits set the pattern in which
the saint would find himself. Ultimately, Magnus could trace his
lineage back to Orkney's first earls, who in turn reckoned descent
from Rognavald of More, Norway. The succession of earls eventually led to Magnus's great-grandfather, Sigurd the Stout Hlodvirsson
(d. 1014). The significance of Sigurd's reign is obvious by at least
one count, since he was allegedly the first to formally accept Christianity – albeit in a grudging and probably cursory manner. This
occurred between 995–6, as a result of the intervention of the future
king of Norway, Olaf Tryggvason (d. 1000).

Saga tradition states that Olaf had been in the British Isles and
Ireland, and during a stop at the Scillies in 993, was baptized by an
anchorite.[17] This same hermit prophesied that Olaf was destined to
become king and help in spreading the Word of God. Later, sailing
from Ireland in an effort to return home and win for himself the
crown of Norway, Olaf visited in succession the Hebrides and the
Orkneys. At this time, Sigurd's fleet was anchored at Osmundwall,
said to be at South Ronaldsay, but actually at Hoy. As the all too
often harsh weather of the Pentland Firth blocked Olaf's passage,
safe anchorage was sought in the Orkneys. The future king then
summoned Sigurd, making the proverbial 'offer he could not refuse':

> 'I want you and all your subjects to be baptised,' he said when they
> met. 'If you refuse, I'll have you killed on the spot, and I swear that I'll
> ravage every island with fire and steel.'
>
> The Earl could see what kind of situation he was in and surrendered
> himself into Olaf's hands. He was baptised and Olaf took his son,
> called Hvelp or Hundi, as a hostage and had him baptised too under
> the name of Hlodvir. After that, all Orkney embraced the faith.[18]

Undoubtedly, Olaf's zeal was in part fuelled by the words of the soothsayer: if he took on the role of evangelist, surely too he would become king. Nevertheless, this account suggests that during Sigurd's reign Christianity was literally forced upon Orkney.

The saga's account is generally confirmed by Theoderic's *Historia de Antiquitate Regum Norwagiensium*. As a monk at Nidarholm, Theoderic wrote possibly between 1177–80, so that his history is probably the oldest Norwegian work of its kind. Though similar to *Orkneyinga*'s account, Theoderic offers some noteworthy divergences:

> Olaf ... called upon earl Sigurd ... to become Christian. And when he ... objected, Olaf pressed him more. But [Sigurd] promised that he would be subject to [Olaf] ... if [Olaf] did not force him to [accept] Christianity. And after a long contest ... Olaf seized [Sigurd's] son ... a little boy of three years ... protesting that he would kill him in his father's sight, and moreover threatened perpetual enmity, if [Sigurd] did not consent ... [T]he earl dreaded both things ... and ... was baptised, with all the people subject to him: and afterwards he was confirmed in the faith, and remained faithful, and all his successors.[19]

Theoderic thus presents an affable Olaf, who only 'plays his trump card' when pressed by Sigurd's stubbornness. This is in some ways similar to the portrayal of Olaf in *Flateyjarbók*'s recounting of the earl's *þáttir*, in which Olaf and Sigurd debate the issue at hand, and only then does Olaf repay the earl's steadfastness with threats. Eventually the two come to terms, with the familiar outcome. So completely won over was the earl, that 'they, king Olaf and Sigurd, parted with friendship.'[20] How, then, do we account for the difference of this portrait of Olaf Tryggvason from that of the sagas?

Theoderic's *Regum Norwagiensium* is, of course, a history written about the kings of Norway by a Norwegian cleric. Therefore it is unlikely that he would make many disparaging comments about a Norse king, especially one who went on record for having promoted 'the faith.' Theoderic asserts that so affable and convincing was Olaf, that Sigurd and Orkney remained true to the faith. *Flateyjarbók*'s authors, however, were less convinced of the long-term success of Olaf's efforts. Upon the untimely death of the earl's hostaged son, 'Sigurd showed king Olaf no service.'[21] Yet Olaf's lengthy speech to Sigurd, recorded in *Flateyjarbók*, is an example of one of the 'many clerical additions' present in that work (see above), since

it not only relates Olaf's right to rule, but also his right as a godly
ruler to punish ungodly idolaters. An earthly king like Olaf who
vigorously furthered the Kingdom of God was an attractive concept
to the priestly authors of *Flateyjarbók*.

The saga versions of Sigurd's 'conversion' tend to indicate that
the earl, at first opportunity, repudiated his alliance with the king.
Orkneyinga relates that Sigurd married the daughter of 'Malcolm
King of Scots,' a move which served to weld a new alliance for himself to replace that which he had had with Olaf.[22] We might also
question if Sigurd broke his religious vows, even though his marriage to the daughter of a Christian king was likely facilitated by his
having been baptized. Prior to baptism, the earl presumably was a
pagan. *Orkneyinga Saga* talks of his *gunnefan* (war-banner), which
had the image of a raven embroidered into it.[23] The raven, as a symbol of war, was closely associated with the Norse god of the dead,
Odin,[24] and it appears that baptism did not cause Sigurd to cast
away this pagan-inspired war-banner. At the fateful Battle of Clontarf (1014), in which the earl perished, Sigurd arrived brandishing
his *gunnefan* in support of the Norse king of Dublin, Sigtrygg
Silken-Beard.

This episode on its own does not prove that Sigurd returned to
the pagan way of life. Perhaps he retained the banner purely because
it had proven lucky in the past. Yet, given the way he was 'force-fed'
Christianity, it is hard to believe that Sigurd was a true, total convert; probably, he retained many pagan ideas. Initially, he likely
underwent the usual style of 'conversion' for this period, which
often entailed simply making the sign of the cross over the 'convert'
as a sort of pre-baptism.[25] Such a ritual hardly guaranteed a full
purging of pagan vestiges from a person long used to such. Theoderic maintains Sigurd was later confirmed in the faith, but little
supporting evidence exists for this suspect claim. Moreover, if Sigurd was ever truly baptized by having water poured over his head,
then this action has parallels in pagan naming ceremonies.[26]

The supposition concerning Sigurd the Stout's religious beliefs
agrees with the general theory regarding the pattern of conversion
in the Scottish Northern Isles. It seems clear that there existed a
long period during which the two religions overlapped and were
coincidentally practised.[27] Paganism probably existed in Orkney
even after the incident between Olaf and Sigurd. Similarly there
would have been Norse Christians in Orkney before that same inci-

dent, as contacts with Ireland and Scotland were frequent. Also, despite it not being 'officially' Christian, Norway had at least one ruler prior to Olaf Tryggvason who personally accepted the Christian faith. Though not successful, Hakon the Good (d. 961) first tried to Christianize Norway, so that any contact between his kingdom and the earldom might have resulted in some nominal Orcadian conversions.

Prior to religious reform, which included the introduction of a system of tithes within the Scandinavian sphere of influence (generally by the twelfth century, though in Iceland during the late eleventh),[28] communal involvement in the building of churches was limited at best.[29] 'The king was head of the early twelfth-century [Scandinavian] church,'[30] and here the word 'earl' could be substituted for 'king.' Without regal promotion in the eleventh century, it seems unlikely that the faith had any chance of thriving. Thus, in order to classify Norse Orkney as Christian, evidence is needed of an earl who built churches and acquired a bishop's services, as was the case during the time of Sigurd's son Thorfinn.

Orkney's first bishop may have been Henry, previously Cnut's treasurer in England, and later appointed to the Danish see of Lund in 1060.[31] Possibly he served Orkney only briefly c. 1035, by authority of the archbishopric of York.[32] Though ecclesiastical authority over Orkney was claimed by both York and Hamburg-Bremen, the latter played the most influential role in the period following Earl Sigurd's death. Adam of Bremen's *History of the Archbishops of Hamburg-Bremen* (c. 1070) reports that Archbishop Adalbert 'consecrated Throlf bishop of ... Birsay.'[33] This was probably instigated by Thorfinn the Mighty (d. 1064), who after visiting the new Norse king Harald Sigurdarson (reigned 1047–66) and new Danish king Svein Ulfsson (reigned 1047–74), went on to Rome to receive absolution for his numerous sins. Along the way, he visited the Empire,[34] where it is likely he petitioned Hamburg-Bremen for a bishop: 'Bremen was ... devoutly sought ... especially by all the peoples of the north. Among those who came the longest distances were the ... legates of the Orkney Islanders. They begged that he [Adalbert] send preachers thither, which he did.'[35] Thus Thorfinn is normally accredited for establishing a residence and minster at Birsay.[36] It was here that *Orkneyinga Saga* placed 'the seat of the first bishop of Orkney.'[37] Probably this refers to Thorolf, who was appointed to the see c. 1050,[38] the earlier ineffective Henry notwithstanding.

This push by Thorfinn to create an ecclesiastic seat and provide a Christian temper to his realm has to be seen in relation to the rest of his life's activities. A career Viking, especially in his early years, Thorfinn spent a lifetime ruthlessly eliminating the opposition. The sagas relate the fall of Thorfinn the Mighty's political rivals, including his half-brothers Sumarlidi, Brusi, and Einar Wry-Mouth (d. 1020). Then, after defeating in battle Karl Hundason, King of Scotland, *Orkneyinga* overly optimistically relates that Thorfinn pursued the Scots deep into their homeland, 'conquering as far as Fife, and laid the region under his rule.'[39] With his nephew Rognavald Brusason's (d. c. 1045) Norwegian-backed challenge successfully stemmed, Thorfinn acquired sole title to the earldom. An awe-struck *Orkneyinga Saga* overstates the case that nobody could then stand up to him.[40]

Thorfinn then assumed the role of benevolent prince by providing the islands with good government and the passage of new laws, in addition to creating a bishopric. It is easy to see his new-found zeal for the Church as an attempt to further his power in matters both secular and religious, facilitated by the relative control Norse rulers had over the Church within their realms. However, Christianity was the vehicle for Thorfinn's entry into the Western world at large. Though an accomplished individual in his own right, he was prince of only a comparatively remote northern land. Nevertheless, as an aspiring member of the Christian community, Thorfinn was welcomed into both the German provinces and Rome, the very hubs of Western society. This is similar to the earlier case of King Cnut, another reputable 'barbarian' prince who, having embraced the faith and maintained good government, received an invitation to Conrad II's imperial coronation ceremony of 1027.[41] Thus, by zealously embracing the faith, great prestige fell to ambitious rulers like Thorfinn.

After Thorfinn's death, the earldom was divided between his sons Paul and Erlend, who in 1066 were 'conscripted' into King Harald Sigurdarson's ill-fated plans for the conquest of England. Harald sought out the brothers because of the earldom's reputation, established by Thorfinn.[42] However, the earls' enthusiasm for the venture might be questioned. The *Anglo-Saxon Chronicle* states that only one of them accompanied Harald,[43] the likeliest candidate being Paul, the more ambitious of the two brothers.[44] Clearly, the Thorfinnsons' reign was strife-ridden, and it appears they allowed their father's considerable conquests to slip away. Noteworthy, however, is the fact that Paul and Erlend were the respective fathers of Hakon and Magnus.

Magnus Erlendsson not only was a descendant of Orcadian earls, but also had impressive roots thanks to his mother. She was Thora, daughter of Sumarlidi Ospakson, whose grandmother Thordis was Hall of Sida's daughter. This same Hall appears in *Njal's Saga* and seems to have been an Icelandic chieftain of certain ability, being lawspeaker to the Althing and influential in establishing Christianity in Iceland, c. 1000.[45]

The sagas mainly indicate that Magnus was a peaceful man. The exception to this stems from *Longer Magnus Saga*, which still extols his virtuous character even though

> many turn their customs after those with whom they live ... so when Magnus had come to be about fullgrown ... placed among grim and wicked men who were ill-willed ... and disobedient to God's commandments; he seemed for some winters like wicked men, and as a viking with robbers and warriors he lived by robbery and plunder, and stood by at manslaughters ... But it is to be believed that he did this more from wickedness and egging on of bad men than from his own badness. Men think it likely that Magnus did this at that time when he and Hakon and Erling ... were all together ... for afterwards no time can be found for it.[46]

The inclusion of this episode from Magnus's earlier life has been used in the past to vindicate *Longer Magnus Saga* as being more than hagiography, or solely a type of Christian panegyric.[47] This may be true, and certainly *Longer Magnus Saga* is much more than panegyric or hagiography. However, the episode it relates of a young Magnus being tempted by worldliness resembles the Gospel of Saint Matthew, possibly the first piece of hagiography ever produced.[48] Matthew 4:1–11 speaks of Jesus wandering the wilderness (likely a metaphor for walking evil's dark path) and being tempted by Satan's worldliness. As the Son of God was tested by and triumphed over evil, so too Magnus, who presumably found Christlike strength and inspiration to throw off the fetters of violent ways. The similarity between the stories is unlikely to be a coincidence. If Magnus had trod the Viking path in earlier life before adopting the way of peace, then probably his biographers noted a

similarity to the story of the youthful Jesus' wanderings. This
would have provided the saga's creators with the inspiration needed
to enhance Magnus's story.

From thenceforth, Magnus Erlendsson seemed destined for sainthood. As indicated above, the sagas depicted Magnus as being a far
gentler sort than his brother Erling or cousin Hakon. The real test
for the three came in 1098 when the Norse king Magnus Barelegs
materialized, looking to muster support for an Irish Sea campaign.[49]
According to *Orkneyinga* and both *Magnus Sagas*, upon arrival in
Orkney, the king seized the reigning earls, Paul and Erlend, and sent
them to Norway. 'King Magnus declared that the earls would never
rule in Orkney as long as he was King of Norway'[50] – prompting
him to install his own son Sigurd as earl. That done, the king
departed, taking with him Hakon Paulsson, and Magnus and Erling
Erlendsson.[51]

From the start of the campaign, Magnus Erlendsson proved a
reluctant participant. Rather than fight for the Menai Strait, Magnus, citing religious conviction, 'took out his psalter and chanted
psalms throughout the battle, and though he refused to take cover,
he wasn't wounded.'[52] Magnus Barelegs, however, was not impressed: 'If you haven't got the guts to fight ... and in my opinion
this has nothing to do with your faith, get below.'[53] No doubt, however, this episode proved to his later followers that Magnus Erlendsson was indeed God's servant. Yet pragmatism probably also
motivated the future saint. It was certainly convenient that his
faith should guide him to act in such a way as to hinder the actions
of his political enemy.

After the battle, King Magnus and his Orcadian namesake never
again saw eye-to-eye, and when opportunity arose, the son of Erlend
made his escape. The sagas maintain he hid variously in England,
Wales, and Scotland, ever reluctant of venturing back to Orkney
while the king remained alive. On his way back to Norway, however, Magnus Barelegs revisited Orkney, where talk was of the
exiled earls' deaths.

Yet King Magnus again grew restless for conquest, so he made a fatal
decision: After ruling Norway for nine years, King Magnus sailed west
over the sea to plunder in Ireland. He spent the winter in Connaught
and was killed the following summer in Ulster ... As soon as news of
his father's death reached Sigurd in Orkney, he set out for Norway

where he was accepted as joint ruler along with his brothers Eystein and Olaf.[54]

After the death of Magnus Barelegs, Hakon Paulsson, having been loyal to the king, visited the Magnussons in Norway and received title to the earldom. Shortly after Hakon's return to Orkney, Magnus Erlendsson reappeared, and became so well liked that many believed he should rule the earldom. Hakon, of course, was not pleased, and a stand-off ensued. It was agreed that Magnus Erlendsson should do as Hakon had done, and travel to Norway to petition the Magnussons. In Norway, Kings Eystein and Olaf[55] were suitably enough impressed with Magnus that they granted him half the earldom. Magnus sailed home to begin joint rule with Hakon, and initially there was friendship between them.

Snorri Sturluson's recollection of these events differs somewhat. *Heimskringla* mentions nothing of King Magnus's abduction of the sons of Paul and Erlend while en route to Menai Strait. However, Snorri does goes into far greater detail concerning the lands in which King Magnus campaigned: Lewis, Uist, Skye, Tiree, Mull, Iona, Islay, Kintyre, Man, and adjacent areas of Ireland, Wales, and Anglesey. At the conclusion of this endeavour, King Magnus returned directly to Norway. However, after a nine-year rest, the king became eager for new conquest and once more set off for Ireland in 1102.[56] En route he visited Orkney to collect Magnus and Erling Erlendsson (but no mention of Hakon Paulsson). According to Snorri, the saint-to-be experienced little crisis of faith; instead, within sight of the Scottish coast and without warning, 'Magnus Erlendsson at night jumped overboard from the king's ship and swam to land. Then he hid in the forest and finally came out to the court of the king of Scotland. Afterwards King Magnus sailed to Ireland and harried there.'[57] Shortly thereafter on Saint Bartholomew's Feast (24 August) 1103, Magnus Barelegs died battling the Ulstermen. Though many fled the ensuing rout, some stood and fell with the king, one of whom was Erling Erlendsson. Thus Snorri concluded his account of the earldom as it was during Saint Magnus's early life.

Probably Snorri's narrative differs largely because his main task was to relate the deeds of King Magnus Barelegs, rather than those of the Orkney earls. His prime purpose did not include promoting Magnus Erlendsson's sanctity. Also, the information he had at his disposal concerning the earls came from the earlier version of *Orkneyinga Saga*. It therefore might not have been a case of his simply neglecting to talk of the sons of Paul and Erlend. Rather, he may have told all he knew at the time. On the other hand, Snorri certainly may have got some of his details wrong, or neglected to verify them as they related to the earls of Orkney.

The extant version of *Orkneyinga* has a different agenda when relating the earls' involvement in King Magnus's campaigns. The saga even attempts to play the role of unbiased factual repository by stating that 'according to some people, Erling, the son of Earl Erlend, was killed at the Battle of Menai Strait, but Snorri Sturluson says he met his death with King Magnus in Ulster.'[58] Is the saga's compiler attempting here to correct Snorri, or rather 'some people' instead? Or is he himself confused, having encountered two opposing traditions? There is just no way of saying for certain. Yet the presence of such equivocal statements as this helps support the claim that *Orkneyinga*'s author had at his disposal information not available to Snorri. Clearly much of this additional material was of a quasi-hagiographic nature, and appears to include the episode concerning Saint Magnus's spiritual awakening that prevented his participation in battle. Perhaps this had the dual design of deflecting opinion that Magnus had cowardly avoided fighting at Menai Strait, while at the time imparting religious significance to his actions.

Thus the sagas emphasize that no better man could be found in all Christendom than the son of Erlend:

> As a leader, Magnus was outstanding, courteous ... and strict in morals, wise, victorious, eloquent and majestic. Everyone sang his praises. He was open-handed with money and sound with advice, brave in battle and loyal to his friends. He punished theft, plundering and other crimes with severity, and robbers and vikings he put to death. Often he gave lavish gifts to great men, but to the poor he always offered deep consolation for the sake of God. God's commandments he observed strictly ...[59]

Magnus's saintly ways even extended to the marriage bed. Though he allegedly married a young aristocratic Scottish woman, the sagas offer little detail concerning Magnus's bride, not even her name or specific lineage. This indeed arouses suspicion, since the men who composed the sagas were generally obsessed with genealogies. A standard feature of virtually every saga is great ancestral lists for almost all significant (and some not so significant) characters therein. Therefore it might be prudent to question the episode's truthfulness, even though a non-Scandinavian source does ascribe to Magnus's wife the name Ingigerd.[60] However, it remains curious that additional detail concerning this 'purest maid of the noblest stock of Scotland's chiefs'[61] is not forthcoming. Truthfully or not, though, the sagas say that on his wedding night, and for ten years thereafter, Magnus would not allow either himself or his wife to 'suffer by way of their lusts, and so remaining chaste, without stain of lechery.' But as illustrated earlier, even the godly could be overwhelmed with temptation. When lustful desires became more than the saint could manage relying upon faith alone, supplementary methods of a less ethereal nature were sought: 'Whenever the urge of temptation came upon him, he would plunge into cold water and pray to God for aid.'[62]

His chastity assured, Magnus settled down to the business of joint rule with Hakon, which included the repression of potential usurpers:

> Poems composed in their honour tell how they fought against a chieftain named Dufniall ... and killed him. There was a man of some importance called Thorbjorn whom they killed at Burra Firth in Shetland. People say they attacked him in his house and burnt him to death inside.[63]

This account from *Shorter Magnus Saga* appears to be based upon orally transmitted skaldic poetry,[64] and might have been designed to counter allegations that Magnus was a weakling who hid behind religion, as Magnus Barelegs had alleged. *Longer Magnus Saga* also enacted this type of 'damage control,' while remaining true to its claim that Magnus only briefly flirted with the Viking way of life. This may have been to reverse any negative opinion concerning his involvement in burning to death men in their own homes – an unsavoury act, judging by sentiments expressed in stories like *Njal's Saga*.[65] Thus, after repeating *Shorter Magnus Saga*'s claim that the killing of Dufniall and Thorbjorn was recorded in verse, *Longer Magnus Saga* qualifies matters by adding:

> These things Saint Magnus hath done not as a viking or robber, but rather as lawful ruler of the realm and a keeper of the laws, the lover of

peace, to restrain bad customs of men and to chastise wrongdoing, to free and relieve his subjects and his realm from the ... onslaughts of wicked men ...[66]

The exact content of the skaldic poems' accounts has not been preserved. This is curious since typically a saga will often interpolate supporting verse, which was regarded as having been composed by men (and occasionally women) who witnessed the events described.[67] Writers of sagas containing alleged historical fact often incorporated skaldic poetry as a means of supporting their narrative, 'the verses acting as a scholarly citation, or footnote.'[68] Yet verse describing Magnus and Hakon's joint campaign is nowhere to be found, and perhaps never existed. Instead, maybe it was the intent of the authors to concoct authority for an unsubstantiated claim being made for Magnus, even though it stands to reason that his supremacy might have been contested.

The amicable relationship between the cousins did not last. Perhaps it was a question of their no longer having a common enemy with which to contend, though the sagas offered this explanation:

> When the kinsmen had been ruling ... for some time, it so happened, as it often does, that malicious tongues set out to destroy their friendship, and it was to Hakon that the more luckless men were drawn, for he was very envious of the popularity and splendour of his cousin Magnus.[69]

As initially noted, the sagas often employed foreshadowing, and many clues suggested that a falling-out between the cousins was inevitable. The stage was set when it was noted that Magnus was gentle, while Hakon aggressive. Adding to this was Hakon's unease with Magnus's return from exile in Scotland, and the trend that joint rule of the earldom was usually strife-ridden. It was thus agreed shortly before Palm Sunday that the two earls should meet on Egilsay to settle their differences. Strict limitations were made on the number of supporters each was allowed to bring. Magnus happily agreed to these terms, being 'trusting, honest and without ambition.' Predisposed toward accepting advice from bad men, Hakon set sail with a sizeable contingent. On Egilsay, Magnus, having had visions of his own death, saw the predicament he was in and threw himself upon his cousin's mercy, which was not forthcoming. Then, 'as cheerfully as if he'd been invited to a feast,' Magnus prostrated himself before God.[70] After much debate, Hakon ordered his cook, a remorseful and reluctant Lifolf, to strike the fatal blow. In Christ-like fashion, Magnus forgave his killers before being put to death on 16 April 1116 (or 1117).[71]

After his martyrdom, numerous miracles were attributed to Magnus Erlendsson. A cult devoted to his veneration emerged not only in Orkney, but in other places of Norse influence. Like many others, his cult was strongly chauvinistic, being inward-looking and based upon local traditions, yet was not necessarily locale specific. Thus Magnus attracted devotees in Iceland, possibly as early as the mid-thirteenth to early fourteenth centuries. In 1298 some of Magnus's relics were transferred to the southern episcopal see of Skálaholt. *Shorter Magnus Saga* describes Kelduhverfi in northern Iceland as home to Eldjarn Vardason, a mortally stricken farmer cured by Magnus.[72] This tale appears to be the product of specific, rather than general, tradition since it is not related in either *Longer Magnus Saga* or *Orkneyinga Saga*.

Iceland's affinity for Saint Magnus might be related to political tensions that peaked during 1262-4, when the Free State fell and supremacy of the Norse Crown was established. This stimulated fears among some Icelanders that a new era had begun which resembled the old, when King Harald Fine-hair (d. c. 933) allegedly made life unbearable enough that many Norse people were forced to flee to places like Orkney, Shetland, and Iceland.[73] The healing powers of Magnus, who was of partial Icelandic lineage, might have served as a bulwark against the ever popular cult of Saint Olaf, a Norse king. *Shorter Magnus Saga* relates that Magnus helped the farmer because Olaf was busy healing another distressed Icelander. Effectively, the Orcadian saint rescued Eldjarn because the Norse saint had insufficient resources to help all who called upon him.

King Olaf was the first Scandinavian canonized largely for political reasons,[74] and the strength of his cult was unceasing throughout Scandinavia, Northern Europe, and Britain.[75] To overcome the influence of such a powerful figure would have been a tall order for any holy man, but the martyred Magnus seems to have made inroads. Thus the political message central to Magnus's cult might contend that since a Norwegian saint could not help all dependent Icelanders, might the Norse Crown likewise lack sufficient resources to help all Iceland?

The growth of Magnus's cult in the Northern Isles probably also had political overtones, thanks to the machinations of his successors. As his cult spread, Orcadians and Shetlanders seemingly counted Magnus as their protector. Interestingly, a large number of his miracles were said to have occurred in Shetland. Half of the twenty-two miracles recorded in *Longer Magnus Saga* were performed there. The tally from *Orkneyinga Saga* is even more impressive, where eleven of seventeen helped by the saint were inhabitants of Shetland. Of course, there is a good deal of overlap in these accounts, as *Orkneyinga* and the two *Magnus Saga*s in many cases relate the same occurrence. This appears as the most conclusive evidence for the existence of a separate miracle book. Yet it is questionable if all miracles related by the three sagas were culled from this source. Certainly some, such as the healing of old Eldjarn, were non-typical, appearing in only one of the three sagas. These isolated tales of Magnus's healing powers could have been the product of independent tradition.

The fame Magnus achieved as a healer in Shetland is probably attributable to the political actions of his nephew and successor, Kali Kolsson, better known as Rognavald Kali (d. 1158). After Magnus's martyrdom, Hakon ruled till his own death, when Paul Hakonarson (d. c. 1137) and his half-brother Harald assumed title. The familiar pattern re-emerged as friction developed between the earls, only ending when Harald fell ill and died. Paul's reign was soon challenged by Kali, the son of Saint Magnus's sister Gunnhild. Kali had been befriended by the Norse king Sigurd Magnusson (d. 1130), who bestowed the name Rognavald upon him because 'Gunnhild claimed Earl Rognavald Brusason to have been the most able of all the Earls ... and people saw this as a sign of good luck.'[76] Earl Kali received title to the half of Orkney once ruled by Saint Magnus.

Back in Orkney, Earl Paul dug in his heels, bitter over the Norse Crown's intervention, and vowed to fight against that which he saw as the first step toward wrestling from him the entire earldom. A lengthy struggle thus ensued; however, its essential feature was that on two separate occasions, Rognavald employed Shetland as a staging post. This was facilitated when he exploited his relationship with Saint Magnus, thanks to his father Kol's advice to seek 'support where men will say the true owner of the realm granted it to you, and that's the holy Earl Magnus, your uncle.' Thus Kali sailed to Shetland, where his party 'and the local people were delighted to see each other.'[77]

The warm welcome which the Shetlanders extended to Rognavald surely was dependent upon Magnus's fame. Successful saints were God's special elect.[78] A person who attached himself to the healer might also garner God's favour, and so could command respect. With rumours of his uncle's miracles spreading, an astute Rognavald likely played up his relationship to him, all the while propagating and enhancing local knowledge of Magnus's healing powers. This would have been especially true on his second visit to the Shetlanders, when he seems to have completely won them over to his side.[79] This may account for a number of miracles recorded in the sagas that allegedly occurred in Shetland.

Rognavald eventually won sole title to the earldom, and he made good on the vow made under Kol's recommendation,

> that should he grant you your family inheritance and his own legacy, and should you come to power, then you'll build a stone minster at Kirkwall more magnificent than any in Orkney, that you'll have it dedicated to ... holy Earl Magnus and provide it with all the funds it will need to flourish. In addition, his holy relics and the episcopal seat must be moved there.[80]

Work began on that stone minster in Kirkwall c. 1136–7, when Rome officially recognized Magnus's sanctity.[81] A funding shortage was overcome when Rognavald allowed local farmers to buy back their lands.[82] According to saga tradition, Earl Turf-Einar previously had acquired title to all farmlands in exchange for paying Harald Fine-hair's tax upon Orkney.[83] However, *Orkneyinga*'s ultimate redactor was forgetful that Sigurd the Stout was said to have returned the farmers' land rights.[84] The fact that Rognavald later received credit for this act might support the claim that it was he who started the entire tradition to further his scheme for procuring funds.[85] If true, it certainly underscores an assumption that, for Rognavald, the building of the minster was really an exercise in demonstrating his worth.

Certainly one way an Orcadian earl expressed his means was to build a church.[86] Upon the completion of such a project, an earl could take pride in having demonstrated both Christian piety and the ability to organize manpower and finances. These religious houses would serve as a lasting testament to their builders, being projects no mere upstarts could undertake. Thus the cathedral at Kirkwall stands as a memorial not only to Saint Magnus, but also to his nephew's status. That Rognavald nearly went 'broke' financing his minster probably speaks not only of its relative grandeur, but also of his 'spare no cost' mentality.[87]

Another factor impacting upon Rognavald's decision to commission a cathedral is that the first half of the twelfth century seemed important for starting or completing religious houses. Likely this is connected with the spirit of reform which the Church was undergoing. Thus, when work began in Kirkwall, a new church had been dedicated by Bishop John of Glasgow to Saint Kentigern (Saint Mungo), while Saint Mary's Abbey at Melrose was also founded in 1136.[88] It seems highly possible that the construction of Saint Mungo's Church (the future Glasgow Cathedral) served to inspire the Orcadians.[89]

Rognavald was not the first church-building earl; that title belongs to Thorfinn the Mighty. Hakon Paulsson probably built the round, Templar-style church at Orphir after returning from pilgrimage.[90] Though every church was the house of God, Thorfinn's and Hakon's churches do not appear to have been dedicated to an earthly saint. The first earl to build a church commemorating a holy relative seems to have been an earlier Rognavald. The individual in question was the son of Brusi, whose name, it will be remembered, was bestowed upon the son of Kol. Rognavald Brusason seemingly chose to honour his stepfather, Olaf Haraldsson, by founding Saint Olaf's Kirk.[91] Rognavald Brusason was at Olaf's side during the fateful Battle of Stiklarstaðir (1030), where the king and future saint fell despite his retinue's optimistic war cry 'Forward, forward, Christ's men, cross men, king's men!'[92] Olaf's sanctity was first recognized by people living in the royal seat of Trondheim, because of the 'many miracles [which] had come to pass testifying to his sainthood.'[93] Because of his relationship with Olaf, Rognavald won over the saint's son, King Magnus the Good, who favoured the earl's challenge to Thorfinn the Mighty's rule.[94] It thus seems that by appropriating his name, the later Rognavald Kali also acquired Rognavald Brusason's ideas on promoting saints' cults for personal benefit.

Little remains of Saint Olaf's Church in modern-day Orkney. Tradition states that it survives solely as a gate leading to a walled-in back garden along Olaf's Wynd, Kirkwall. The disuse this church has suffered is perhaps strange, since when intact it might have temporarily housed Saint Magnus's relics. Though Orkney never forgot Saint Olaf himself, the unfortunate fate of his church seemingly attests to the thoroughness of Rognavald's promotion of Magnus by moving the saint's earthly remains to the new minster.

It took some time before Magnus's remains found their way to his cathedral. The site of the earl's death is said to be marked on Egilsay by the stone-towered church dedicated to him, dated c. 1135.[95] Hakon Paulsson at first barred Magnus's burial. Later, while intoxicated, he relented upon encountering the martyred saint's grief-stricken mother. The remains were taken to Thorfinn the Mighty's minster at Birsay, where the first evidence of holiness was observed – together with a common attribute of saintly remains – 'a heavenly fragrance near his grave.'[96] Thorfinn's minster was then the seat of Bishop William, who in a likely bid to sustain Earl Paul Hakonarson's favour, was initially sceptical of Magnus's saintliness. However, William underwent something of a Saul / Saint Paul conversion. After being struck with blindness and great fear (not unlike Saul on his way to Damascus), the bishop relented and had the martyred earl's remains enshrined. Thereafter, William proclaimed the earl's holiness and eventually moved the relics to Kirkwall in grand style.[97]

The transferral of the relics, sanctioned by William, seems the fulfilment of Rognavald's successful bid for power. It also signifies a shift in power away from Birsay to Kirkwall, even though earlier earls like Rognavald Brusason might have maintained residences in the latter locale.[98] Geographically central, Kirkwall was always important since earliest times. The town overlooks Scapa Flow, and with good reason in modern times the British Home Fleet called it home. The Flow offers safe anchorage,[99] with ready links to the North Sea, Irish Sea, English Channel, and North Atlantic. Journeying overland from east to west Mainland, the traveller passes through the isthmus on which Kirkwall is situated. In this central location, Rognavald Kali centralized his power. Concurrently, the Orcadian church could also take the first steps toward true consolidation. By moving to Kirkwall to become the guardian of Magnus's relics, William could 'establish a central and local church organisation in a more systematic fashion.'[100]

The bishop's change of heart toward Magnus might indicate that he sensed the upcoming power shift. William was installed as bishop in 1102 by either King Magnus Barelegs, or his son Sigurd[101] – the latter was also responsible for making Rognavald Kali an earl. If William remained friends with Sigurd Magnusson – and there is little contrary evidence – he would have been aware of Rognavald's amicable relationship with the king. Thus when Rognavald went on pilgrimage (1151–3), William was there at his side.

Since Thorfinn the Mighty's time, pilgrimage had been an essential activity of the earls. Hakon Paulsson went on pilgrimage after Magnus's death, probably with the hope of deflecting any lingering negative opinion concerning his order to kill the saint. The anticipated results seem to have been realized, since after visiting Rome and Jerusalem, where he bathed in the River Jordan, Hakon returned to an Orkney more predisposed toward him.[102] However, never to be outdone, Rognavald Kali one Christmas revealed 'his plan to go abroad and visit the Holy Land.'[103] Being skilled at foreign languages, Bishop William accompanied the earl as his translator.[104] It is tempting to think that this journey helped spread news of Magnus's holiness, as it stands to reason that Rognavald would stress his relationship to the martyred Orcadian saint. It is difficult to say what impact this had upon godly men outside of the earldom. However, during the Reformation some of Magnus's relics were allegedly transferred from Kirkwall to Aix-la-Chapelle, and to Saint Vitus in Prague.[105] If true, this might be attributed to a knowledge of the saint dating to Rognavald's time, at least in Prague, since the earl visited Bulgaria and Galicia, and went 'to Rome, then follow[ed] the usual pilgrim route ... to Denmark.'[106] Certainly, then, Rognavald was at least in the vicinity of Prague. Notwithstanding, Magnus also won support in the west, as affirmed by dedications to him in Orkney, Shetland, Caithness, England, the Faeroes, Iceland, and Norway.[107]

Few saints command strong followings for political reasons alone. A saint that also filled the role of protector of the people would inevitably enjoy broad appeal. In this capacity, veneration of the saint becomes an expression of communalism, readily apparent in songs reaffirming that Magnus was the pride of his homeland:

This glory we sing, and by miracles wrought,
The Lord Christ is blessed, and the Church doth rejoice,

And praise high ascendeth with thee as its theme;
How blessed Orcadia from henceforth appear![108]

This hymn is an expression of communalism, even though it was
written in Latin by a cleric.[109] Further community support for a
saint was assured when he assumed a niche formerly reserved for
certain traditional beliefs:

> The king-saints of Scandinavia and the earl-saints of Orkney embody
> older, pre-Christian concepts of sacral kingship, when the king as
> descendant and successor of the gods exercised a supreme priestly
> function. These ideas were slow to disappear ...[110]

This 'sacral kingship' might have been realized in the goðar (chieftain-priests) who formed the ruling caste in Iceland, and administered matters both secular and religious. Though not titled 'king' or
'earl,' the goðar still reckoned themselves to be of kingly stock, and
probably represented an earlier Scandinavian concept of kingship.
In Orkney, these chieftain-priests may have formed a political elite
during the reign of certain earls.[111]

As mentioned, the office of sacral ruler originated in pagan times.
Though the names of the Norse gods might be familiar, the day-to-
day appeasement of these entities is poorly comprehended. Yet it
seems safe to say that Norse paganism was regional in nature,
likely structured around the preferences of local chieftains. Thus
the paganism practised in one district could have been vastly different to that in another. Throughout, however, many functions of the
sacral ruler probably revolved around ensuring fertility. The Scandinavians had their own fertility god and goddess, Frey and Freyja
respectively. Some Icelandic sacral rulers counted the fertility god
their patron, the prime example being the title character of The
Saga of Hrafnkel Frey's goði. This saga talks of Hrafnkel sacrificing
to the gods, but most of all venerating Frey. As a chieftain, Hrafnkel
possessed much land but distributed it to farmers in exchange for
their loyalty.[112] Presumably this meant supporting Hrafnkel in both
political and religious affairs. In effect, this would probably result in
a good measure of religious uniformity within the area. Tales like
The Saga of Hrafnkel seem to stress the fertility deity's importance.[113]

However, Scandinavian paganism seemed sufficiently flexible to allow for other gods and goddesses to assume the role of fertility deity. As a sky god, Thor provided life-giving rain, essential for successful harvest, and was universally popular in most areas inhabited by pagan Scandinavians. Thorolf the Large Bearded honoured Thor by allegedly building a temple administered by a priest and supported through a tax levied against local farmers. It is unlikely, however, such a precise arrangement existed. More likely, this picture was the creation of thirteenth-century authors, reflecting upon the increasing level of organization within Scandinavian Christianity, particularly in Iceland.[114] Yet the same account seems accurate when concluding that area farmers had a duty 'to support the temple priest in his missions, just as farmers nowadays have to support their chieftains.'[115] Still, the essential point is once again the localized nature of Scandinavian paganism.

However, religion in early Christian Scandinavia probably also was influenced by local preference. As shown, the Church's initial strength and character was dependent upon the efforts of individual notables. In such an environment, the cults of locally popularized saints like Magnus could continue to thrive. Thus, when examining a saint's cult and the functions it served, it is probably more useful to comprehend its fulfilment of communal needs, rather than any role it played serving a Christian or pagan mindset.

Though many routine tasks asked of a holy man like Magnus had pagan trappings, they were really designed to fulfil a specific communal need. Successful harvest was important to both pagans and Christians. Yet the formula for ensuring fertility was established in heathen times, so that the Christian saint was summarily factored into that process. Thus some hymns devoted to Magnus contained the hope that he would placate nature:

Lift our flocks to the hills,
Quell the wolf and the fox,
Ward from us spectre, giant, fury,
And oppression.

Surround cows and herds,
Surround sheep and lambs;
Keep from them the water-vole,
And the field vole.

Sprinkle dew from the sky upon kine,
Give growth to grass, and corn, and sap to plants,
Watercress, deer's-grass, ceis, burdock,
And daisy.

O Magnus of fame,
On the barque of heroes,
On the crests of waves,
On the sea, on the land,
Aid and preserve us.[116]

Collected during the nineteenth century, and possibly originating
in the Hebrides,[117] this hymn contains older sentiments that are
reminiscent of ancient land charms. So essential were these, that
they survived the old gods' disappearance from many lands. Many
were given a Christian colouring,[118] and one thirteenth-century
German manuscript instructs clerics on accomplishing this.[119]
Thus, to facilitate the spread of Christianity, the church fathers
conceded certain territories to traditional practice. Though often
appearing as an attempt to incorporate paganism, in actual practice
it was a case of universal thought coming to terms with localism
employing varying levels of Christian and pagan ideology. This atti-
tude resulted in a hybrid religion which merged both Christian and
pagan, and universal and local ideologies. In this atmosphere, Christianity blended with many outside rites and rituals, and in no
aspect was this more true than with the earliest saints' cults.[120] Yet
it is important to realize that though one function of Magnus's cult
was to satisfy the need for fertility ritual, it is doubtful if the saint's
followers – especially by the nineteenth century – thought of themselves as bowing to pagan-inspired wisdom. Rather, Magnus was
fulfilling a need which had remained constant throughout time. He
had proven himself as capable of healing the land, as he was at healing the people.
    Healers of a more earthly origin also roamed the Northern world.
These guardian spirits were the metaphysical remains of departed
ancestors, who in many cases held greater importance for ordinary
people than the major gods.[121] Odin was a shadowy, fickle character,
who preferred poets and potentates. Farmers and mariners depended
upon Thor to favourably control the skies. But guardian spirits and

land spirits were often turned to when the troubles of everyday life overwhelmed ordinary people. The guardian spirit's popularity is reflected in tales like *Bárðar Saga*. A resident of Snófellsás, Iceland, when Bárðar died 'people virtually worshipped him in those parts and called on him in their need. He became the greatest of guardian spirits to men.'[122] This was religion with an affable 'human face,' and perhaps the Church's growing legions of healing saints were perceived as Christian successors to local land spirits. These Christian successors, however, still had to pass muster.

'Christianity was born into a world ... familiar with wandering healers ... it developed in an atmosphere heavy with magic and miracle.'[123] In the competition for devotees, a 'sorcerers' contest' was waged between the respective holy men of the old and new religions. The contest in which the druid Broichan's magic was defeated by Saint Columba's faith[124] demonstrated that God's healers possessed great skill. A holy man desiring to usurp another had to prove he possessed a special relationship with a god that was incomparably powerful.[125] Thus miracles were ultimately performed by God working through the individual, who functioned as a conduit. The saint as mediator between Christians and God[126] mimicked the land spirit acting as mediator between pagans and the supernatural elements.

With the establishment of Christianity, a healer still had to prove himself, though his rivals were now other Christians. Saint Magnus was tested and evidently passed, since the sagas suggest that God deemed the earl a suitable channel through which to work his mercy. *Shorter Magnus Saga* maintains that after Eldjarn was healed, people recognized the Almighty's intervention, so that they 'praised God for the mercy he had shown, to honour the Holy Earl Magnus.'[127] *Longer Magnus Saga* finishes with the saint aiding two Norwegian brothers who were attacked by the male relatives of a woman they seduced. One was killed, the other blinded and mutilated. The survivor prayed to God, who sent Magnus to help. After the dead brother was revived and the wounded one healed, the two gave 'thanks to God and to saint Magnus'[128] – suggesting that the miracle was worked by God acting through Magnus. Thus saints were superior miracle workers, demonstrating God's might to the Northern peoples.[129]

Magnus's cult was built upon numerous Christian, pagan, universal, and local traditions. It was influenced by earlier earls' activities, general Church reform, and local miracle-working traditions. To his earliest advocates, Saint Magnus's martyrdom was only one phase in a divine life, destined for holiness from the outset. Rognavald's minster in Kirkwall is a testament to the recognition of Magnus's holiness, and his immortality. Through deeds attributed to him, Magnus Erlendsson has achieved another form of immortality spelled out in the Norse *Havamal*:[130]

Cattle die, kinsmen die,
the self must also die;
I know one thing which never dies:
the reputation of each dead man.[131]

Notes

1 *OS*, 78 (chapter 34).

2 The medieval Scandinavian's bloodthirstiness has recently been re-evaluated by C. Morris; see S. Fraser, 'Vikings Lose Violent Image,' *Scotland on Sunday*, 27 June 1999 [News], 10.

3 The discussion is furthered in P. Schach, *Icelandic Sagas* (Boston, 1984); C.J. Clover, *The Medieval Saga* (Ithaca, 1982); T.M. Andersson, *The Problem of Icelandic Saga Origins* (New Haven, 1964); and P. Hallberg, *The Icelandic Saga*, trans. P. Schach (Lincoln, 1962).

4 *The Orkneyinga Saga*, trans. A.B. Taylor (Edinburgh, 1938) [*OS* (Taylor)], 9–11.

5 F. Guðmundsson, 'On the Writing of *Orkneyinga Saga*,' in *The Viking Age in Caithness, Orkney and the North Atlantic*, ed. C.E. Batey, J. Jesch, and C.D. Morris (Edinburgh, 1993), 206.

6 *OS* (Taylor), 16. 'Þættir' ('þáttir,' singular) may be thought of as being (roughly) synonymous with 'short stories.'

7 *Icelandic Sagas and Other Historical Documents Relating to the Settlements and Descents of the Northmen on the British Isles*, ed. G. Vigfusson and G.W. Dasent, 4 vols, RS (London, 1887–94) [*Icelandic Sagas*], i, ix–x.

8 For example, *Orkneyinga Saga*, ed. F. Guðmundsson, Íslenzk Fornrit, no. 34 (Reykjavik, 1965); *OS* (Taylor); and *OS*.

9 *OS* (Taylor), 17–18.

10 'Magnus Saga the Longer,' in *Icelandic Sagas*, iii, 239 (chapter 1). The author appears to be boasting about the advanced level of Latin scholar-

ship in his native land. On the social and political ramifications of this, see G.M. Brunsden, 'Politics and Local Tradition within the Cult of Saint Magnus of Orkney,' *Northern Studies* 32 (1997), 131–2.

11 'Magnus Saga the Longer,' in *Icelandic Sagas*, iii, 268 (chapter 28).

12 *OS* (Taylor), 36.

13 P. Bibre, 'Magnúss saga helga eyajarls,' in *Medieval Scandinavia: An Encyclopaedia*, ed. P. Pulsiano and K. Wolf (New York, 1993), 401.

14 W.M. Metcalfe, *Lives of the Scottish Saints* (Paisley, 1895; repr. Lampeter, 1990), 7. Metcalfe incorrectly stated that the saga was a strict translation of the *vita*. He provides a 'Life of S. Magnus,' which appears to be *Longer Magnus Saga* with *Shorter Magnus Saga*'s chapters 15–18 interpolated.

15 *Magnus' Saga: The Life of St Magnus, Earl of Orkney 1075–1116*, trans. H. Pálsson and P. Edwards (Oxford, 1987), 45–6.

16 Bibre, 'Magnúss saga helga eyajarls,' in *Medieval Scandinavia*, 401. Bergr might also have been the author of one Icelandic version of Thomas Becket's life; see A. Jackobsen, 'Thómas saga erkibiskups,' in *Medieval Scandinavia*, 643–4.

17 Snorri Sturluson, *Heimskringla*, trans. L.M. Hollander, paperback ed. (Austin, TX, 1991) [*Heimskringla*], 171 ('Saga of Olaf Tryggvason,' chapter 31).

18 *OS*, 37 (chapter 12); cf. *Heimskringla*, 189 ('Saga of Olaf Tryggvason,' chapter 47).

19 'Theoderic, Historia de Antiquitate Regum Norwagiensium' (chapter 9), in *ES*, i, 507–8.

20 'Flatey Book,' in *Icelandic Sagas*, iii, 338; also in *ES*, i, 509.

21 'Flatey Book,' in *Icelandic Sagas*, iii, 338.

22 *OS* (Taylor), 357n.

23 *OS*, 37 (chapter 11).

24 The relationship between Odin, the raven, and war is explored in H.R.E. Davidson, *Myths and Symbols in Pagan Europe: Early Scandinavian and Celtic Religions* (Syracuse, 1988), 98–9.

25 This ritual of *primum signum* (prime-signed) as it existed in Iceland is described in *Laws of Early Iceland: Grágás I*, trans. A. Dennis, P. Foote, and R. Perkins (Winnipeg, 1980) [*Grágás*], 26 and note.

26 *The Poetic Edda: A New Translation*, trans. C. Larrington (Oxford, 1996), 247 and 295n.

27 B. and P. Sawyer, *Medieval Scandinavia: From Conversion to Reformation circa 800–1500* (Minneapolis, 1993), 103–5.

28 On tithes in Iceland, see *Grágás*, 36.

29 P. Sawyer, 'Dioceses and Parishes in Twelfth-Century Scandinavia,' in
   St Magnus Cathedral and Orkney's Twelfth Century Renaissance, ed.
   B. Crawford (Aberdeen, 1988), 40.

30 K. Helle, 'The Organisation of the Twelfth-Century Norwegian
   Church,' in *St Magnus Cathedral*, ed. Crawford, 46.

31 *ES*, ii, 229; B. Crawford, 'Bishops of Orkney in the Eleventh and Twelfth
   Centuries: Bibliography and Biographical List,' *Innes Review* 47/1
   (Spring 1996), 1–13.

32 W.P.L. Thomson, *History of Orkney* (Edinburgh, 1987), 52.

33 Adam of Bremen, *History of the Archbishops of Hamburg-Bremen*, ed.
   F.J. Tschan (New York, 1959), 216 (book. 4, chapter 35).

34 *OS*, 74–5 (chapter 31).

35 Adam of Bremen, *History*, 134 (book 3, chapter 23); cf. book 3, chapter 72.

36 The exact location of Thorfinn's minster is discussed in A. Ritchie,
   Viking Scotland (London, 1993), 53–4; Thomson, *History of Orkney*, 53;
   and B. Crawford, *Scandinavian Scotland* (Leicester, 1987) 81.

37 *OS*, 75 (chapter 31).

38 C.A.R. Radford, 'St Magnus Cathedral, Kirkwall, and the Development
   of the Cathedral in Northwest Europe,' in *St Magnus Cathedral*, ed.
   Crawford, 17–18.

39 *OS*, 55 (chapter 20).

40 *OS*, 71 (chapter 30).

41 R.A. McDonald, '"Far is Rome from Lochlong": Gaels and Scandinavians on Pilgrimage and Crusade, *c.*1000–*c.*1300,' *Scripta Mediterranea*
   18/3 (1997), 11, stresses that for individuals like Cnut, pilgrimage
   demonstrated a desire to play the role of just-minded Christian
   prince.

42 Thomson, *History of Orkney*, 54.

43 *The Anglo-Saxon Chronicle*, trans. G.N. Garmonsway (London, 1953;
   new ed., 1972), 155 ('Worcester Chronicle,' 1066); *The Anglo-Saxon
   Chronicle*, ed. and trans. M. Swanton (London, 1996), 199.

44 Florence of Worcester, *A History of the Kings of England*, trans. J. Stevenson (London, 1860; repr. Lampeter, 1990), 134, mentions only
   Paul's presence; while *OS*, 76 (chapter 33), talks of his energies.

45 *Njal's Saga*, trans. M. Magnusson and H. Pálsson (Harmondsworth,
   1960; repr. 1974), 216–26 (chapters 100–5).

46 'Magnus Saga the Longer,' in *Icelandic Sagas*, iii, 247 (chapter 8).

47 J. Mooney, *St. Magnus, Earl of Orkney* (Kirkwall, 1935), 46.

48 One theory holds that the oldest Gospel is really that of Mark, which
   relates an abridged version of this story.

49 Florence of Worcester, *History of the Kings of England*, 157, provides the date for King Magnus's venture; see also *SAEC*, 120.

50 *Magnus' Saga*, 23 (chapter 3).

51 *Heimskringla* says nothing of Hakon Paulsson's or the Erlendssons' involvement in the king's first campaign. However, Theoderic says Earl Erlend and an eighteen-year-old Magnus were with King Magnus; see 'Theoderic, Historia de Antiquitate Regum Norwagiensium,' in *ES*, ii, 110.

52 *Magnus' Saga*, 23 (chapter 3).

53 *OS*, 84 (chapter 39).

54 *OS*, 88 (chapter 43).

55 *Longer Magnus Saga* and *Orkneyinga* neglect to mention the whereabouts of Olaf, but all three agree that Sigurd was away to the Holy Land.

56 'Annals of Ulster' and 'Icelandic Annals,' in *ES*, ii, 126.

57 *Heimskringla*, 683 ('Saga of Magnus Barelegs,' chapter 23).

58 *OS*, 88 (chapter 42).

59 *Magnus' Saga*, 26–7 (chapter 7).

60 William of Worcester's *Itineraria*, described in *OS* (Taylor), 375n.

61 'Magnus Saga the Longer,' in *Icelandic Sagas*, iii, 254 (chapter 15).

62 *OS*, 90 (chapter 45).

63 *Magnus' Saga*, 27 (chapter 7).

64 The skalds may be thought of as court poets who accompanied notables on their ventures.

65 *Njal's Saga*, 263–73 (chapters 28–30).

66 'Magnus Saga the Longer,' in *Icelandic Sagas*, iii, 253–4 (chapter 14).

67 On the historical accuracy of skaldic poetry, see P. Hallberg, *Old Icelandic Poetry: Eddic Lay and Skaldic Verse*, trans. P. Schach and S. Lindgrenson (Lincoln, 1962; trans., 1975), 105–72.

68 H. O'Donoghue, *The Genesis of a Saga Narrative: Verse and Prose in Kormaks Saga* (Oxford, 1991), v.

69 *OS*, 90–1 (chapter 46).

70 *OS*, 94 (chapter 50).

71 A summation of evidence favouring one or the other date is in *ES*, ii, 160–1n.

72 *Magnus' Saga*, 43 (chapter 20).

73 *Egil's Saga*, trans. H. Pálsson and P. Edwards (Harmondsworth, 1976), 26 (chapter 4), is but one that talks of Harald Fine-hair's 'tyranny.'

74 T. Jexlev, 'The Cult of Saints in Early Medieval Scandinavia,' in *St Magnus Cathedral*, ed. Crawford, 188.

75 B. Dickins, 'The Cult of S. Olave in the British Isles,' *Saga-Book of the Viking Society* 12 (1937–45), 53–80, lists those British locations where Olaf has been honoured.

76 *OS*, 116 (chapter 61).

77 *OS*, 130–1 (chapter 68).

78 A. Mirgeler, *Mutations of Western Christianity*, trans. E. Quinn (London, 1961; tr. 1964), 49.

79 A pivotal episode that helped assure victory occurred when three Shetlanders assisted in extinguishing Paul's signal beacon on Fair Isles; see *OS*, 131–3 (chapters 69–70).

80 *OS*, 130–1 (chapter 68).

81 Mooney, *St Magnus, Earl of Orkney*, 10.

82 *OS*, 142 (chapter 46).

83 *OS*, 32 (chapter 8).

84 *OS*, 37 (chapter 11). Here is further evidence suggesting the saga's composite nature, and perhaps its hasty assembly. The *jarla þáttir* provides the story of Einar's acquisition, then Sigurd's return, of the farmers' rights. Rognavald's *þáttir* provides the competing tale.

85 Thomson, *History of Orkney*,16.

86 C.D. Morris, 'Viking Orkney: A Survey,' in *The Prehistory of Orkney B.C. 4000–1000 A.D.*, ed. C. Renfrew (Edinburgh, 1985), 234–45.

87 Thomson, *History of Orkney*, 63, suggests that given the style of Rognavald's minster, and stonemasons' marks contained therein, that either the workmen were 'recruited directly from Durham, or were Durham men who had previously been working on Norwegian churches.'

88 See 'Chronicle of Melrose,' in *ES*, ii, 195–6 and note.

89 D.E.R. Watt, 'The Church in Scotland,' in *St Magnus Cathedral*, ed. Crawford, 28.

90 L. Laing, *Orkney and Shetland: An Archaeological Guide* (London, 1974), 195. Laing also believes that the architectural inspiration for Orphir was the Church of the Holy Sepulchre. The details of Hakon's pilgrimage, but no mention of his having built Orphir, are found in *OS*, 97 (chapter 52).

91 Mooney, *St Magnus*, 243n. Mooney certainly believed that Rognavald Brusason was the builder of Saint Olaf's; whereas Thomson (*History of Orkney*, 63) says the earl 'may have been responsible.' The people who researched Kirkwall's (relatively recent) 'Heritage Guide' share Mooney's earlier certainty and optimism.

92 *Heimskringla*, 511 ('Saint Olaf's Saga,' chapter 226).

93 *Heimskringla*, 526 ('Saint Olaf's Saga,' chapter 240).

94 *OS*, 58 (chapter 21).

95 Laing, *Orkney and Shetland*, 196; and E. Fernie, 'The Church of St Magnus, Egilsay,' in *St Magnus Cathedral*, ed. Crawford, 119.

96 *OS*, 96 (chapter 52).

97 *OS*, 105 (chapter 57).

98 Thomson, *History of Orkney*, 63.

99 Safe from the elements, though not from the attacks of submarines like U-47, as 833 officers and crew onboard HMS *Royal Oak* fatally discovered on the night of 13–14 October 1939.

100 P.A. Anderson, 'The Orkney Church of the Twelfth and Thirteenth Centuries – a Stepdaughter of the Norwegian Church?' in *St Magnus Cathedral*, ed. Crawford, 60.

101 Crawford, 'Bishops of Orkney,' 10.

102 *OS*, 97 (chapter 52). The passage of a new legal code also helped Hakon win new approval among the Orcadians.

103 *OS*, 161 (chapter 85).

104 For a discussion of William's command of tongues, see I. McDougall, 'Foreigners and Foreign Languages in Medieval Iceland,' *Saga-Book of the Viking Society* 22 (1986–9), 193 and 217.

105 Mooney, *St Magnus*, 253. However, Mooney (261–3) is careful to qualify that there were a few other venerated holy-men named Magnus, besides the Orcadian earl.

106 *OS*, 181 (chapter 89).

107 A full list of dedications is found in Mooney, *St Magnus*, 269–83.

108 'Hymn to Saint Magnus,' in J. Beveridge, 'Two Scottish Thirteenth-Century Songs, with the Original Melodies, Recently Discovered in Sweden,' *Proceedings of the Society of Antiquaries of Scotland* 73 (1939), 284 (stanza 6). The piece's creator was thoroughly familiar with the Magnus legend, since he mentions the earl's chaste marriage and his 'crafty foe, Hakon.' The first four stanzas of the Latin original are preserved in Mooney, *St Magnus*, 291–2; there is a new translation in *The Triumph Tree: Scotland's Earliest Poetry A.D. 550–1350*, ed. T.O. Clancy (Edinburgh, 1998), 292–4.

109 The hymn may have been written in an Orcadian Minorite friary, according to Beveridge, 'Two Scottish Thirteenth-Century Songs,' 284.

110 Thomson, *History of Orkney*, 66.

111 L.K. Shei and G. Moberg (*The Orkney Story* [London, 1985]), 52) believe such an institution existed in Thorfinn the Mighty's time,

probably basing their claim on *Orkneyinga Saga*'s observation that he promoted good government.

112 *Hrafnkel's Saga and Other stories*, trans. H. Pálsson (Harmondsworth, 1971), 36–7 (chapter 2).

113 Sagas which talk of Frey worship include *The Saga of Gisli the Outlaw*, trans. G. Johnston (Toronto, 1963); *Viga-Glums Saga*, trans. J. McKinnell (Edinburgh, 1987); and *The Fljotsdale Saga and the Droplaugarsons*, trans. E. Haworth and J. Young (London, 1990). See also Adam of Bremen, *History*, 207–8 (book 4, chapters 26–7).

114 Sawyer, *Medieval Scandinavia*, 105.

115 *Eyrbyggja Saga*, trans. H. Pálsson and P. Edwards (London, 1989), 29 (chapter 4).

116 'Magnus of My Love,' in *Carmina Gadelica*, ed. Alexander Carmichael, 6 vols (Edinburgh, 1900–83), i, 179–81 (no. 72). Reprinted as Alexander Carmichael, *Carmina Gadelica*, with an introduction by J. MacInnes (Hudson, NY, 1992), 82 (no. 72).

117 Mooney, *St Magnus*, 292.

118 See, for example, 'For Unfruitful Land,' in *Anglo-Saxon Verse Charms, Maxims and Heroic Legends*, trans. L.J. Rodrigues (Pinner, Middlesex, 1993), 130–5.

119 F. Grendon, 'The Anglo-Saxon Charms,' *Journal of American Folklore* 22 (April–June 1909), 148.

120 T.J. Heffernan, *Sacred Biography: Saints and Their Biographers in the Middle Ages* (New York, 1988), 143–4.

121 Davidson, *Gods and Myths*, 214.

122 *Bárðar Saga*, ed. and trans. J. Skaptason and P. Pulsiano (New York, 1984), 31–3 (chapter 6).

123 R.C. Finucane, *Miracles and Pilgrims: Popular Beliefs in Medieval England* (London, 1977), 17.

124 Adomnan of Iona, *Life of St Columba*, trans. R. Sharpe (London, 1995), 181–4 (book 2, chapters 33–4).

125 Finucane, *Miracles and Pilgrims*, 20; see also Mirgeler, *Mutations of Western Christianity*, 46 and 48.

126 K. McCone, *Pagan Past and Christian Present in Early Irish Literature* (Maynooth, 1990), 188.

127 *Magnus' Saga*, 43 (chapter 20).

128 'Magnus Saga the Longer,' in *Icelandic Sagas*, iii, 280 (chapter 34).

129 Mirgeler, *Mutations of Western Christianity*, 49.

130 *Poetic Edda*, trans. Larrington, 24 ('Sayings of the High One,' ll. 76–80).

131 Since this article was written, a new edition of *Morkinskinna* appeared
in translation: *Morkinskinna: The Earliest Icelandic Chronicle of the
Norwegian Kings (1030–1157)*, trans. T.M. Andersson and K.E. Gade
(Ithaca, NY, 2000). Chapters 57–9 offer yet another portrayal of the
earls' involvement in Magnus Barelegs's British and Irish campaigns,
and I intend to revisit this episode in the future, taking into account
the testimony of *Morkinskinna* and the relationship between its
manuscripts and those of *Heimskringla*.

3

'Soldiers Most Unfortunate': Gaelic and Scoto-Norse Opponents of the Canmore Dynasty, c. 1100–c. 1230

R. ANDREW McDONALD

In 1211 William king of Scotland sent a huge army together with all the nobles of the kingdom into Ross against Guthred MacWilliam. The king himself followed when he was able to come ... On the way he built two castles, laid waste pretty well all of Ross, and took or killed as many of the said Guthred's supporters as he could find. But Guthred himself always avoided the king's army, meanwhile laying ambushes for it whenever he could by night or day, and driving off booty from the lord king's land.[1]

Guthred MacWilliam, as this passage from the fifteenth-century chronicler Walter Bower so vividly demonstrates, was one of several individuals against whom the Scottish kings of the twelfth and thirteenth centuries were forced to flex their military muscle from time to time. Indeed, as one historian has remarked, 'a recurrent note of hostility can be detected' throughout the reigns of these kings.[2] This paper takes up the theme of hostility toward the Scottish monarchs from the peripheral regions of their kingdom, analyses who their enemies were and what motivated them, and reflects on the significance of this hostility for Scottish political culture of the central Middle Ages.

Twelfth-century Scotland was moving into a new era as a self-confident medieval kingdom. From 1097 until 1286 it was ruled by the descendants of King Malcolm III 'Canmore' (1058–93) and his second wife, Queen Margaret (d. 1093) – the so-called Canmore or MacMalcolm dynasty. After a brief civil war following the deaths of Malcolm and Margaret, their son Edgar gained the kingship in 1097 (to 1107); he was followed by his brothers Alexander I (1107–24) and

David I (1124–53). David was succeeded by his grandsons Malcolm IV (1153–65) and William I (1165–1214); and William by the two Alexanders (II, 1214–49, and III, 1249–86), his son and grandson respectively. The early Canmore kings (particularly David I) initiated, and their successors consolidated, a thoroughgoing transformation of Scottish society, characterized by a process of 'Europeanization'[3] or modernization of the kingdom. David's reign was the turning point; by his death in 1153, although much remained to be done, all the hallmarks of the process were clearly visible. Colonists from England and the Continent (conveniently termed 'Anglo-Normans') settled in Scotland. Lands (mostly south of the Forth) were granted out in return for military service, and knights and castles, the joint symbols of contemporary European society, also appeared for the first time.[4] The growth of towns (burghs) and the introduction of coinage signalled economic transformation, while the construction of churches and monasteries for the reformed religious orders marked ecclesiastical change.[5]

Largely because the Europeanization of Scotland was undertaken at the initiative of native kings, rather than foreign conquerors, and through invitation rather than military conflict, the introduction of foreign ideas, institutions, and settlers is seen as an essentially peaceful process – a 'peaceful Norman conquest,' as it has been called.[6] Indeed, the twelfth-century kingdom of the Scots has been regarded as representing a balance between old and new – so much so that by the thirteenth century, it has been described as a hybrid in which native Scottish and European elements were successfully synthesized.[7] Yet, despite the relative harmony that prevailed in the twelfth-century kingdom, not to mention the power and prestige of its kings, there were disaffected elements, too; individuals who, for various reasons, stood against the Canmore kings. Although relatively neglected in the past, resistance to the Canmore dynasty is increasingly regarded by some historians as an important theme in medieval Scottish kingship and political culture. As one authority succinctly put it, 'the history of Scottish kingship from the eleventh century to the thirteenth is a mixture of consolidation and internal challenges.'[8]

Without doubt, the most stubborn and potentially deadly opposition to the twelfth-century kings of Scots came from the rugged and inhospitable northern reaches of their kingdom, Moray (the large but ill-defined region around the Moray Firth that stretched from the Grampians to the western seaboard) and Ross (the province north of Moray, encompassing the territory between the River Oykel and the Dornoch Firth to the north and the Cromarty Firth to the south) – these were 'the remotest territories of Scotland' according to one chronicler.[9] The Scottish kings faced threats from the north between 1124 and 1230, led by two families about whom relatively little is known: the MacHeths and MacWilliams. Generally speaking, the MacHeths were in the forefront of insurrection from 1124 until 1157, and then, from the late 1170s, the MacWilliams became prominent until their extinction in 1230.

David I faced insurrections in 1124 and 1130, both orchestrated, it would seem, by an individual named Malcolm MacHeth. Two battles were fought in 1124, but this did not completely eliminate the danger because in 1130 Malcolm, operating this time in cooperation with Angus, the ruler of Moray, clashed with the Scottish army at Stracathro in the Mearns. Angus was slain in what Irish chroniclers described as the 'slaughter of the men of Moray,'[10] but Malcolm escaped, only to be captured in 1134 and incarcerated at Roxburgh, a royal stronghold, for over twenty years.[11] Stracathro's legacy was the annexation of Moray to the Crown, and the initiation of a policy of vigorous colonization, but the large northern region remained a 'turbulent marchland'[12] down to the very end of the twelfth century. David, meanwhile, was remembered by one chronicler as 'a most unconquered king, who had reduced to himself so many barbarous races, and who had triumphed with little labour over the men of Moray and of the Isles.'[13]

David I's death in 1153 triggered further insurrections. That year, Malcolm's sons joined forces with their powerful uncle, the mighty Somerled, and assaulted the Scottish kingdom.[14] The uprising dragged on for several years but seems to have lost momentum by 1157, by which time one of MacHeth's sons had been captured, Somerled had become embroiled in conflict with the Manx kings, and Malcolm MacHeth had come to terms with the Scottish king (see below).[15] Malcolm died in 1168 (outliving both King Malcolm IV and Somerled), and of both himself and his sons little more is known.[16]

It did not take long for a new nemesis to emerge for the Scottish kings. Within a decade of the death of Malcolm MacHeth, the mantle of the MacHeths as the opponents of the Scottish kings fell squarely upon the shoulders of new champions: the MacWilliam kindred. As early as 1179, King William I was forced to undertake a campaign in the north, during which he constructed two castles at strategic locations on the Beauly and Cromarty Firths. This expedition was said to have been undertaken against Donald MacWilliam.[17] In 1181, MacWilliam, 'by the mandate of certain powerful men of the kingdom of Scotland,' invaded with a large army, and even though the king campaigned against him, he remained at large. It was not until 1187 that Donald met a much more unhappy fate than Malcolm MacHeth when a contingent of the royal army, based at Inverness, smashed his forces at the unknown site of 'Mam Garvia' (possibly Strath Garve near Dingwall). Donald's severed head was presented to the king as a grisly trophy.[18] 'And thus,' a contemporary chronicler wrote, 'when he was laid low, a great peace arose in the kingdom of Scotland.'[19]

For the next twenty-five years, little is heard of either MacHeths or MacWilliams. Then, in 1211, another MacWilliam appeared on the scene – Guthred, the son of Donald. After a major series of military campaigns in Ross, led by William Comyn, Guthred's forces were engaged, defeated, and scattered. But as soon as the king departed, Guthred besieged a royal castle in Ross and was on the verge of capturing it when the garrison surrendered; the use of siege machines by Guthred is interesting and reveals something of the capacity of the MacWilliam armies. In response, King William sent his son, Alexander, with a large army to Ross at the start of the next campaigning season (June 1212). But before any military action could be taken, Guthred was betrayed by his own followers, put in chains, and taken to the king's justiciary in Moray, William Comyn (who was made earl of Buchan c. 1212 for his role in defeating Guthred).[20] Comyn, with the prisoner in tow, set out to meet the king, but 'when he learned the king's will, which was that he did not want to see him [Guthred] alive, they beheaded Guthred, dragged him along by the feet, and hung him up.'[21]

A few years later, in 1215, the MacWilliams joined forces with the MacHeths and staged another attack. The leaders of the invasion were Donald Bán MacWilliam, probably a son of Guthred, and Kenneth MacHeth, who were said to have been accompanied by the son of an Irish king.[22] In a pattern that was becoming increasingly predictable, the uprising was quashed, only this time not by the king or a royal army, but rather a northern dignitary named Farquhar MacTaggart, who cut off the heads of the leaders and presented them as gifts to the new king, Alexander II. As a reward for his loyal service, Farquhar was knighted by the king, and later made earl of Ross.[23]

Nonetheless, another insurrection seems to have broken out in the early 1220s, led by Gillescop MacWilliam, a son of Donald Bán or Guthred. He was still active in 1228, when Thomas de Thirlestane, a northern landholder, was attacked in his wooden castle, part of Inverness burnt, and some royal lands plundered; since Thomas also held lands in Lauderdale, in the southwest, it might be that the attack on his northern fief represented retribution for the Gallovidian role in suppressing the MacWilliam insurrection in 1187.[24] Gillescop was killed in 1229,[25] but resentment lingered until 1230, when the MacWilliams were snuffed out forever. A contemporary English chronicler recorded the fate of the last of this unfortunate kindred: '... the same MacWilliam's daughter, who had not long left her mother's womb, innocent as she was, was put to death in the burgh of Forfar ... her head was struck against the column of the [market] cross and her brains dashed out.'[26]

What made the MacHeths and the MacWilliams such implacable foes of the Canmore kings that they had to be eliminated down to the last child? To answer this question, we must turn to both the identity of the individuals concerned and to the question of Scottish kingship in the twelfth century.

Malcolm MacHeth was associated in the 1130 uprising with Angus of Moray. Angus was a grandson and heir of King Lulach, slain by David's father, Malcolm III, in 1058. As such, he was a legitimate claimant to the Scottish kingship, but Malcolm's genealogy is much more uncertain; indeed, his identity is an important unsolved mystery of medieval Scottish history.[27] Modern opinion on this question splits along two main lines: one view is that he was a member of the important Cenél Loairn dynasty, from which the rulers of Moray (like Angus) and some Scottish kings had been drawn in the past; while another view holds that he was a member of an important family from Ross, the province north of Moray that stretched from Drumalban eastward to the Beauly Firth, and separated Moray from Caithness and Sutherland, which were under the control of the Scandinavian earls of Orkney.[28] The evidence, as far as it goes, will sustain both views. The name 'MacHeth' represents the Gaelic 'mac Aed' (son of Aed),[29] and Aed (Aodh) was a common Gaelic name.[30] Coincidentally, there was an earl of this name who

witnessed one charter (probably) of King Alexander and two early
ones of David, but he is, unfortunately, given no territorial designation.[31] It may be that this Earl Aed was Malcolm's father, but there
is no indication whether he was an early earl of Ross, or some relation to Angus of Moray, who was slain in 1130, or whether he was
an ally or an enemy of the Scottish king.

Fortunately, several other facts are known about MacHeth that
leave no doubt of his importance and standing in society. First, he
married a sister of Somerled, the king of the Isles, and a daughter of
this union married Earl Harald Maddadsson of Orkney and Caithness.[32] These matrimonial alliances are proof of MacHeth's high
status, since medieval princes and nobles intermarried at their own
social levels or even higher; MacHeth's pedigree and standing in
society must have been well known to both Somerled and Earl
Harald, or the matches would never have taken place. Second, we
know that MacHeth finally came to terms with Malcolm IV in
1157, after one of his sons had been captured and after Somerled
had all but abandoned the MacHeth cause.[33] The terms of the agreement are not known but hinge on a third fact about MacHeth: when
he died in 1168, he was styled earl of Ross, a title which he also
held when he witnessed a royal charter to the abbey of Dunfermline
sometime in the late 1150s.[34] These last two pieces of evidence suggest that, as part of the agreement of 1157, MacHeth was awarded
the province of Ross, probably in compensation for giving up whatever claims he had to the Scottish kingship or else to Moray. If such
an arrangement seems inherently unlikely, it is worthwhile bearing
in mind that at least one other prominent kindred, the mormaers of
Fife, had probably abandoned their claims to the royal office in the
tenth century, receiving in return the status of premier nobles of
the kingdom and the privilege of inaugurating new Scottish monarchs.[35] Moreover, such an arrangement had practical appeal for
both the Scottish king and Malcolm MacHeth: the former got a sta-
ble northern frontier, governed by a native noble now bound to the
monarchy, while the latter maintained something of his status –
not to mention his head. What is not clear is whether the earldom
of Ross was actually created at this time, being carved out of Moray,
or whether Malcolm was installed in an existing province whose
previous holders are unknown.[36]

In contrast to Malcolm MacHeth, the lineage of the MacWilliams
is clear. They descended from William, a son of King Duncan II,

who ruled briefly in 1094 and was the eldest son of Malcolm III by his first marriage to Ingibjorg of Orkney. William fitz Duncan, as he was known – and the Norman form of his name is significant – was the lord of Allerdale, a close companion and a supporter of David I who often witnessed royal charters and who seems to have accommodated himself to the modernizing policies of the Scottish kings, his status as a potential claimant to the kingship notwithstanding.[37] A thirteenth-century genealogy names William as 'earl of Moray,' a title by which he is not otherwise known and which, if correct, could be explained by a marriage into the Moray dynasty, giving him a claim to the Scottish kingship as well as the earldom of Moray.[38] But, despite this enigmatic reference, William is not known to have harboured any enmity toward David I, which makes the sudden appearance of his son, Donald, on the scene as an enemy of the king in 1179–81 difficult to explain. Several factors may do so. First, William himself was very young, if he had even been born, when his father was killed in 1094, and, in the ensuing round of civil wars, would have been in no position to stake any claim. Indeed, it is not even certain that he was in Scotland at all in these years: he was probably residing at the English court. Second, it seems clear from what is known of William fitz Duncan that he had achieved prominence within Scottish society and was little inclined toward pressing a claim of his own. In this respect, it is interesting to note that the chroniclers loyal to the Canmore kings regarded Duncan II as illegitimate, thereby strengthening the case of their patrons and weakening the claims of rivals descended from Duncan II.[39] If, however, Donald, as the Gaelic form of his name – MacWilliam – suggests,[40] was not raised at court but was fostered out to a Gaelic household, his assimilation is less likely; his position to press a claim, stronger. Thus, despite the difficulties of the source material, the MacHeths and MacWilliams are best regarded as dynastic rivals.

In the twelfth century, under the Canmore kings, and as part and parcel of the large-scale transformation of Scottish society that took place under their aegis, an older, more inclusive system of kingship started to break down. Between the ninth and eleventh centuries, Scottish kingship alternated among different branches of the royal line, representatives of which took turns holding the royal office in alternating reigns; thus, a father might be succeeded by a son under this system, but not directly – another kinsman, like an uncle or a cousin, usually held power in-between. In the eleventh century, kings like Malcolm II (1005–34) tried to alter the system – Malcolm industriously spent the latter part of his reign killing off potential rivals so that his grandson, Duncan, could succeed. This he did in 1034, as Duncan I, only to be slain in 1040 by Macbeth, who represented a branch of the royal line excluded by the succession of Duncan I. This led to one of the more famous episodes in Scottish history, when Malcolm III slew Macbeth in 1057 and then his stepson, King Lulach, in early 1058, paving the way for the triumph of the Canmore dynasty. After a brief civil war following the death of Malcolm III in 1093, the kingship passed in an orderly fashion among his descendants. This happened as much by accident as by design, at least at first, but the end result was the same: the older, more inclusive system of succession had broken down, and the kingship was now monopolized by a single lineage; eventually, primogeniture came to prevail. Those who had, in the past, been eligible to compete for the royal office now found themselves on the outside, looking in. As D. Ó Corráin explained in the Irish context (where a similar pattern of succession operated), 'the passing of the kingship from one segment to another, from one dynastic base to another, upset as many as it satisfied.'[41] That explains both why the MacHeths and MacWilliams can be considered dynastic rivals – they seem to have belonged, as far as the evidence shows, to royal lineages – and why they were such implacable enemies: they were fighting for a prize which they fully believed to be theirs by right and tradition. As one historian remarked, '... the case for the claimants was that of rightful heirs against "modern" usurpers and in the end it narrowed down to MacWilliam *versus* William. At no time was there a straight issue: Gael *versus* Norman.'[42]

The MacHeths and MacWilliams, with their strong, apparently dynastic, claims, represented the most tenacious and perhaps the most dangerous opposition that the Scottish kings faced. But there were others. Beyond any doubt, one of the greatest foes that King William I had to face, and one who had links with both the MacHeths and the MacWilliams, was Harald Maddadson, the earl of Orkney and Caithness (d. 1206). Earl Harald was the son of the earl of Atholl (who was a kinsman of David I) and an Orkney woman. He became nominal joint ruler of Orkney and Caithness in 1139 (at the age of five) and married a daughter of the earl of Fife. In 1159 he became sole ruler of the earldom, and sometime after that, probably around 1168, he put aside his first wife and married the daughter of Malcolm MacHeth, with whom he had several children. This marriage, which was perhaps intended to provide a claim to the earldom of Ross after the death of MacHeth in 1168, led Earl Harald into collaboration with the MacHeths and MacWilliams and eventually to conflict with King William. There can be little doubt that Harald was one of those unnamed powerful men who instigated the 1181–7 insurrection of Donald MacWilliam, but if so, he soon moved into the forefront of events in the 1190s. In 1196, Earl Harald led a force into Moray and, in that year or the next, fought a battle with the king's vassals near Inverness. In retaliation, in the summer of 1197, King William invaded the province of Caithness, and his army destroyed the earl's castle at Thurso. Harald was forced to submit, and had to give up half of the earldom to a rival (Harald Ungi) and deliver hostages, including his son Thorfinn, to the king. Thorfinn seems to have had little inclination toward this arrangement and led a revolt which resulted in further campaigns; later in the year, as a result of this intransigence, Harald was removed to Edinburgh or Roxburgh castle in chains and deprived of the earldom of Caithness until Thorfinn surrendered. Thorfinn soon came to terms and took his father's place in prison, while Harald returned to Orkney and eliminated his rival in a brief but intense conflict. Caithness, however, seems to have been given by the Scottish king to Ragnvald, the king of Man, and administered by stewards.

In 1201 Harald launched a bid to recover his mainland possessions, possibly at the instigation of King John of England, or else possibly with his help (the two main sources for the event differ considerably in their presentation of it). King William undertook yet another campaign to Caithness and brought Harald to heel in 1202. For a payment of £2000, he was restored to the earldom; his son, meanwhile, had been blinded and castrated by the king for his father's intransigence. Harald died in 1206, and he was reckoned by the author of the *Orkneyinga Saga*, a saga-history of the earls of Orkney, as one of the three most powerful earls.[43]

This brief sketch hardly does justice to the mighty earl of Orkney and Caithness who gave the Scottish king plenty of opportunity to test his military mettle. His activities in the 1190s clearly cannot be dissociated from the activities of the MacHeths and MacWilliams, and, whether or not he sought the earldom of Ross through his marriage connections to the MacHeths, there can be little doubt that his position in Caithness would have been strengthened by attacks which eroded the power and authority of the Scottish monarchs. Whatever the case, from about 1180 Earl Harald had joined the ranks of those ranged against the Scottish kings, playing a behind-the-scenes role, aiding, abetting, and instigating the MacWilliams, but also taking centre stage in the events of 1196–1202.

An occurrence of 1197 may well be connected to Earl Harald's activities. The English chronicler Roger of Howden records that, in this year, King William,

> ... made the men of his kingdom swear that they would preserve peace to the extent of their power, and they would not be robbers nor thieves nor outlaws, nor receivers of them, and they would not in anything consent with them; and that when they should be able to know of malefactors of this kind, they would to the extent of their power take and destroy them.[44]

The passage is interesting for a number of reasons. At the general level, it is suggestive of rather more internal disorder than is normally admitted to be the case for the late twelfth-century kingdom, although it would be dangerous to push this conclusion too far solely on the basis of this episode. Yet in the context of opposition to the Scottish kings, the passage assumes further significance, since it is interesting, and surely not coincidental, that William's attempt to preserve the peace came in the very year that saw a substantial conflict between the king and the earl of Orkney, and only a decade after the defeat of Donald MacWilliam at Mam Garvia. Indeed, it is tempting to suppose that behind the generic robbers, thieves, and outlaws of Howden's passage there lay individuals like the MacHeths, MacWilliams, and Earl Harald, who had, by 1197, caused considerable disruption to the internal peace and stability of the Scottish kingdom.

By the time the infant MacWilliam was slain in 1230, what might be called the 'Scottish conquest of the north' had been largely completed. Yet the Scottish kings also faced challenges from other peripheral regions of the kingdom, including the far west, where, by the 1150s, a new power had emerged: the mighty Somerled, king of the Isles, every bit as formidable as Earl Harald Maddadson. Somerled, of mixed Gaelic-Norse background, had risen to power on the western seaboard – a political power vacuum in the early twelfth century – and carved out an insular and mainland kingdom held together by war galleys that plied the seaways. He possessed regal standing – Irish sources called him *rí Innse Gall*, 'king of the Isles' – and his position was less that of a client or subordinate of the king of Scots than an independent ruler in his own right in an age when several native dynasties could still be found in northern Britain. Somerled's expansionary impulses were aimed primarily at another one of those dynasties: between 1154 and 1156 he annexed the Isle of Man, driving out the Manx king, who sheltered for a while at the Scottish court.[45] But there is no evidence of enmity between Somerled and David I; in fact, Islesmen participated in the Battle of the Standard in 1138, suggesting cooperation and mutual good relations between the two rulers.[46]

This situation seems to have changed on the death of David in 1153, when Somerled backed his nephews, the sons of Malcolm MacHeth, in their struggle with Malcolm IV; a Scottish chronicle lamented that they 'perturbed and disquieted Scotland in great part.'[47] If Somerled lost interest and abandoned the cause of his nephews, as the capture of Donald MacHeth in 1156 suggests, it was not until 1160 that a formal treaty was made.[48] Then, in 1164, Somerled gathered a massive fleet of some 160 vessels, filled them with warriors from Dublin and the Hebrides, and invaded the Scottish kingdom. The fleet landed near Renfrew and the warriors plundered the land until they were defeated, and their leader killed, by what seems to have been a hastily organized local militia. A clerk at the cathedral of Glasgow who was an eyewitness to these events composed a lengthy Latin verse in which he described the death of Somerled:

> The deadly leader, Somerled, died. In the first great clash of arms
> he fell, wounded by a spear and cut down by the sword.[49]

After his death, Somerled's numerous brood fell to internal squabbling, and, although there was plenty of political violence in the Hebrides after 1164, none of it was aimed, directly, at least, at the Scottish kings. Only from the 1220s did the kings of Scots turn their attention to the western seaboard, finally annexing it by the Treaty of Perth in 1266.[50]

Twelfth-century Galloway in the southwest of Scotland (roughly modern Kirkcudbrightshire and Wigtownshire), like Argyll and the Isles, was home to a powerful native dynasty, represented in the first half of the century by Fergus. Fergus's ancestry and his rise to power are obscure, but there is no doubt that he was well established by the 1140s and that, like Somerled, he possessed regal standing. One of his own charters styled him *rex Galwitensium*, king of the Gallovidians,[51] and he married an illegitimate daughter of King Henry I of England (1100–35). Fergus was a patron of the Church, and like Somerled there is no evidence of enmity between him and the Scottish king. Gallovidians fought at the Battle of the Standard in 1138, perhaps as mercenaries, suggesting close and cooperative relations between Galloway and the Scottish kingdom.[52] As with Somerled, it was not until after the death of David I that relations between Fergus and the kings of Scots seem to have soured.[53]

In 1159 the young King Malcolm IV travelled with King Henry II of England (1154–89) to Toulouse in the south of France, in the hope of winning the spurs of knighthood, which he coveted. When he returned home, in 1160, he was met by a decidedly cold reception from a number of his native earls, who besieged him at Perth.[54] It is not entirely clear what the objective of the so-called revolt of the earls was, although it might well have been related to the king's perceived dependence and subservience with respect to his formidable English counterpart, but it seems highly likely that Fergus was involved.[55] This is deduced from the fact that, once the earls' revolt was defused, the Scottish king immediately launched a series of campaigns in Galloway: 'In 1160, king Malcolm led an army into Galloway three times. And he conquered his enemies there, and made a treaty with peace, and returned without loss.' Fergus was captured and sent off to retirement at the Augustinian abbey of Holyrood near Edinburgh, where he died in 1161.[56]

But even after the capture and confinement of Fergus, Galloway remained a threat. In 1174, following the capture of the Scottish king at Alnwick, Fergus's two feuding sons apparently set aside their differences long enough to go on a rampage, expelling Scottish bailiffs, killing all the 'English and French' they could lay their hands on, and destroying castles. Not until about 1200 did the situation stabilize; by then, the Lords of Galloway, Roland (1185–1200) and Alan (1200–34), were prominent supporters of the Scottish kings – it was Roland who hunted down Donald MacWilliam in 1187.[57]

If the enmity of the MacHeths and MacWilliams toward the Canmore kings was dynastically driven, then what motivated the assaults launched by Fergus and Somerled upon the Scottish king? One of the characteristics of the modernization of Scotland was an influx of foreign settlers, from England and the Continent, who were granted lands in return for military service, so that the process of colonization was accompanied by the spread of fiefs, castles, and knights. In the north, Flemish colonists helped consolidate the conquest of Moray (sometimes displacing the native inhabitants), while in the west and southwest of Scotland the Scottish kings granted out large tracts of land to loyal supporters in a deliberate bid to encircle Galloway and Argyll, creating buffer zones equivalent to marcher lordships between these peripheral regions and the Scottish kingdom itself. The process was a gradual one, beginning early in the reign of David I and continuing into the 1150s, but it was well enough advanced by 1160 that the threat to Somerled and Fergus was clear. Galloway in particular found itself isolated, because in addition to the process of encirclement just described, the Scottish kings had also controlled Cumbria from the 1130s until 1157. Thus, Fergus and Somerled were not dynastic rivals of the kings of Scots, like the MacHeths and MacWilliams. Their enmity was rooted in the dynamics of Scottish internal expansion in the early twelfth century, which, by 1160, pressed uncomfortably close to the autonomous rulers of the marginal regions in the west and southwest.[58] Indeed, some historians have postulated the existence of an 'anti-feudal faction' in the twelfth century,[59] of which Fergus and Somerled were members, and whether or not this terminology is accepted, it is difficult to see the invasion of Somerled in 1164 and the insurrection of Fergus in 1160 as anything but conservative reaction against the shifting balance of power in the north of Britain, which was increasingly tilting toward the side of the Scottish kings at the expense of their neighbours. As with the MacHeths and MacWilliams, to interpret these insurrections in ethnic terms – 'Celt' versus 'Norman' – is oversimplified; this is demonstrated by the fact that Fergus himself was open to some European influences, since he was a patron of the reformed religious orders.[60]

Of all the enemies of the Scottish kings in the twelfth century, the most difficult to make sense of is Wimund, whose bizarre career was described by the contemporary English chronicler William of Newburgh, who claimed to have met and spoken with him. Said to have been born in an obscure spot in England and trained as a monk at Furness Abbey in Lancashire, Wimund went to the Isle of Man, where he soon became bishop, and not long thereafter he claimed that he was the son of the earl of Moray, wrongfully deprived of his inheritance by the king of Scots. His charisma and eloquence seem to have won him a large following, with which he attacked the Scottish mainland and forced David I to yield to him a 'certain province,' possibly part of Cumbria in the northwest of England (then under Scottish control). But in the end, it was his own arrogance that proved to be Wimund's undoing, and it was his own followers who laid a trap for him, captured and mutilated him, and sent him off to monastic confinement at Byland Abbey in North Yorkshire. He seems to have remained intransigent, however, and even toward the end of his life is said to have remarked that, 'had he only the eye of a sparrow, his enemies should have little occasion to rejoice at what they had done to him.'[61] These events are not easy to date, but probably took place in the second half of the 1140s, with Wimund's deposition and mutilation occurring between 1148 and 1151.[62]

It is hard to know what to make of this warrior-bishop who seems to have had a substantial chip on his shoulder and a grudge against the Scottish king. Most perplexing of all, however, is his claim to have been the son of the earl of Moray – presumably a reference to Angus, who was killed in 1130 at Stracathro. Most historians have dismissed this story as fraudulent, but even if that is the case it does little to explain how Wimund managed to generate so much support for his cause. Contemporaries clearly accepted that Wimund had some grudge against the Scottish king, and it is worth reflecting that David I, who was certainly in a position to know the truth of the matter, seems to have treated the threat seriously.

Although it is easy to classify the MacHeths and MacWilliams as 'dynastic' rivals and Fergus and Somerled as 'political' opponents, it would be very misleading to suggest that there was no interaction whatsoever among these various enemies of the Scottish kings, and that each individual or group operated in a vacuum. In fact, there is a considerable amount of evidence to suggest quite the opposite – justifying, perhaps, the notion of an anti-feudal, or at least anti-Canmore, faction. It has already been noted how Somerled came to the aid of Malcolm MacHeth's sons in 1153, demonstrating close contact between political and dynastic rivals, and showing how such categories could easily become blurred along the lines of kinship. Also important are the connections between Somerled's descendants (the MacSorleys) and the MacWilliams. The 1223 MacWilliam uprising is said to have included a certain 'Roderick,' who can almost certainly be identified with Ruairi, the son of Ranald, one of Somerled's sons.[63] His association with the MacWilliams suggests that they obtained aid from the Hebridean chieftains, and there can be little doubt that this was an important motivating factor in Scottish efforts to subdue the western seaboard from the 1220s onward. The aid probably took the form of galloglasses (galloclaig), those renowned Hebridean mercenary soldiers who were often employed by the Irish in their struggles against the English from the fourteenth century. Although the galloglasses appear on the record in the late thirteenth century, it is entirely possible that they had been the major form of Hebridean aid to the MacWilliams from as early as about 1200.[64] The use of Hebridean troops by the MacWilliams reveals not only the way in which leaders from one region of the Gaelic-Norse Irish Sea world were able to use troops from another,[65] but is also indicative of the complex web of connections that linked the various regions rimming the Irish Sea.[66]

In fact, the tentacles of resistance to the Canmore kings extended right across the Irish Sea to Ireland itself, and it is almost certain that Gaelic Ireland served as a staging-point for many of the MacWilliam incursions. The chronicler Walter Bower reported that Guthred had come to Moray and Ross from Ireland in 1211, a statement which helps makes sense of earlier descriptions of MacWilliam armies landing in Scotland and devastating the sea-coast.[67] English sources show that the MacWilliams relied heavily on Ireland for aid, and Irish contingents made up part of their armies on several occasions.[68] Indeed, the Chronicle of Melrose stated that the son of an Irish king participated in the 1215 insurrection.[69] As one authority has remarked, 'there were always men in Ireland ready and willing to throw their military muscle about in Scotland and the islands ... The underdog, the pretender, and the malcontent in Scotland all found Irish support.'[70] Moreover, the Irish dimension to the MacWilliam threat meant that its significance stretched beyond the bounds of the Scottish kingdom. It is surely noteworthy that an

Anglo-Scottish treaty in 1212 was followed by what has been seen as a 'coordinated campaign' to impose English control in northern Ireland; these English campaigns relied heavily on Scottish, especially Gallovidian, forces and 'look like determined efforts to strike out bases of MacWilliam support.'[71]

That the kings of Scots were ultimately victorious owed much, it has been observed, to their possession of a solid landed base with firm territorial definition and ready access to England and Europe.[72] The superior resources of these kings included, by the reign of David I, heavily armoured knights, which could be used to devastating effect against their foes on the lesser-developed margins. The point is nicely illustrated by a speech put in the mouth of Robert de Brus (an ancestor of King Robert I) in 1138 by the English chronicler Ailred of Rievaulx, in which Brus reminds the Scottish king of the Anglo-Norman aid he received against Malcolm MacHeth in 1134:

Remember when in a past year you requested the aid of the English against Malcolm, the heir of paternal hatred and persecution, how joyful, how eager, how willing to help, how ready for danger came Walter Espec and very many other nobles of the English to meet you at Carlisle: how many ships they prepared, how they made war, with what forces they made defense; how they terrified all their enemies, until they took Malcolm himself ...

Ailred has Brus go on to say, 'So did the fear of us while binding his limbs bind still more the courage of the Scots, and by quenching all hope of success remove the presumption to rebel.'[73] Ailred's words remind us of something that is often forgotten: namely, that if the Anglo-Normans who settled in Scotland during the reign of David I came as friends and allies, their potential role as enforcers for the Canmore dynasty should not be underestimated.[74] Moreover, generally good Anglo-Scottish relations meant that English aid was often available to the Scottish kings. King John (1199–1216) sent Brabantine mercenaries to help suppress the 1211 invasion,[75] and by 1212, as we have seen, a coordinated Anglo-Scottish effort was under way to destroy the MacWilliam bases in northern Ireland. In military terms, then, the deck was heavily stacked against the MacWilliams, as it was against other opponents of the Scottish kings. Men like Roland of Galloway and Farquhar MacTaggart were still another asset possessed by the Scottish monarchs. Whereas once they might

have backed the MacWilliams and MacHeths, by the early thirteenth century they were supporting the Canmore dynasty, and
adding their resources to those ranged against the opponents of the
Scottish kings. Roland of Galloway and his retainers crushed the
MacWilliams in 1187, and Farquhar MacTaggart single-handedly
quashed the 1215 invasion. Once native dignitaries and potential
supporters like Roland and Farquhar abandoned the MacHeths and
MacWilliams, their cause was doomed.

Yet the question remains, did the likes of Malcolm MacHeth,
Donald MacWilliam, Somerled, and Wimund really represent a serious threat to the Scottish kings? Although the insurrections led by
these figures are often dismissed as little more than a series of
haphazard, piratical raids, closer scrutiny suggests that a very real
danger existed. Take, for example, Somerled's 1164 invasion of the
Scottish mainland, said to have been undertaken with 160 vessels.
Assuming some forty to fifty warriors per ship, Somerled may have
commanded between six and eight thousand men. This figure,
although almost certainly inflated, nonetheless represents a formidable assault force, made up, as we are told, of fierce warriors from
Dublin, the Hebrides, and Kintyre.[76] That the invasion ended in
disaster for Somerled and his forces is not in doubt, but the most
detailed description of the seemingly easy rout of the Islesmen is a
piece of Scottish propaganda (considered below) and needs to be
treated with more caution than is usually the case. Like Somerled,
Guthred MacWilliam could also recruit from across the Irish Sea
(noted above), but the composition of his army is instructive for
another reason as well: Walter Bower relates how he was able to uti-
lize siege engines of an unspecified type to force the garrison of a
royal stronghold to surrender in the course of his insurrection in
1211–12. Such weapons were potentially expensive, and this is
hardly the sort of equipment that we would expect to find in the
possession of a rag-tag rebel army.[77] Not only in terms of numbers,
then, but also in terms of equipment, should the armies that faced
down the forces of the Scottish kings be regarded as potentially dangerous. Moreover, there are many indications that the MacHeths
and MacWilliams commanded considerable support among certain
segments of the population. During the course of the 1187 campaign
against Donald MacWilliam, for instance, the leaders of the army
polarized into those who supported the king and those who did not,
while not only this insurrection but also that of Guthred in 1211–12

was said to have enjoyed the support of powerful nobles in Moray and Ross. Stronger evidence still comes from an inventory of Scottish documents, now lost, which stated that there once existed a roll containing 'recognitions and old charters of the time of King William and King Alexander his son [concerning] those to whom the said kings formerly gave their peace, and those who stood with MacWilliam.'[78] All of this hints at a substantial amount of support for the MacHeth/MacWilliam cause, support which translated into insecurity for the Scottish kings. Indeed, as one critic has pointed out, events could easily have taken a different turn in 1187 if William I had been killed in favour of his rival, Donald MacWilliam, and how else are we to account for the brutal slaying of an infant MacWilliam in 1230 if not through the insecurity of the ruling dynasty?[79]

Finally, the timing of many of the MacHeth and MacWilliam assaults is significant: those of 1124, 1153, and 1215 coincided with the death of a Scottish king, a time when the kingdom was always vulnerable. Moreover, the attacks of 1130 and 1181 were launched when the king was absent from his realm, and that of 1211 occurred at a time when the king was ageing and feeble and so unable to 'pacify the interior districts of his kingdom, disturbed by revolt.'[80] The timing of these insurrections more than anything else shows that, although they might appear in the various chronicles and annals which recorded them as little more than random and haphazard events, they actually represented 'carefully timed, and presumably orchestrated, predatory strikes against the Canmore kings in their weakest moments.'[81] Perhaps an English chronicler came closest to capturing the essence of the MacWilliam uprisings when he recorded that 'Guthred was of the ancient line of Scottish kings; and, supported by the aid of Scots and Irish, had practised long hostility against the modern kings, now in secret, now openly, as had also his father Donald.'[82]

The kings of Scots, then, were hedged around by some powerful and potentially dangerous enemies in the twelfth century. That this is not a better developed theme of Scottish historical writing is the result, in large measure, of both the nature and the tone of the chronicles in which accounts of opposition are preserved. Indeed, as one historian put it in a very different context but in words that ring no less true in the present examination, 'we may fairly accuse the historical record of having failed us not only in the familiar way, being simply insufficient, but through being also distorted.'[83]

In the first place, no chronicler devoted very much attention to the uprisings of the MacHeths and MacWilliams, the invasion of Somerled, or the demise of Fergus; our knowledge of these events must be painstakingly pieced together from a variety of sources.[84] This is partly a result of the nature of the chronicle genre itself, but partly, it is to be suspected, also a result of a deliberate policy of omission on the part of the chroniclers, since almost without exception, they were the devoted partisans of the kings of Scots descended from Malcolm III and Queen Margaret.[85] These kings, because of their descent from an English princess, their close contacts with the Norman kings of England, and their Europeanizing policies, were held in high regard by English and Scottish chroniclers. William of Newburgh, for example, describes David I in a memorable passage as 'a king not barbarous of a barbarous people' (rex non barbarus barbarae gentis).[86] The opponents of these rulers, however, were held in contempt, discredited, and painted in broad strokes as troublemakers, pirates, and ruffians who disturbed the internal peace of the kingdom. Consider, for instance, the vilification of Somerled in William of Glasgow's Latin poem 'Song on the Death of Somerled.' In the first stanza of the poem, William writes of the 'treachery of scheming Scots,' and describes the 'Norsemen and Argyllsmen who leaned on Scotsmen's might, raging, slaughtered righteous men with cruel hands.' Somerled's army is portrayed as the 'treacherous thousands,' while Somerled himself is described as 'foul with treachery, the cruellest of foes.'[87] And Somerled was not alone in being vilified by the contemporary writers; some of Roger of Howden's most vitriolic comments were reserved for Donald MacWilliam:

> ... because of the evils he had wrought neither grief nor lamentation, neither any sorrow was caused by his death. And no wonder: 'For the praise of the wicked is short, and the joy of the hypocrite as a moment; if his pride ascend to the sky, and his head touch the clouds, like a dung-heap shall he perish in the end.'[88]

History, so the axiom goes, and as the words of Howden poignantly remind us, is written by the victors. In the end, the scales are weighted heavily against the opponents of the Scottish kings in the twelfth and thirteenth centuries; not only must their story be pieced together from a bewildering array of contemporary and later

chronicles, annals, and other documents, but many of these same
sources are distinctly partisan in nature and biased against figures
like Donald MacWilliam – the eventual 'losers' in the dual processes of internal colonialism in Scotland and the dynastic consolidation pursued by the descendants of Malcolm III and Margaret.
Professor Robin Frame, summing up the achievement of the Canmore kings, remarked, 'The weight of the house of Canmore was
irresistible, and its brand of kingship inimitable.'[89] This statement
rings true, yet these kings did not always have things their own
way, and their eventual triumph must not be regarded as a foregone
conclusion. The peripheral regions of the Scottish kingdom raised
up some formidable opponents, and judging by the effort required to
hunt down Malcolm MacHeth in 1130-4, the vacillation of some of
the Scottish nobles before the battle of Mam Garvia in 1187, William's law of 1197 requiring the men of his kingdom to preserve the
peace, or the existence of a now lost document which listed those
who stood with the MacWilliams, these opponents had a cause
which commanded sympathy. A different turn of events at almost
any one of the encounters between the Scottish kings and their
opponents might well have substantially altered the subsequent
course of Scottish medieval history.[90]

Notes

1 *Scotichronicon*, iv, 464–5.
2 R.L.G. Ritchie, *The Normans in Scotland* (Edinburgh, 1954), 91.
3 See R. Bartlett, *The Making of Europe: Conquest, Colonization and
   Cultural Change, 950–1350* (London and Princeton, 1993) for the term
   and its broader application.
4 Whether or not Scotland was 'feudalized' in this period depends largely
   upon where one stands in relation to the current debate about the
   value of the term 'feudalism' in historical studies. Some scholars advocate expunging it altogether from the vocabulary of the historian,
   while others regard it as 'an appropriate means of describing a particular form of social organisation which was found widely throughout
   western Europe and came increasingly into prominence in Scotland in
   the twelfth century' (A.D.M. Barrell, *Medieval Scotland* [Cambridge,
   2000], 15). An important work dealing with the debate over feudalism

   is S. Reynolds, *Fiefs and Vassals: The Medieval Evidence Reinter-preted* (Oxford, 1994).

5 See the important works of Ritchie, *Normans in Scotland*; A.A.M. Duncan, *Scotland: The Making of the Kingdom* (Edinburgh, 1975); G.W.S. Barrow, *The Anglo-Norman Era in Scottish History* (Oxford, 1980) and *idem, Kingship and Unity: Scotland 1000–1306* (London, 1981); D. Walker, *The Normans in Britain* (Oxford, 1995); and R. Frame, *The Political Development of the British Isles 1100–1400* (Oxford, 1990). A good recent survey is Barrell, *Medieval Scotland*, cited above, note 4.

6 Ritchie, *Normans in Scotland*, xi, xiv.

7 See G.W.S. Barrow, *David I of Scotland (1124–1153): The Balance of New and Old* (Reading, 1985), reprinted in *Scotland and Its Neighbours in the Middle Ages* (London, 1992); and A. Grant, 'Scotland's "Celtic Fringe" in the Late Middle Ages: The MacDonald Lords of the Isles and the Kingdom of Scotland,' in *The British Isles 1100–1500*, ed. R.R. Davies (Edinburgh, 1988), 119 (for the hybrid kingdom).

8 Quotation from B. Webster, *Medieval Scotland: The Making of an Identity* (Basingstoke and London, 1997), 22. Challenges are mentioned by Duncan, *Scotland*, and Barrow, *Kingship and Unity, passim*. There is more discussion in J.L. Roberts, *Lost Kingdoms: Celtic Scotland and the Middle Ages* (Edinburgh, 1997); and A. Grant, 'The Province of Ross and the Kingdom of Alba,' in *Alba: Celtic Scotland in the Medieval Era*, ed. E.J. Cowan and R.A. McDonald (East Linton, 2000). See also R.A. McDonald, '"Treachery in the Remotest Territories of Scotland": Northern Resistance to the Canmore Dynasty, 1130–1230,' *Canadian Journal of History* 33 (1999), 161–92. I am preparing a much more detailed monograph on the subject of resistance to the Scottish kings in the twelfth and thirteenth centuries.

9 *ES*, ii, 471.

10 *ES*, ii, 173.

11 *SAEC*, 158, 166–7; *ES*, ii, 173–4, 183.

12 K.J. Stringer, *Earl David of Huntingdon: A Study in Anglo-Scottish History* (Edinburgh, 1985), 32.

13 *SAEC*, 230n1.

14 *ES*, ii, 223–4.

15 *ES*, ii, 232.

16 *ES*, ii, 266.

17 *ES*, ii, 301–2; *CGS*, i, 268; ii, 263.

18 *Gesta Regis Henrici Secundi*, ed. W. Stubbs, 2 vols, RS (London, 1867), i, 277–8; ii, 7–8 (trans. in *SAEC*, 278–9, 294–5; *ES*, ii, 312–13).

19 *SAEC*, 295.

20 A. Young, *Robert the Bruce's Rivals: The Comyns, 1212–1314* (East Linton, 1997), 22–3.

21 *Scotichronicon*, iv, 464–7.

22 *ES*, ii, 404.

23 *ES*, ii, 403–4; R.A. McDonald, 'Old and New in the Far North: Farquhar MacTaggart and the Early Earls of Ross,' in *Native Kindreds*, ed. S. Boardman (East Linton, forthcoming).

24 *Scotichronicon*, v, 116–17, 142–3.

25 *Scotichronicon*, v, 144–5.

26 *ES*, ii, 471.

27 Duncan, *Scotland*, 166.

28 Ritchie, *Normans in Scotland*, 400–6, and Duncan, *Scotland*, 166, associate Malcolm with Moray. Compare their views to G.W.S. Barrow, *The Acts of William I King of Scots 1165–1214*, Regesta Regum Scottorum II (Edinburgh, 1971), 12–13; and Grant, 'The Province of Ross and the Kingdom of Alba,' in *Alba*, ed. Cowan and McDonald.

29 *A Scottish Chronicle Known as the Chronicle of Holyrood*, ed. and trans. M.O. Anderson (Edinburgh, 1938), 129n1.

30 W.F. Skene, *The Highlanders of Scotland*, 2nd ed., ed. A. MacBain (Stirling, 1902), 404–5; see also *Early Scottish Charters prior to A.D. 1153*, ed. Sir A.C. Lawrie (Glasgow, 1905) [*ESC*], notes on 283–4. An important recent work, which partially replaces that of Lawrie, is *The Charters of David I: The Written Acts of David I King of Scots, 1124–53 and of His Son Henry Earl of Northumberland, 1139–1152*, ed. G.W.S. Barrow (Woodbridge, 1999).

31 *ESC*, nos. 36, 49, and 94; see also notes on 283–4.

32 *ES*, ii, 223–4; *OS*, chapter 109.

33 *ES*, ii, 232.

34 *ES*, ii, 266; G.W.S. Barrow, *The Acts of Malcolm IV King of Scots 1153–1165*, Regesta Regum Scottorum I (Edinburgh, 1960), no. 157.

35 See J. Bannerman, 'MacDuff of Fife,' in *Medieval Scotland: Crown, Lordship and Community*, ed. A. Grant and K.J. Stringer (Edinburgh, 1993), 20–38.

36 A landmark paper is Grant, 'The Province of Ross and the Kingdom of Alba,' in *Alba*, ed. Cowan and McDonald.

37 *ESC*, nos. 32, 35, 50, 57, 82, 83, 99, 100, 109, 117, 121, 141, 142, 153,

163, 172, 176, and notes on 271–2; see also Barrow, *Acts of Malcolm IV*, nos. 2, 22, 29, 25, 41.

38 See Barrow, *Acts of William I*, 12–13; but note Duncan's comments in *Scotland*, 193.

39 *ES*, ii, 89; *SAEC*, 119; discussed by W.C. Dickinson, *Scotland from the Earliest Times to 1603*, 3rd ed., revised and edited by A.A.M. Duncan (Oxford, 1977), 64n12.

40 G.W.S. Barrow, 'MacBeth and Other Mormaers of Moray,' in *The Hub of the Highlands: The Book of Inverness and District*, ed. L. MacLean (Edinburgh, 1975), 119.

41 D. Ó Corráin, 'Irish Regnal Succession: A Reappraisal,' *Studia Hibernica* 11 (1971), 8. For early Scottish kingship and succession, see A.P. Smyth, *Warlords and Holy Men: Scotland A.D. 80–1000* (London, 1984), 218–27, and *passim*; and B.T. Hudson, *Kings of Celtic Scotland* (Westport, CT, and London, 1994).

42 Ritchie, *Normans in Scotland*, 406.

43 See Roger of Howden, trans. in *SAEC*, 316–18; and *OS*, especially chapters 109–12. For modern comment, see Duncan, *Scotland*, 192–6; B. Crawford, 'The Earldom of Caithness and the Kingdom of Scotland, 1150–1266,' *Northern Scotland* 2 (1976–7), 97–118 (reprinted in *Essays on the Nobility of Medieval Scotland*, ed. K.J. Stringer [Edinburgh, 1985]); and P. Topping, 'Harald Maddadson, Earl of Orkney and Caithness, 1139–1206,' *SHR* 62 (1983), 105–20.

44 *SAEC*, 318.

45 Evidence for Somerled is collected in *ES*, ii, 137, 223–4, 230–3, 239, 252–8; see also R.A. McDonald, *The Kingdom of the Isles: Scotland's Western Seaboard c.1100–c.1336* (East Linton, 1997), chapter 2. *The New History of the Isle of Man, Volume III: The Medieval Period 1000–1405*, ed. S. Duffy (Liverpool, forthcoming), will also shed further light on this maritime region.

46 *SAEC*, 200.

47 *ES*, ii, 224.

48 *Acts of Malcolm IV*, no. 175.

49 'Carmen de morte Sumerledi' [Song on the Death of Somerled], in Symeon of Durham, *Opera Omnia*, ed. T. Arnold, 2 vols, RS (London, 1882–5), ii, 386–88; trans. in *The Triumph Tree: Scotland's Earliest Poetry A.D. 550–1350*, ed. and trans. T.O. Clancy (Edinburgh 1998), 212–14. The quotation in the title of this paper is taken from this work: 'While Somerled stood with a thousand of our enemies / ready to make

war against a mere one hundred innocents / our few men advanced and made assault upon the ranks / of treacherous Argyllsmen, soldiers most unfortunate' (213).

50 See McDonald, *Kingdom of the Isles*, chapters 3–5.

51 R. Dodsworth and W. Dugdale, *Monasticon Anglicanum*, 3 vols (London, 1660–73), ii, 551; see also *The Knights of St. John of Jerusalem in Scotland*, ed. I.B. Cowan, P.H.R. Mackay, and A. Macquarrie (Edinburgh, 1983), xxvi.

52 *SAEC*, 198, 202–3; contemporary writers sometimes called the Gallovidians 'Picts' and almost always characterized them as barbarians.

53 Basic material on Fergus is in *ES*, ii, 137, 204, 245, and 247. Fergus, though in greatly distorted form, became the central figure in an Arthurian romance composed in Scotland: Guillaume le Clerc, *Fergus of Galloway: Knight of King Arthur*, ed. and trans. D.D.R. Owen (London, 1991). Two important modern works on Galloway are R.D. Oram, 'Fergus, Galloway and the Scots,' in *Galloway: Land and Lordship*, ed. G.P. Stell and R. Oram (Edinburgh, 1991); and D. Brooke, *Wild Men and Holy Places: St. Ninian, Whithorn, and the Medieval Realm of Galloway* (Edinburgh, 1994).

54 *ES*, ii, 240–4.

55 Brooke (*Wild Men and Holy Places*, 93–5) argues against Fergus's involvement, suggesting the expeditions were the result of internal disputes that spilled over into border raiding by the Gallovidians.

56 *ES*, ii, 245, 247.

57 See *SAEC*, 256, for the 1174 uprising; and Brooke, *Wild Men and Holy Places*, chapters 5–6, for the Lords of Galloway after Fergus.

58 Settlement in these regions is discussed by Barrow, *Anglo-Norman Era*, *passim*, and also in *Acts of Malcolm IV*, 39. For Fergus and Somerled as reactionaries against the westward thrust of Scottish settlement, see R.A. McDonald, 'Rebels without a Cause? The Relations of Fergus of Galloway and Somerled of Argyll with the Scottish Kings, 1153–1164,' in *Alba*, ed. Cowan and McDonald.

59 E.J. Cowan, 'The Historical MacBeth,' in *Moray: Province and People*, ed. W.D.H. Sellar (Edinburgh, 1993), 131.

60 See R.A. McDonald, 'Scoto-Norse Kings and the Reformed Religious Orders: Patterns of Monastic Patronage in Twelfth-Century Galloway and Argyll,' *Albion* 27/2 (1995), 187–219; and K.J. Stringer, 'Reform Monasticism and Celtic Scotland: Galloway, c. 1140–c. 1240,' in *Alba*, ed. Cowan and McDonald.

61 William of Newburgh, *Historia Rerum Anglicarum*, in *Chronicles of*

the Reigns of Stephen, Henry II, and Richard I, ed. R. Howlett, 4 vols, RS (London, 1884–9) [Chron. Stephen], i, 73–6; trans. in The History of English Affairs, Book I, ed. and trans. P.G. Walsh and M.J. Kennedy (Warminster 1988), 103–7.

62 See R.A. McDonald, 'Monk, Bishop, Imposter, Pretender: The Place of Wimund in Twelfth-century Scotland,' TGSI 58 (1993–4), 247–70.

63 McDonald, Kingdom of the Isles, 82.

64 On the galloglasses, see G.A. Hayes-McCoy, Scots Mercenary Forces in Ireland (1563–1603) (Dublin and London, 1937), 4–35; and J. Lydon, 'The Scottish Soldier in Medieval Ireland: The Bruce Invasion and the Gallowglass,' in The Scottish Soldier Abroad, 1247–1967, ed. G.G. Simpson (Edinburgh, 1992); McDonald, Kingdom of the Isles, 154–6.

65 K.J. Stringer, 'Periphery and Core in Thirteenth-century Scotland: Alan Son of Roland, Lord of Galloway and Constable of Scotland,' in Medieval Scotland, ed. Grant and Stringer, 87.

66 See R.A. McDonald, 'Matrimonial Politics and Core-Periphery Interactions in Twelfth- and Thirteenth-century Scotland,' JMH 21 (1995), 227–47.

67 Scotichronicon, iv, 466–7; SAEC, 278.

68 Memoriale Fratris Walteri de Coventria, ed. W. Stubbs, 2 vols, RS (London, 1872–3) ii, 206; trans. SAEC, 330n6.

69 ES, ii, 403–4.

70 S. Duffy, 'The Bruce Brothers and the Irish Sea World,' Cambridge Medieval Celtic Studies 21 (1991), 63.

71 Stringer, 'Periphery and Core in Thirteenth-century Scotland,' in Medieval Scotland, ed. Grant and Stringer, 88.

72 Frame, Political Development, 105.

73 Ailred of Rievaulx, De Standardo, in Chron. Stephen, iii, 193; trans. (in somewhat archaic English) in SAEC, 193–4 (I have modernized the translation).

74 A point that is seldom recognized, but see Grant's remark in 'Scotland's "Celtic Fringe" in the Late Middle Ages' (cited in note 7 above): '... they [Scotland's Anglo-Normans] upheld the power of the native Scottish kings, against the latter's Celtic opponents' (118–19).

75 SAEC, 330.

76 The numbers are, of course, contentious since medieval chroniclers were notoriously unreliable on such matters. The figure of 160 ships led by Somerled is given in Cronica Regum Mannie & Insularum / Chronicles of the Kings of Man and the Isles BL Cotton Julius Avii, ed. G. Broderick (Douglas, 1991), f.39r. An entry in the Irish Annals of

Ulster for 1098 which describes how the men of Ulster destroyed three ships of Foreigners from the Isles, totalling about 120 men, gives some indication of how many warriors a galley might hold. See *ES*, ii, 114; and, for more discussion, see E. Roesdahl, *The Vikings* (London, 1991), 192. Ultimately, I would suggest that these figures simply reveal a degree of magnitude rather than anything approaching the actual size of the forces involved. A passage from Gerald of Wales, who describes an attack by the Islesmen on Dublin in 1171, indicates that these warriors could be formidably equipped: 'They were warlike figures, clad in mail in every part of their body after the Danish manner. Some wore long coats of mail, others iron plate skilfully knitted together, and they had round, red shields protected by iron round the edge' (Giraldus Cambrensis, *Expugnatio Hibernica / The Conquest of Ireland*, ed. and trans. A.B. Scott and F.X. Martin [Dublin, 1978], 76–7).

77 *Scotichronicon*, iv, 464–7; a good overview of the various types of medieval siege engines is found in J. Bradbury, *The Medieval Siege* (Woodbridge, 1992), especially chapter 9.

78 *APS*, i, 114.

79 D.P. Kirby, review of *Scotland: The Making of the Kingdom*, by A.A.M. Duncan, *English Historical Review* 91 (1976), 840.

80 *SAEC*, 330n6. However, William did personally campaign against Guthred in 1211, according to Bower, *Scotichronicon*, iv, 464–5.

81 McDonald, 'Treachery in the Remotest Territories,' 183.

82 *SAEC*, 330n6.

83 R. MacMullen, *Christianity and Paganism in the Fourth to Eighth Centuries* (New Haven and London, 1997), 3.

84 One exception is the English chronicler Roger of Howden, who had good first-hand information on Scotland; see J. Gillingham, 'The Travels of Roger of Howden and His Views of the Irish, Scots and Welsh,' *Anglo-Norman Studies* 20 (1997), 151–69.

85 See B. Webster, *Scotland from the Eleventh Century to 1603* (Ithaca, 1975), 38.

86 William of Newburgh in *Chron. Stephen*, i, 72; trans. *SAEC*, 230 (again updated by the author); many other examples could be cited. Professor John Gillingham has explored English attitudes toward their Celtic neighbours, who were generally regarded as barbarians: 'The Beginnings of English Imperialism,' *Journal of Historical Sociology* 5/4 (1992), 392–407; 'Foundations of a Disunified Kingdom,' in *Uniting the Kingdom: The Making of British History*, ed. A. Grant and K.J. Stringer (London, 1995), 48–64; and now *The English in the Twelfth Century: Imperial-*

ism, *National Identity, and Political Values* (Woodbridge, 2000). I suggest that the kings of Scots encouraged similar attitudes toward the peoples on the margins of their kingdom.

87 *Triumph Tree*, ed. and trans. Clancy, 212–14.

88 *SAEC*, 294–5. I am preparing a more detailed study, 'The Defamation of the Enemies of the Scottish Kings in the Twelfth Century,' which takes up this theme at greater length.

89 Frame, *Political Development of the British Isles*, 104.

90 I am grateful to Elizabeth Ewan and Ben Hudson for their perceptive and helpful comments on an early draft of this paper. I must also thank Drs Simon Taylor, Alex Woolf, and Judith Green for discussing various facets of the subject with me at the Leeds International Medieval Congress in July 1999, and again in July 2000.

4

'Off quhat nacioun art thow?'
National Identity in Blind Hary's *Wallace*

RICHARD J. MOLL

A recent anthology on medieval nationalism begins by establishing Benedict Anderson as a sort of straw man. Quoting his *Imagined Communities: Reflections on the Origins and Spread of Nationalism*, the editors take issue with Anderson's position that concepts of national identity were not possible in the Christian Middle Ages.[1] For Anderson, and for several scholars before him, the universal 'religious community' of Christendom, bound together by a 'sacred language' (i.e., Latin), suppressed any emerging sense of loyalty to, or identity with, a particular nation.[2] This view has recently been challenged in numerous studies using various peoples and texts as case studies. R.R. Davies, for example, explored emerging national identities in Britain and Ireland in his four presidential addresses to the Royal Historical Society,[3] and, more recently, Adrian Hastings examined England for evidence of a medieval nationalism in the 1996 Wiles Lectures at Queen's University of Belfast.[4] Medieval Scotland has also been fruitful ground for those who wish to examine national identity in pre-modern Europe. The Wars of Independence in particular have been seen as important in the development of a Scottish national consciousness in opposition to a common foe. In 1874, long before the current debate on nationalism arose, J. Clark Murray wrote:

> The history of the Scots, as one distinct people, begins properly with this war; and in the enthusiasm which the common resistance to Anglo-Norman oppression created, may be recognized the force which welded together the different tribes that peopled Scotland.[5]

Although Barron long ago reminded us, throughout his work, of the oversimplification this statement represents,[6] R. James Goldstein can still correctly state that the 'prolonged period of Anglo-Scottish warfare, known as the Wars of Independence, rapidly accelerated the growth of national consciousness at all levels of Scottish society.'[7] It is not surprising, therefore, that texts written in the decades following the Wars of Independence, such as John Barbour's *Bruce* (c. 1375) and John Fordun's *Chronica Gentis Scotorum* (c. 1380), have been seen to exhibit an early form of Scottish national consciousness.[8]

Although the exact nature of concepts like national identity or nationalism is difficult to define, these studies do indicate that late medieval Scotland recognized itself as a nation, that many of the Scottish people identified themselves with the land and its inhabitants, and that this recognition was expressed in both Latin and vernacular literary traditions.[9] National identity in Scotland, however, had the potential to be fragmented as the land itself was divided by mountains and waterways,[10] just as the people were divided by language and culture. The land which was ruled by the king of Scots in the fifteenth century was home to highlanders and men of the Isles, both speaking a Gaelic language, lowlanders, speaking a dialect of English, and many other ethnic groups, including Norse and Norman French. It is not at all clear, therefore, to which group a glossator of the *Scotichronicon* was referring when he wrote at the end of Walter Bower's work, 'Christ! He is not a Scot who is not pleased with this book!'[11]

Blind Hary, who composed his heroic poem *The Wallace* in the 1470s, had a very clear understanding of who was a Scot. Like John Barbour before him, Hary looks to the Wars of Independence for the action and themes of his work. Ian Walker has noticed that *The Wallace*, unlike *The Bruce*, praises Scottish national independence often at the expense of a universal code of chivalry. For Walker, the poems are written under different circumstances, and 'whereas Barbour can still extol the medieval and truly supranational virtue of chivalry, Harry is sufficiently a man of the Renaissance to prize the narrower national quality of patriotism.'[12] While some would argue with the picture of Blind Hary as the Renaissance man, it is true that his poem rejects any universalizing impulse. In the rare instances where a universal ideal is given voice in *The Wallace* (although it is not the ideal of a supranational chivalry, but of a universal Church), it is immediately rejected. This universalizing tendency, which Anderson argues makes nationalism unthinkable during the Middle Ages, is expressed by Edward's queen, first when she hears of the conflict ('Crystyne thai ar, зone is thar heretage' [They are Christian, yon is their heritage]),[13] and again when she acts as an ambassador for peace:

> 'Зies,' said the queyne, 'for crystyn folk we ar,
> For goddis saik, sen we desyr no mar,
> We awcht haiff pes.'[14]

['Yes,' said the queen, 'for we are Christian folk. For God's sake, since we desire no more, we ought to have peace.']

The sentiment is denied by William Wallace, and implicitly by the poet, in favour of a national conflict based on blood:

> 'Madeym, that I deny.
> The perfyt caus I sall зow schaw, for quhy
> Зe seke na pes bot for зour awn awaill.
> Quhen зour fals king had Scotland gryppyt haill,
> For nakyn thing that he befor him fand
> He wald nocht thoill the rycht blud in our land,
> Bot reft thar rent, syne put thaim selff to ded.'[15]

[Madam, that I deny. The perfect cause I shall show you, why you seek no peace except for your advantage. When your false king had gripped Scotland wholly, for no thing that he found before him would he endure the right blood in our land, but he took away their rents, and then put them to death.]

There can be no peace, Wallace informs the queen, until the Scots have taken revenge 'Off зour fals blud that has our elderis slayn' [of your false blood that has our elders slain].[16] For both the poem's hero and its author, the ideal of a universal Christian Church takes a back seat to the opposing ideal of national independence.

At first glance, Blind Hary presents a simplistic binary image of the Scottish and English nations in which, to paraphrase a pattern established by crusading literature, Scots are good, Southron evil.

As R. James Goldstein has shown, this pattern is most clearly defined in terms of blood.[17] When Wallace describes Scotland's conflict with England to the French king, he expresses it solely in terms of blood:

'Our barnat land has beyn our-set with wer
With Saxonis blud that dois ws mekill der,
Slayn our eldris, distroyit our rychtwys blud ...'[18]

[Our battered land has been over-set with war against Saxon blood that does much harm to us, slain our elders and destroyed our right-wise blood.]

Indeed, in the opening lines of the poem, the audience is reminded that 'Our ald Ennemys cummyn of Saxonys blud' [our old enemies come of Saxon blood].[19] According to this dichotomy, participation in the war requires nothing more than lineage, and Wallace justifies his own actions purely in terms of his descent:

'Becaus I am a natyff Scottis man
It is my dett to do all that I can
To fend our kynrik out off dangeryng.'[20]

[Because I am a native Scottish man, it is my debt to do all that I can to defend our kingdom from all dangers.]

In contrast, the English are consistently viewed as 'Scotlandis aduersouris' [Scotland's adversaries]. While Wallace and his men refuse to harm women and children, 'Quham euir thai mett was at the Inglis fay / Thai slew all doun with-out langar delay. / Thai sparyt nane that was off Inglis blude' [whomever they met that was of the English faith, they slew down without longer delay. They spared none that was of English blood].[21] Indeed, when the Scots sack one castle, they 'slew that was tharin; / Off Sotheroun blud thai Scottis thocht na syn' [slew those that were therein; the Scots did not think it a sin (to kill those) of Southron blood].[22]

   The conflict between rival blood is nowhere felt more strongly than in the dramatic meeting between William Wallace and Robert Bruce which follows the battle of Falkirk. Although Wallace is defending Bruce's right to the throne of Scotland, Bruce himself fights for the English, and during the battle the loyal subject watches as his king raises the royal banner of Scotland on the English side:

> Quhen Wallace saw battallis approchyt ner,
> The rycht lyon agayn his awn kynryk,
> 'Allace,' he said, 'the warld is contrar-lik!
> This land suld be ӡon tyrandis heretage,
> That cummys thus to stroy his awn barnage.'[23]

[When Wallace saw battle lines approached near, the true lion against his own kingdom, 'Alas,' he said, 'the world is turned upside-down! This land should be yon tyrant's heritage, that comes thus to destroy his own baronage.']

The barons of Scotland do suffer at the hands of their rightful king as Bruce enters the battle:

> Bathid in blud was Bruce suerd and his weid
> Throw fell slauchtyr off trew men off his awn.[24]

[Bathed in blood was Bruce's sword and his clothes through the fierce slaughter of his own true men.]

After the battle, Wallace and Bruce find themselves on opposite sides of a ravine, and they converse briefly. When Bruce admits that the English have lost more men on the day, Wallace rebukes his king:

> Wallace ansuerd, 'Allace, thai war ewill cosyt,
> Throuch thi tresson, that suld be our rycht king,
> That willfully dystroyis thin awn off-spryng.'[25]

[Wallace answered, 'Alas, they were evilly bought through your treason that should be our right king, that wilfully destroys your own off-spring.']

Wallace's verbal assault is unrelenting, and his imagery returns to one of the central themes of the poem:

'Schamys thow nocht that thow neuir ʒeit did gud,
Thow renygat deuorar off thi blud?'[26]

[Does it not shame you that you never did good, you renegade
devourer of your blood?]

What Goldstein terms 'the Saturnian image of a father who devours
his own children'[27] is literally realized in the following scene. Leav-
ing Wallace at the ravine, Bruce returns to the English camp:

Bludyt was all his wapynnys and his weid.
Sotheroun lordys scornyt him in termys rud.
Ane said, 'Behald, ʒon Scot ettis his awn blud.'
The king thocht Ill thai maid sic derisioun.
He bad haiff watter to Bruce off Huntyntoun.
Thai bad hym wesche. He said that wald he nocht:
'This blud is myn. That hurtis most my thocht.'
Sadly the Bruce than in his mind remordyt
Thai wordis suth Wallace had him recordyt.
Than rewyt he sar, fra resoun had him knawin
At blud and land suld all lik beyn his awin.[28]

[Bloody were all his weapons and his clothes. The Southron lords
scorned him in rude terms. One said, 'Behold, yon Scot eats his own
blood.' The king thought ill that they made such derision of him. He
ordered water to be brought to Bruce of Huntingdon. They bade him
wash. He said that he would not: 'This blood is mine. That hurts my
thoughts the most.' Sadly, the Bruce regretted in his mind the true
words that Wallace had said to him. Then he sorely repented, for reason made known to him that blood and land should together be his
own.]

In a poem not given to introspection, the scene is remarkable as
Hary portrays for us the moment when Bruce resolves to claim the
crown. Bruce is persuaded not only by Wallace's words, but also by
the blood of Scottish barons, which was shed on the battlefield and
which remains unwashed in the English camp. The unwashed
blood weighs on Bruce until he recognizes his own debt to both the
blood and the land of Scotland. A reader interested in Bruce's rise to

the throne must look to John Barbour's poem, but the seeds of that narrative are planted here, with Wallace as the sower. McDiarmid, commenting on Walter Bower's account of the exchange between the heroes, notes that '[i]f Wallace has lost the day, he has won Bruce.'[29]

As Bruce resolves to seek the crown, he sees his claim in terms of 'blud and land' — people and territory. The title which Bruce will claim as his own, King of Scots, begs the question: who is a Scot? On several occasions, this question is raised openly in the poem. When Jop asks a fisherman, 'Off quhat nacioun art thow?' [Of what nation are you?], he receives the firm reply: 'A Scot.'[30] Similarly, when meeting a woman, 'Wallace sperd of Scotland giff scho be' [Wallace asked if she were of Scotland][31] before he resolves to trust her, and the occupants of a stronghold in Rannoch Muir must identify themselves as Scots to avoid Wallace's sword:

'All Scottis we ar that in this place is now.
At ʒour commaund all baynly we sall bow.'
Off our nacioun gud Wallace had pete,
Tuk aythis off thaim and syne meit askyt he.[32]

['We are all Scots that are now in this place. We shall all bow readily to your command.' Good Wallace had pity of our nation, took oaths of them and then asked for meat.]

As we have seen, Hary divides the combatants according to blood, but when the Scots and their enemies are so indistinguishable that Wallace must ask whomever he meets to identify themselves with a nation, blood becomes as much a measure of political opinion as descent. Edward I, for example, felt that William Douglas was loyal to England because he had married an Englishwoman, yet Hary assures us that 'Ay Scottis blud remaynyt in-to Douglace; / Agayn Ingland he prewyt in mony place' [Scottish blood always remained in Douglas; he proved that in many places against England].[33] That Douglas was born in Scotland is never questioned, but his Scottish blood is proven by his continued animosity against the 'Southron.'

Scotland's diverse population, however, did have the potential to raise questions about descent: when blood is divided along ethnic lines, the identification of a Scot becomes problematic. This diversity was a recognized fact, yet Hary describes all of the ethnic groups of Scotland as 'trew Scottis,' as long as they support the ideological ideal of Scottish independence.[34] This is not surprising, as contemporary founding myths tended to define peoples in terms of political boundaries rather than ethnic groups.[35] Susan Reynolds observes that 'medieval people took it for granted that each "people" of their own day – and that increasingly seems to mean the whole population of an area, and quintessentially of a kingdom – was of one descent.'[36] Founding myths describe the ancient origins of a nation, but this imagined community extends into the not-so-distant past as well, as the poem blurs the lineage of the hero at his first introduction to the audience. For Blind Hary, William Wallace is a true Scot, and there is no mention of his Norman ancestors who had entered Scotland with David I:

And hensfurth I will my proces hald
Of Wilȝham Wallas ȝhe haf hard beyne tald.
His forbearis, quha likis till understand,
Of hale lynage and trew lyne of Scotland.[37]

[And henceforth I will proceed to tell of William Wallace. You have heard stories being told. His forebearers, whoever wishes to understand, are of whole lineage and true line of Scotland.]

The question 'Off quhat nacioun art thow?' is difficult enough to answer when the 'trew lyne of Scotland' is divided by opposing political allegiances, but at the time of the Wars of Independence it was also broken into different ethnic groups and intersected by an immigrating Norman nobility. Hary seems aware of the difficulty of establishing to which nation an individual belongs, and, as we have seen with Robert Bruce, the simple dichotomy of Scottish and English blood is not easy to maintain. Blood, therefore, becomes more than a simple means of delimiting descent, and political orientation within the complex web of Anglo-Scottish relations is, for Hary, as much a determinant of blood as is one's place of birth.

The Wallace, therefore, while maintaining its focus on the conflict between the Scots and the English, devotes a great deal of attention to answering the question 'Off quhat nacioun art thow?' The second half of the poem is loosely organized around the three campaigns required to free Scotland from English rule. After Wallace's first major victory at Biggar, he is made Guardian and we are told that

> Fra Gamlis peth the land obeyt him haill
> Til Vr wattir, bath strenth, forest and daill.
> Agaynis him in Galloway hous was nayne
> Except Wigtoun byggyt off lyme and stayne.[38]

[The whole land obeyed him from Gamelspath to the Urr water, both fortress, forest and dale. There wasn't a house against him in Galloway, except Wigtownshire, built of lime and stone.]

In the notes to his edition of Hary's poem, Matthew McDiarmid remarks that 'these bounds exclude Wigtownshire where Wallace now proceeds, and Berwickshire with East Lothian which he will recover from Patrick, Earl of Dunbar, in Book VII.'[39] These successes are foretold in a vision which Wallace receives while sleeping in a church. Wallace dreams that he is visited by two figures, one of whom is an elderly man who shows him Scotland and gives him a sword. The man leads Wallace to a mountain from which he could see all of Scotland:

> Tharwith he saw begyne a felloune fyr
> Quhilk braithly brynt on breid throu all the land,
> Scotland atour fra Ros to Sulway sand.[40]

[Therewith he saw begin a fierce fire which violently burned abroad through all the land, over Scotland from Ross to Solway sand.]

Upon Wallace's awakening, a cleric interprets the dream. He states:

> 'Saynct Androw was, gaiff the that suerd in hand.
> Off Sanctis he is wowar off Scotland.'[41]

[It was Saint Andrew that gave you that sword in your hand. Of the saints he is the patron of Scotland.]

The fire is interpreted as 'fell tithingis' [fierce tidings] of what will engulf Scotland before Wallace departs.[42] Indeed, Book VII provides details of Wallace's campaigns throughout Scotland, against both the English invaders and rebellious Scots.

In his first campaign, Wallace avenges the Barns of Ayr atrocity, but he then turns against his fellow Scot. Wallace is resting when 'tithandis come him till / Out off the hycht' [tidings come to him out of the highlands].[43] An uprising is led by Macfadyan, who 'till Inglismen was suorn ... / Thus falsly he gaiff our his heretage / And tuk at London off Eduuard grettar wage' [was sworn to Englishmen ... Thus falsely he gave over his heritage and took greater pay from Edward at London].[44] Hary goes to extreme lengths to demonize both Macfadyan and his men:

Barnys nor wyff thai peple sparyt nocht,
Waistyt the land als fer as thai mycht ga.
Thai bestly folk couth nocht bot byrn and sla.[45]

[That people spared neither children nor wives, and wasted the land as far as they might go. That beastly folk did nothing but burn and slay.]

Wallace also wishes to suppress Macfadyan, both for his misplaced allegiance and for his low birth:

Wallace awowide that he suld wrokyn be
On that rebald or ellis tharfor to de.
Off tyrandry king Eduuard thocht him gud.
Law born he was and off law simpill blud.[46]

[Wallace vowed that he would be avenged on that rascal or else die trying. King Edward thought that he was good for oppression. He was low born and from low, simple blood.]

Macfadyan fights with a large force, many of whom are 'out off Irland brocht' [brought out of Ireland].[47] In addition to these men, Macfadyan also fights 'With Yrage men hardy and curageous' [with hardy and courageous highlanders].[48] As Wallace 'began to tak the hicht, / Our a montayne' [began to enter the highlands over a mountain], his army consists of two thousand Scots, including five hundred 'westland men.'[49]

When the two armies meet among the 'mos and crag,'[50] Hary

again draws attention to Macfadyan's army of 'Yrage men.' Macfadyan begins to lose the long battle, as Wallace's troops are of a
hardy will:

> Off Yrage blud full hardely thai spill,
> With feyll fechtyn maid sloppys throuch the thrang.
> On the fals part our wicht wer-men sa dang
> That thai to byd mycht haiff no langar mycht.[51]

[They spilled highland blood full hardily, and with fierce fighting they
made a breach through the press of battle. Our strong men of war
struck so hard on the false part that they might no longer have any
strength to bide.]

As the battle concludes, Hary once again describes Macfadyan's
army in terms of the nationality of his troops:

> The Irland folk than maid thaim for the flycht,
> In craggis clam and sum in wattir flett,
> Twa thousand thar drownyt with-outyn lett.[52]

[The Irish folk then put themselves to flight, climbed into craigs and
some floated in water. Two thousand drowned there at once.]

The rest of Macfadyan's army, however, submits to Wallace's
authority:

> Born Scottis men baid still in-to the feild,
> Kest wappynnys thaim fra and on thar kneis kneild.
> With petous woice thai criyt apon Wallace
> For goddis saik to tak thaim in his grace.
> Grewyt he was bot rewth off thaim he had,
> Rasauit thaim fair with contenance full sad.
> 'Off our awne blud we suld haiff gret pete.
> Luk ʒhe sla nane off Scottis will ʒoldyn be.
> Off outland men lat nane chaip with the liff.'[53]

[Born Scottish men remained still in the field, cast weapons from
themselves and kneeled on their knees. With piteous voice they cried
upon Wallace to take them in his grace for God's sake. He was grieved,

but had pity upon them, and received them fairly with a grave countenance. 'Of our own blood we should have great pity. Look that you slay none of the Scots that will yield. Of the outland men, let none escape with their life.']

Since Hary has already said that the 'Irland folk' had fled, the 'Born Scottis men' must be the highlanders who make up the rest of Macfadyan's army. Thus Gaelic highlanders, once 'Yrage men' who performed beastly deeds, are transformed into 'Born Scottis men' who accept Wallace and his grace; 'Yrage blud,' spilled on the battlefield in opposition to Wallace, becomes 'our awne blud' through an act of political will. Later, these same 'blessit men that was off Scotland born' [blessed men that were of Scotland born] are restored to their lands by the beneficent Wallace.[54] In contrast, Wallace treats the 'outland men' (presumably the 'Irland folk' who have fled) as he treated the English: none are allowed escape with their lives. Macfadyan himself does not fare well, as he is killed after fleeing the battlefield. Duncan of Lorn chases Macfadyan and, as befits a traitor, severs his head from his body. He returns to Wallace with the traitor's head, and 'Apon a sper throuch-out the feild it bar' [bore it upon a spear throughout the field].[55]

It is Hary's precise use of language which distances the Scots from the rebellious Macfadyan, even though his army includes Scottish soldiers. Through careful attention to the ethnic diversity within Macfadyan's rebellious army, Blind Hary sorts the once 'bestly folk' into distinct groups of 'outland men,' who are to be killed, and 'Scottis men,' who are received into Wallace's peace. Hary's use of the phrase 'Yrage men' insulates Wallace's army from the rebellious highlanders until they identify themselves as Scots by abandoning the 'fals part' and accepting the ideal of Scottish independence. Only after the political transformation does Hary abandon the distancing adjective 'Yrage' in favour of the unifying 'Scottis' and 'our awne.' What appears to be a transformation of blood, therefore, is actually a political metamorphosis as Hary ignores the ethnic and linguistic differences between the highlands and lowlands and presents an image of united Scottish 'blud.'

It would be overly simplistic, of course, to argue that the ethnic divisions within Scotland were not recognized, and it might be useful to return to Anderson's definition of a nation as an 'imagined community' to examine how the Scots themselves perceived the

linguistic and ethnic diversity of their realm, and how they ratio-
nalized that diversity within a single nation. The chronicler John
Fordun, writing about a century before Hary, clearly states in his
ethnographic introduction that 'the manners and customs of the
Scots vary with the diversity of their speech.'[56] While the chronicler claims that those who speak the Teutonic language 'are of
domestic and civilized habits,' the highlanders, who speak a Scottish language, 'are a savage and untamed nation.'[57] The Gaelic population, claims Fordun, are 'hostile to the English people and their
language, and, owing to diversity of speech, even to their own
nation, and exceedingly cruel.'[58] Despite the animosity between the
Gaelic- and English-speaking peoples of Scotland, and their obvious
cultural differences (Fordun does state that each group represents a
different *gens*), he identifies both highlanders and lowlanders as
members of the same nation. Fordun may be critical of the Gaelic
Scots, but he never attempts to diminish their position within the
realm of Scotland. He is careful to set apart the 'highland Scot'[59]
who fell on his knees to recite Alexander III's genealogy at his coronation in 1249; but after tracing the descent of the king to Fergus,
'then the said Scot, going on with the said pedigree, from man to
man, read through until he came to the first Scot – namely Iber
Scot. This Iber was the son of Gaithel Glas ... and was begotten of
Scota.'[60] Alexander's genealogy, as represented at his coronation,
associated him with the founding myth of Scotland and the Gaelic
highlands.

Other authors were not always positive about the Gaelic population of Scotland. The *Buke of the Howlat* (*Book of the Owl*), a mid-
fifteenth-century allegorical poem, describes the political unity of
Scotland (it briefly relates that Douglas campaigned in Galloway
and 'maid it ferme, as we fynd, till our Scottis fay' [made it firm, as
we find, to our Scottish faith]),[61] but the rustic image of the Gaelic
Scots is also affirmed: the 'bard owt of Irland' [bard out of Ireland;
i.e., the highlands], who speaks a muddled mixture of Scots-Gaelic
and Scots, is ridiculed and abused by the more refined birds who
attend the pope's court.[62] Hary's account of Macfadyan's campaign
seems to conform to the pattern of recognizing the diversity of
Scotland even while viewing the realm as a single nation. Like Fordun, Hary shows the highlanders in conflict with their fellow Scots,
but that conflict is resolved when the warring factions unite under
Wallace and the ideological program he espouses.

Hary's willingness to transform rebels into true Scottish men is
not limited to the Gaelic population. The same concern for a Scottish foe is shown for Earl Patrick's army during the suppression of
his rebellion in Book vıı. After the battle at Stirling Bridge, Wallace
holds a council at Saint Johnston to settle the land. The three
estates assemble, 'clerk, barown and bowrugie, / Bot Corspatrik
wald nocht cum at thar call' [clerk, baron and burgesses, but Patrick
would not come at their call].[63] When summoned personally,
Patrick again refuses, claiming that he owes no allegiance to
Wallace, and that he will hold his lands in Scotland free from any
lord. Wallace is determined to march against Patrick and 'ger him
grant quhom he haldis for his lord' [make him admit whom he
holds for a lord].[64] As they approach Dunbar, Wallace regrets that it
is necessary to attack Patrick with force:

'A hardyar lord is nocht in-to Scotland.
Mycht he be maid trew, stedfast, till a king,
Be wit and force he can do mekill thing,
Bot willfully he likis to tyne him sell.'[65]

[A hardier lord is not in Scotland. If he could be made true and stead-
fast to a king, he could do many things by wit and force. But wilfully
he likes to ruin himself.]

Wallace's army meets Patrick near Innerwick, and they join battle
immediately. Concerning the initial battle, Hary writes:

The stour was strang and wondyr peralous,
Contenyt lang with dedis chewalrous.
Mony thar deit off cruell Scottis blud.
Off this trety the mater is nocht gud,
Tharfor I ces to tell the destruccioun.
Pete it was, and all off a nacioun.[66]

[The battle was strong and wonderfully perilous, it lasted long with
chivalric deeds. Many of fierce Scottish blood died there. The matter
of this negotiation is not good, and therefore I cease to tell of the
destruction. It was a pity, and all of a nation.]

The brief description of the battle is unusual in a poem which relishes military action, and Goldstein, when discussing this scene, writes that 'Hary's refusal to portray this history of Scot against Scot is just one form of the suppression of an unpleasant truth that we will come to recognize as characteristic of the author.'[67] According to Goldstein, Hary's desire 'to provoke his contemporaries' hatred against the English ... leads him to skip over atrocities committed by Scots against their own kind, since the emotions these incidents would incite could distract attention from the central aim of the poem.'[68] Although Goldstein's interpretation of the battle with Patrick is attractive, it does not account for the poem's treatment of the Macfadyan rebellion, in which, as we have seen, the battles between Scots were described in great detail. The interpretation becomes even more problematic when it is remembered that the conflicts with Macfadyan and Patrick have no basis in history. Goldstein does not attempt to explain why Hary would invent two rebellious Scottish lords if he did not want to depict the internal strife of Scotland. Obviously, Hary did intend to depict conflict among the Scots, and he did not feel that the depiction of internal strife distracted attention from the central aim of the poem. Goldstein is correct to assume that these scenes do not focus hatred against the English, but does this mean that they are meant to be glossed over by the reader? The key to understanding this passage lies in Hary's statement that the two armies are 'all off a nacioun.'

Earl Patrick's army is described as being of 'Scottis blud,' just as Macfadyan's army of highlanders is made up of 'born Scottis men.' In the same way, when Patrick makes peace, 'With full glaid hart Wallace resauit him thar' [with full glad heart Wallace received him there],[69] just as he had accepted the highlanders who fought with Macfadyan but not the 'outland men.' By describing the rebellious armies of Patrick and Macfadyan as being 'all off a nacioun' with Wallace and his 'trew Scottis,' Hary demonstrates that the national ideology of a unified and independent Scotland could overcome the ethnic, linguistic, and political differences which had the potential to divide Scotland and make it vulnerable to English aggression.

The significance of these rifts in Scottish unity is demonstrated by Wallace's activities after the defeat of Patrick. It is only after this battle that Wallace 'tuk state to gowern all Scotland' [took state to govern all Scotland][70] and finally, after the peace with Patrick and the return of Roxburgh and Berwick into Scottish hands, Hary states:

Scotlande atour fra Ros till Soloway sand
He raid it thrys and statut all the land.[71]

[Over Scotland, from Ross to Solway sand, he rode it thrice and established all the land.]

The prophecy of Wallace's dream is recalled here through verbal
repetition. The 'felloune fyr' which burned brightly throughout the
land, 'Scotland atour fra Ros to Sulway sand,'[72] is here realized in
Wallace's threefold ride around Scotland. The fulfilment of the
prophecy occurs after the submission of the rebellious Patrick,
rather than after the battle at Stirling Bridge, where Wallace first
drives out the English. The prophecy that Wallace will free the land
'fra Ros to Sulway sand,' therefore, applies both to freedom from the
aggression of the English and to the submission of rebels within
Scotland itself. The expulsion of the English is an important step,
but the Scots must also adhere to the ideal of an independent Scotland before they can be 'all off a nacioun,' and before Bruce can
truly claim that 'blud and land suld all lik beyn his awin.'

Hary's emphasis on the unity of the land and its people may have
had particular relevance for his contemporary audience. As mentioned earlier, the events of both campaigns against rebellious Scots
in Books VII and VIII are entirely fictitious. McDiarmid notes that the
account of Macfadyan's rebellion draws heavily from Barbour's
description of Bruce's campaign against John of Lorn, but that it also
recalls the recent rebellion of John, Lord of the Isles and Earl of
Ross.[73] The campaign against Earl Patrick is also fictitious, and
McDiarmid argues that it is inspired by the raids of the earl of March
in the early fifteenth century.[74] By recalling recent internal conflict
within Scotland, Hary focuses the attention of the reader on the need
for a united realm which is free not only from the influence of the
Southron, but also from civil discord. Such an interpretation contra-
dicts Goldstein's view that the incitement of hatred against the
English is the central aim of the poem. Certainly this is one of the
aims of the poem, and many of Hary's authorial asides warn against
trusting the old enemy: in the opening lines of Book I, Hary com-
plains that 'Till honour Ennymyis is our haile entent' [to honour enemies is our whole intent],[75] a sentiment assumed to refer to James
III's policies of alliance with England.[76] Hary would have disapproved
of any policy which warmed relations with England, and he warns:

Our ald Ennemys cummyn of Saxonys blud,
That neuyr ʒeit to Scotland wald do gud ...[77]

[Our old enemies come of Saxon blood, that never yet would do good
to Scotland ...]

Many of Hary's apostrophes, however, do not incite hatred of the
English, but encourage unity among the Scots or bewail civil discord. In Edward's first campaign against Scotland, for example, Earl
Patrick is already fighting against his fellow Scot, and Hary warns,
'Is nayne in warld at scaithis ma do mar / Than weile trastyt in-
born familiar' [There is none in the world that may do more harm
than a well trusted, native associate].[78] Hary's longest digressions
are not devoted to inciting anti-English sentiment, but to condemn-
ing envy among the Scots themselves. To Hary, the Scots who fight
against their own land are motivated by envy, and this allows
England to complete the third conquest of Scotland. The description of that conquest is remarkably brief:

The fals Inwy, the wicked fell tresoun,
Amang thaim selff brocht feill to confusioun.[79]

[The false envy, the wicked fierce treason, brought many to confusion
among themselves.]

The same concern is revealed in France, where Wallace is forced
to fight with a lion because of the envy of the king's courtiers. Hary
uses this episode to direct another short sermon against envy:

Lordis, behald, Inwy the wyle dragoun,
In cruel fyr he byrnys his regioun;
For he is nocht that bonde is in Inwy,
To sum myscheiff It bryngis hym haistely.
Forsaik Inwy, thow sall the bettir speid.[80]

[Lords, behold, envy the vile dragon, in cruel fire he burns his region;
for there is no one that is bound in envy but it brings him hastily to
some mischief. Forsake envy, you will speed the better.]

Shortly after this episode, the full effects of envy will be revealed

through the pact between Wallange and Mentieth, which will lead
to Wallace's betrayal. Hary uses Wallace's downfall, not to bewail
English aggression and deceit, but the envy and covetousness of
Wallace's fellow Scots:

Thar cowatys was our gret maister seyn.
Nane sampill takis how ane othir has beyn
For cowatice put in gret paynys fell,
For cowatice the serpent is off hell.
Throuch cowatice gud Ector tuk the ded.
For cowatice thar can be no ramed.
Throuch cowatice gud Alexander was lost,
And Iulius als for all his reiff and bost.
Throuch cowatice deit Arthour off Bretane.
For cowatice thar has deit mony ane.
For cowatice the traytour Ganʒelon
The flour off France he put till confusion.
For cowatice thai poysound gud Godfra
In Antioche, as the autor will sa.
For cowatice Menteth apon fals wys
Betraysyt Wallace at was his gossop twys.[81]

[There covetousness was seen to be our great master. No one takes
example of how another has fared, for covetousness put many in great
pains, for covetousness the serpent is now in hell. Through covetousness good Hector took death. For covetousness there can be no rem-
edy. Through covetousness Alexander was lost, and Julius also, for all
his plundering and boasts. Through covetousness died Arthur of Britain. For covetousness there has died many-a-one. For covetousness the
traitor Ganelon put the flower of France to confusion. For covetousness they poisoned good Godfrey in Antioch, as the author will say.
For covetousness Mentieth in a false way betrayed Wallace, who was
his godfather twice.]

The passage is striking for its use of repetition, one of Hary's favou-
rite rhetorical devices, but also for the heroes to which it alludes:
Hector, Alexander, Caesar, Arthur, Charlemagne, and Godfrey of
Bouillon. Wallace has been compared with each of these characters
throughout the text, but here, as Hary demonstrates the cause of
Wallace's downfall, all these men are drawn together, each repre-

senting a national myth which carried the same cautionary element. Goldstein remarks that Hary draws these figures from the 'discourse of the Nine Worthies,'[82] but the choice is more significant than that. Hary's sermon on envy and covetousness is closely parallel to Barbour's sermon on the evils of treachery.[83] However, as Barbour laments that heroes are brought low 'throw tresoune and throw wikkitnes' [through treason and through wickedness],[84] Hary narrows his focus to 'cowatice' and envy as the only motivations for treachery. Throughout *The Wallace*, Scotland is under the constant threat of invasion from England, but it is only because of envy and covetousness that the Scots are unable to withstand their old enemy.

To be sure, Scottish identity in *The Wallace* is most clearly defined in opposition to the English, or the Southron. But the poem also recognizes that Scottish identity need not be expressed purely in contrast to the southern neighbour. In the turbulent years of the 1470s, Hary's poem certainly opposes closer ties with England. Citing the looming Albany rebellion, Goldstein goes so far as to argue that '*The Wallace* begins to read like an antiroyalist allegory, with Wallace loosely standing for Albany and Bruce for James III,' but this reading is too restrictive.[85] It is obvious that Hary disapproved of any policy which led to warmer relations with England, but to call him 'antiroyalist' stretches the evidence and ignores Hary's preoccupation with the evils of internal strife.[86] As we have seen, William Wallace's success in the poem is based on his ability to unite the diverse peoples of the kingdom into a single national group with a single ideal of Scottish independence. This group is most threatened when civil discord within Scotland itself, caused by envy and covetousness, opens it to external forces. The poem demonstrates that a unified Scotland, bound by common descent and political ideals, is necessary to protect the realm from the aggressions of the 'auld enemy,' both in Wallace's day and in the late fifteenth century.

Notes

1 B. Anderson, *Imagined Communities: Reflections on the Origins and Spread of Nationalism*, rev. ed. (London and New York, 1991), 12–19. For an overview of reactions to Anderson, see the preface to *Concepts of*

National Identity in the Middle Ages, ed. S. Forde, L. Johnson, and A.V. Murray, Leeds Texts and Monographs, n.s. 14 (Leeds, 1995), vii–viii.

2 Anderson, *Imagined Communities*, 12–19. See also H. Kohn, *The Idea of Nationalism: A Study of Its Origins and Background* (New York, 1944), 78–85. The early debate surrounding medieval nationalism is usefully summarized in *Nationalism in the Middle Ages*, ed. C.L. Tipton European Problem Studies (New York, 1972), *passim*.

3 Published as R.R. Davies, 'The Peoples of Britain and Ireland 1100–1400,' *Transactions of the Royal Historical Society* 6th ser., 4 (1994), 1–20; 5 (1995), 1–24; 6 (1996), 1–23; 7 (1997), 1–24.

4 Published as A. Hastings, *The Construction of Nationhood: Ethnicity, Religion, and Nationalism* (Cambridge, 1997).

5 J.C. Murray, *The Ballads and Songs of Scotland* (London, 1874), 136.

6 See E.M. Barron, *The Scottish War of Independence* (London, 1914; repr. New York, 1997), *passim*, but especially 485–7.

7 R.J. Goldstein, *The Matter of Scotland: Historical Narrative in Medieval Scotland* (Lincoln, NE, and London, 1993), 23.

8 See, for example, D. Watt, 'Nationalism in Barbour's *Bruce*,' *Parergon: Bulletin of the Australian and New Zealand Association for Medieval and Renaissance Studies* 12/1 (1994), 89–107; H. Utz, 'Traces of Nationalism in Fordun's Chronicle,' *SS* 4 (1984), 139–49; B. Webster, 'John Fordun and the Independent Identity of the Scots,' in *Medieval Europeans: Studies in Ethnic Identity and National Perspectives in Medieval Europe*, ed. A.P. Smyth (New York, 1998), 85–102; J. Schwend, 'Nationalism in Scottish Medieval and Renaissance Literature,' in *Nationalism in Literature / Literarischer Nationalismus: Literature, Language, and National Identity*, ed. H.W. Drescher and H. Volkel (Frankfurt, 1989), 29–42.

9 On the importance of a vernacular literary tradition, particularly biblical translation, for the development of national sentiment, see Hastings, *Construction of Nationhood*, 22–5.

10 See, for example, B. Webster, *Medieval Scotland: The Making of an Identity* (Basingstoke and London, 1997), 9–20.

11 'Non Scotus est Christe cui liber non placet iste' (*Scotichronicon*, viii, 340–1).

12 I.C. Walker, 'Barbour, Blind Harry and Sir William Craigie,' *SSL* 1 (1964), 203.

13 Blind Hary, *Hary's Wallace* (*Vita Nobilissimi Defensoris Scotie Wilelmi Wallace Militis*), ed. M.P. McDiarmid, 2 vols, STS (Edinburgh, 1968–9), vi.293. Hereafter, the poem will be referred to as Hary, *Wallace*, cited by

book and line number, while McDiarmid's commentary will be referred
to by page number as McDiarmid, *Hary's Wallace*.

14 Hary, *Wallace*, viii.1291–3.

15 Hary, *Wallace*, viii.1293–9.

16 Hary, *Wallace*, viii.1396.

17 See R.J. Goldstein, 'Blind Hary's Myth of Blood: The Ideological Closure
    of *The Wallace*,' *SSL* 25 (1990), 70–82; this article is expanded and mod-
    ified in chapter 8 of Goldstein's *Matter of Scotland*, 215–49. Goldstein
    points out that 'blood is endowed with a symbolic meaning that is truly
    remarkable for a poem that is not expressly about Christ' ('Blind Hary's
    Myth of Blood,' 72, and *Matter of Scotland*, 232).

18 Hary, *Wallace*, ix.495–7.

19 Hary, *Wallace*, i.7.

20 Hary, *Wallace*, viii.545–7. Cf. also Wallace's response to the English
    request that he take the crown:

    He said, 'Fyrst, it war a our hie thing,
    Agayne the faith to reyff my rychtwis king.
    I am his man, born natiff of Scotland.
    To wer the croun I will nocht tak on hand.
    To fend the rewm it is my dett be skill.
    Lat God abowe reward me as he will.' (Hary, *Wallace*, viii.639–44)
    [He said, 'First, it would be an over-high thing, against faith to rob my
    rightful king. I am his man, born native of Scotland. I will not under-
    take to wear the crown. To defend the kingdom by skill is my debt.
    Let God above reward me as he will.']

21 Hary, *Wallace*, iv.293, 295–7.

22 Hary, *Wallace*, x.999–1000.

23 Hary, *Wallace*, xi.208–12.

24 Hary, *Wallace*, xi.252–3.

25 Hary, *Wallace*, xi.470–2.

26 Hary, *Wallace*, xi.491–2. The scene is derived from *Scotichronicon*, vi,
    94–7.

27 Goldstein, *Matter of Scotland*, 246.

28 Hary, *Wallace*, xi.534–44.

29 McDiarmid, *Hary's Wallace*, ii, 261.

30 Hary, *Wallace*, x.603–4.

31 Hary, *Wallace*, v.1091.

32 Hary, *Wallace*, xii.689–92.

33 Hary, *Wallace*, x.881–2.

34 As Fiona Watson points out, the ideal of an independent Scotland was

not so clear during the Wars of Independence. It was only after independence had been achieved that it came to be seen as the only worthy alternative. See F. Watson, 'The Enigmatic Lion: Scotland, Kingship and National Identity in the Wars of Independence,' in *Image and Identity: The Making and Re-making of Scotland through the Ages*, ed. D. Broun, R.J. Finlay, and M. Lynch (Edinburgh, 1998), 4–17. The first use of the phrase 'trew Scottis' occurs after the description of Corspatrik's attack at Berwick. While Patrick, a Scot, supports the English side, 'Of trew Scottis chapyt na creatur' [of true Scots escaped no creature] (Hary, *Wallace*, I.96). The Scots who submit to Wallace are also consistently referred to 'trew Scottis'; see, for example, Hary, *Wallace*, VI.778; VIII.995.

35 Hary alludes to the Scottish founding myth in the first book of *The Wallace*. After a brief account of Edward's initial campaigns in Scotland, Hary claims that 'The croune he tuk apon that sammyne stane / At Gadalos send with his sone fra Spane' [He took the crown upon that same stone that Gaythelos sent with his son from Spain] (Hary, *Wallace*, I.121–2). Gaythelos, husband of the eponymous Scota, recalls the myth of descent which argues for a unified nation. For the development of the Scota legend and its use by Fordun, see Goldstein, *Matter of Scotland*, 104–32; and D. Broun, *The Irish Identity of the Kingdom of the Scots in the Twelfth and Thirteenth Centuries* (Woodbridge, 1999), passim.

36 S. Reynolds, 'Medieval Origines Gentium and the Community of the Realm,' *History* 68 (1983), 380.

37 Hary, *Wallace*, I.19–22.

38 Hary, *Wallace*, VI.793–6.

39 McDiarmid, *Hary's Wallace*, ii, 196.

40 Hary, *Wallace*, VII.86–8.

41 Hary, *Wallace*, VII.123–4.

42 Hary, *Wallace*, VII.127.

43 Hary, *Wallace*, VII.618–19.

44 Hary, *Wallace*, VII.627, 631–2.

45 Hary, *Wallace*, VII.644–6.

46 Hary, *Wallace*, VII.735–8.

47 Hary, *Wallace*, VII.643. McDiarmid suggests that 'Irland' may refer to the Hebridean islands, rather than Ireland itself (*Hary's Wallace*, ii, 207).

48 Hary, *Wallace*, VII.833.

49 Hary, *Wallace*, VII.783–4, 776.

50 Hary, *Wallace*, VII.805.

51 Hary, *Wallace*, vII.842–5.

52 Hary, *Wallace*, vII.446–8.

53 Hary, *Wallace*, vII.849–57.

54 Hary, *Wallace*, vII.869–73. McDiarmid assumes that the phrase 'Born Scottis men' 'would seem to imply that some of Macfadyan's men were Irish' (*Hary's Wallace*, ii, 210). This seems unlikely, however, as Wallace accepts these men as his vassals and 'Restorit thaim to thar landis bot les' [restored them to their lands without any less] (Hary, *Wallace*, vII.871). It would also be the only incidence in the poem of the phrase 'Scottis men' referring to anyone but a Scot.

55 Hary, *Wallace*, vII.865.

56 'Mores autem Scotorum secundum diversitatem linguarum variantur' (*CGS* i, 42; ii, 38).

57 '... domestica gens est et cultu ...'; '... ferina gens est et indomita ...' (*CGS*, i, 42; ii, 38).

58 'populo quidem Anglorum et linguae, sed et propriae nationi, propter linguarum diversitatem, infesta, jugiter et crudelis' (*CGS*, i, 42; ii, 38).

59 '... Scotus montanus ...' (*CGS*, i, 294; ii, 290).

60 'Deinde dictam genealogiam dictus Scotus ab homine in hominem continuando perlegit donec ad primum Scotum, videlicet, Iber Scot, pervenit. Qui quidem Iber fuit filius Gaithel Glas ... genitus ex Scota ...' (*CGS*, i, 295; ii, 290).

61 'The Buke of the Howlat,' in *Longer Scottish Poems*, ed. P. Bawcutt and F. Riddy (Edinburgh, 1987), 567 [cited by line number].

62 'Buke of the Howlat,' 795ff.

63 Hary, *Wallace*, vIII.4–5.

64 Hary, *Wallace*, vIII.45.

65 Hary, *Wallace*, vIII.82–5.

66 Hary, *Wallace*, vIII.97–112.

67 Goldstein, *Matter of Scotland*, 222.

68 Goldstein, *Matter of Scotland*, 221.

69 Hary, *Wallace*, vIII.1544. The same phrase is used when Wallace accepts the rebel Wallange into his faith (Hary, *Wallace*, x.326).

70 Hary, *Wallace*, vIII.415.

71 Hary, *Wallace*, vIII.1593–4.

72 Hary, *Wallace*, vII.86–8.

73 See McDiarmid, *Hary's Wallace*, i, xv–xvi, and ii, 206–7. For John, Lord of the Isles, see N. Macdougall, 'Achilles' Heel? The Earldom of Ross, the Lordship of the Isles, and the Stewart Kings, 1449–1507,' in *Alba:*

Celtic Scotland in the Medieval Era, ed. E.J. Cowan and R.A. McDonald (East Linton, 2000), 248–75.

74 McDiarmid, *Hary's Wallace*, ii, 219.

75 Hary, *Wallace*, I.5.

76 See, for example, McDiarmid, *Hary's Wallace*, i, xiv–xxvi; and Goldstein, *Matter of Scotland*, 278–81.

77 Hary, *Wallace*, I.7–8; for other authorial asides which incite hatred of the English, see, for example, II.242, VI.111, and VI.235–8.

78 Hary, *Wallace*, I.111–12. McDiarmid notes that this proverb, originally from Boethius, is probably suggested by its use in Bower's *Scotichronicon* (*Hary's Wallace*, ii, 133).

79 Hary, *Wallace*, XI.983–4.

80 Hary, *Wallace*, XII.287–91.

81 Hary, *Wallace*, XII.833–48.

82 Goldstein, *Matter of Scotland*, 249.

83 John Barbour, *Barbour's Bruce: A Fredome Is a Noble Thing!* ed. M.P. McDiarmid and J.A.C. Stevenson, 3 vols, STS (Edinburgh, 1980, 1981, 1985), I.515–60. Barbour refers to the heroes of Troy, Alexander, Caesar, and Arthur as victims of treachery.

84 *Barbour's Bruce*, I.559.

85 Goldstein, *Matter of Scotland*, 279. Goldstein is forced to this conclusion by the emphasis that he places on the character of Robert the Bruce, an emphasis which leads him to refer to Books XI and XII as the 'denouement' of the poem (*Matter of Scotland*, 247).

86 Goldstein (*Matter of Scotland*, 281) argues that Hary was in favour of the 1488 rebellion which brought James IV to the throne: 'Taking the son's side against the father, Blind Hary was rewarded by the son.' This statement, however, is unfounded. The 'reward' to which Goldstein refers is simply a payment from the Crown recorded in *The Accounts of the Lord High Treasurer of Scotland* (see McDiarmid, *Hary's Wallace*, i, xxviii). There is no indication of what this payment was for; the general consensus is that it was probably for the singing of songs (possibly *The Wallace* itself).

5

Carnival at Court and Dunbar in the Underworld

MARY E. ROBBINS

During the Middle Ages representations of both purgatory and hell achieved a level of gruesomeness so extreme that, to a modern sensibility at least, they would seem scarcely worthwhile. Punishments described in early texts, before the tenth century, for example, were often just graphic enough to indicate the painful nature of the next life for those who fail to prepare themselves spiritually in this one.[1] By the late fifteenth or early sixteenth century, the faithful at all social levels had been well schooled in the elaborately conceived, viscerally intrusive punishments that must be endured by those waiting in purgatory or simmering in hell. Scotland was no exception, according to William Dunbar (c. 1460–c. 1520), the brilliant, if enigmatic, court poet of King James IV (1488–1513). In a dream vision describing events that take place in hell on, or in preparation for, Fasterns Eve, or Shrove Tuesday, Dunbar works both within and against the traditions associated with medieval descriptions of the afterlife. The vision, 'Off Februar the fyiftene nycht,' is in two parts. In the first, the seven deadly sins and their respective bands of followers, dressed as courtiers, dance before Mahoun (the devil) and his fiends. In the second, a bungling shoemaker and tailor try to joust with one another.

The Scots celebrated Shrove Tuesday with the same abandon displayed by their English and Continental neighbours,[2] and the rambunctious action in this poem approximates a carnival atmosphere familiar to Dunbar's contemporaries. Yet this piece offers more than carnival entertainment. It represents a Shrovetide warning, aimed at the court of James IV, that casts a cold eye upon the vanity of earthly things. Dunbar's satire here reflects, indicts, and, of course, exaggerates in carnival fashion the behaviour he observed daily among the Scottish nobility, his primary audience. The demonic dancers follow in death the vices to which they devoted themselves in life. In accord with the topsy-turvy world of this poem, the once noble audience, deprived of social status, becomes the entertainment. And the tournament, bastion of the medieval aristocracy, is overrun with pedestrian rabble led by two inept tradesmen.

Scholars have given attention to this work over the centuries, with the discussion often centring upon whether or not the two sections of the vision, the dance and the tournament, are connected in some way or are two separate poems that bear little relation to one another. Although most scholars agree that the two parts are linked structurally, they are disinclined generally to discuss them as a single work because thematic similarities are not readily apparent. Some early critics, put off by the bawdy aspects of the pieces, recognized little merit in them; later ones found value in Dunbar's 'satire against chivalry' that is 'clearly directed against the false imitators of chivalry, the would-be courtiers' in the tournament section,[3] and admired his use of allegory and the grotesque 'to show the monstrosity of evil, to bring its disgusting and horrifying nature to the surface' in the dance section.[4] Priscilla Bawcutt, in her edition of Dunbar's poetry, prints both the dance and the tournament as one poem;[5] in *Dunbar the Makar* enlightened discussion points to the horror in the poet's notion 'that human vice and its punishment are devised to amuse the devil' in the dance, and she feels that the tournament between the shoemaker and the tailor 'is simply a "bourd," and provokes violent laughter in the poet himself.'[6] I would like to show a more intimate thematic connection between the two sections of this poem than earlier scholars would allow. I believe that this poem presents complementary parts of a unified vision. The thematic connection between the dance and the tournament lies first of all in their combined contribution to the poem's role as pre-Lenten caveat, directed at a courtly audience, that depicts social functions reversed, the high brought low and the low raised high. This unity of purpose is augmented by unity of place: Dunbar's representation of the underworld, the setting for the poem, is odd by medieval standards – odd in the same way for both the dance and the tournament.

Dunbar's hell, it seems to me, is mild by medieval standards and a good bit less grotesque than others have labelled it. Neither section threatens an audience with terror in the afterlife. The dance of the deadly sins may be a grotesquerie that instances Mikhail Bakhtin's carnival culture (see below), yet it presents a spectacle rather than a horror show. The tournament, with its scatological passages, poses more of a threat to the fastidious than to the fearful. As the dream vision begins, the devil cries a dance of 'schrewis that wer nevir schrevin.'[7] At the outset comes the call to spiritual vigilance familiar in medieval poems, including those of Dunbar, who writes, for example, in 'I that in heill wes and gladnes':

> Sen for the ded remeid is none,
> Best is that we for dede dispone,
> Eftir our deid that lif may we:
> *Timor mortis conturbat me.* (No. 62, 97–100)

> [Since for death there is no remedy,
> It is best that we for death make ready,
> So that after our death we may live:
> Fear of death disturbs me.]

In another poem ('In to thir dirk and drublie dayis'), Age says to the poet, 'Remember thow hes compt to mak / Of all thi tyme thow spendit heir' (no. 69, 34–5). And again in another ('*Memento homo quod cinis es*'):

> So speid the, man, and confes
> With humill hart and sobir teiris,
> And sadlye in thy hart inpres
> *Quod tu in cinerem reverters.* (No. 61, 37–40)

> [So hasten thee, man, and confess
> With humble heart and solemn tears,
> And sorrowfully in thy heart imprint
> The fact that you will return to ashes.]

In a poem that urges confession during the forty days of Lent ('O synfull man, thir ar the fourty dayis'), Dunbar admonishes,

> I reid the, man, of thi transgressioun

With all thi hert that thou be penitent;
Thow schrive the clene and mak confessioun
And se thairto that thou be deligent,
With all thi synnis into thi mynde presente,
That every syn ma be the selfe be schawin –
To thyne confessour it ma be kend and knawin. (No. 5, 8–14)

[I counsel thee, man, of thy sin
That thou be penitent with all thy heart.
Confess completely and formally acknowledge thy sin
And see that thou be diligent in this,
With all thy sins directly recalled in thy mind,
That every sin may by itself be revealed,
To thy confessor it may be imparted and known.]

In a variation on this theme, the poet begins another piece, 'O wreche, be war: this warld will wend the fro / Quhilk hes begylit mony greit estait' (no. 60, 1–2), and goes on to say:

Bend up thy saill and win thy port of grace;
For and the deith ourtak the in trespas
Than may thow say thir wourdis with, Allace:
Vanitas vanitatum et omnia vanitas. (No. 60, 13–16)

[Draw up thy sail and win thy port of grace;
For if death overtakes thee in sin
Then may thou say these words with 'Alas':
Vanity of vanities, all is vanity.]

Of course, every medieval Christian would have understood the seriousness of the sentiment voiced in these lines, and in terms of content almost any medieval poet could have written them. In his portrayal of the dance of the seven deadly sins and the tournament between the shoemaker and the tailor, Dunbar cautions those who might ignore the importance of shrift. The force of the poet's communication here lies in the social standing of his audience, who are shown in this poem that the trappings of nobility have meaning only for the short span of man's earthly existence. In the next world, the deadly sins can become courtiers, and craftsmen can be dubbed knights. The raucous enthusiasm of carnival in this work is punctuated by Dunbar's grim portrayal of the permanent effects of sin in the next world on those who seem least vulnerable in this one.

Dunbar establishes the courtly background of the dancers at the outset. Mahoun 'bad gallandis ga graith a gyis / And kast up gamountis in the skyis / That last came out of France' [Mahoun commanded young men to prepare for a masquerade / And cast up capers in the sky / That last came out of France] (no. 52, 10–12). From here the event proceeds almost methodically. Each dancer comes forward in allegorical trappings that have been traditionally associated with his vice. The order of the dancers is Gregorian, a common sequence in medieval texts.[8] Pride begins the dance, dressed in a cloak down to his heels, 'with hair wyld bak and bonet on syd' (17). He and his followers grimace and groan as they skip through scalding fire. Ire follows brandishing a knife. Boasters and braggarts wearing war gear follow him in pairs buffeting and stabbing one another with swords and knives. Envy is next, trembling with hatred, along with his retinue of liars, backbiters, and traitors disguised 'with fenyeit wirdis quhyt' [with false words white] (48). They lie and whisper among themselves, and Dunbar laments, 'Allace, that courtis of noble kingis / Of thame can nevir be quyte' (53–4). Avarice leads a group of usurers and misers who are forced to swallow gold, eject it, and then swallow more. Sloth leads a band of lazy servants who are lashed by an impatient devil when they are slow to dance. Lechery and his group of decayed corpses dance along connected to one another by their privy members. Gluttony takes up the dance leading a band of greasy and obese companions who brandish their wine cups, cry out for 'Drynk!' and are given hot lead to lap (100). Dunbar describes this lead toddy as 'thair lovery' (102), which Kinsley glosses as 'bounty dispensed to a retainer.'[9] The dance ends when the devil calls for a highland pageant, is himself overcome with the clatter of the 'Erschemen' (113), and banishes the highlanders to the deepest part of hell.

The dream vision continues with a tournament between a shoemaker and a tailor.[10] Dunbar systematically describes the procedure followed in a tournament. The dreamer states:

Nixt that a turnament wes tryid
That lang befoir in hell wes cryid
In presens of Mahoun (121–3)

[After that a tournament was attempted
That long before in hell was proclaimed
In the presence of Mahoun.]

Announcement of the tournament long before it takes place mirrors common practice. Once the lists are made ready, the tailor, armed with spear and shield, is conveyed onto the field, followed by a retinue of seam biters, basting thread snappers, and cloth tackers. His banner of multicoloured rags is borne before him. As he eyes the lists, the tailor loses courage until Mahoun comes forward and dubs him knight. This newly made tailor-knight then delivers the traditional boast before his sovereign, Mahoun, that he will strike the shoemaker down, 'thocht he wer strang as mast' (147). As this phrase suggests, Dunbar's language describing the tournament is reminiscent of every tail-rhyme romance one has ever encountered. The odd contrast here is between the framework of the action, which is faithful to what is called for in such an essentially noble event, and the ludicrous nature of the participants, who are oblivious to the traditions that they mimic.

The jousting shoemaker's endeavours are very like those of his opponent. He approaches the field with his band of lice-infested retainers, and he too is portrayed as a romance hero. Dunbar states:

The sowtar to the feild him drest;
He wes convoyid out of the west
As ane defender stout. (157–9)

[A shoemaker took himself to the field;
He was led out of the west
As a champion brave.]

His banner of tanned hide bearing the likeness of a devil, Saint Girnega, is carried before him. When the shoemaker, like his mate, lacks courage, 'the Devill off knychtheid gaif him order' (176). His fear persists, and 'he about the Devillis nek / Did spew agane ane quart of blek / Thus knychtly he him quitt' [he about the Devil's neck / Did spew again a quart of boot blacking / Thus like a knight he comported himself] (178–80). The devil's angry surprise forces the shoemaker onto the field. Both craftsmen spur their horses, they meet, and the tailor falls to the ground, having covered his sad-dle with excrement. Next, the shoemaker's harness breaks, and the terrified horse races its rider toward the wary devil:

> Sum thing frome him the feynd eschewit –
> He went agane to bene bespewit,
> So stern he wes in steill. (199–201)

> [The fiend kept a little away from him –
> He thought he would be spewed upon again,
> So fierce he was in steel.]

Thus Mahoun, expecting to be 'bespewit' again, avenges himself by covering the shoemaker with excrement, as Dunbar states, 'from nek till heill' (203–4). This episode ends, as does the dance of the seven deadly sins, when the devil tires of the foolery and orders the inept jousters to the dungeon.

Although neither part of this dream vision is without its instances of pain, the ones Dunbar chooses lack the truly sensational character of other medieval descriptions of hell. The deadly sins and their followers endure torments along the way, yet they are still willing participants in the dance. In the encounter between the shoemaker and tailor, the most extreme punishment Dunbar describes has to do with excrement and the fall from the horse to the ground. The concept of a vision of hell, however, would have evoked a specific set of expectations on the part of a medieval audience, who would have anticipated the serious punishments they had been taught to fear. Elements in Dunbar's poem indicate knowledge of the traditions associated with medieval descriptions of the underworld on the parts of both poet and audience. Yet, rather than work within the tradition, Dunbar only alludes to it.

A description of the underworld as famous as any in the Middle Ages was the mid-twelfth-century *Vision of Tundale*. In this text, an Irish knight named Tundale is guided by an angel through hell and then is given a look at heaven. As the knight proceeds on his grim journey, he experiences one horror after another. For example, as Tundale progresses through the underworld, the poet tells us,

> He sawe mony a fowle bochere
> Euen amyddys þe fyr stande.
> Some hadde grete axes in her hande;

They wer full loþely on to loke.
Some hadde knyues & some hadde croke,
Some hadde grete toles in her hande
That semede full sharpe bytande.
Off þat sy3te Tundale hadde wonþer
How þey stroke þe sowles asonder.
Some strete of hede & some þyes,
Some [armes & legges by the knees].
Some smote þe bodyes in gobettes small[11]

[He saw many a foul butcher
Standing amidst the fire.
Some had great axes in their hands;
They were very loathsome to look upon.
Some had knives and some had crooks,
Some had large swords in their hands
That seemed to cut very keenly.
At that sight Tundale felt astonishment
At the way they struck the souls asunder.
Some struck off the head and some the thighs,
Some the arms and the legs at the knees.
Some chopped the bodies into small pieces.]

The author later describes the prince of darkness himself, who is bound to an iron griddle in the pit of hell:

Tundale herde & sawe also
How Lucyfere sykkede for wo
For þat he was bownden so faste,
And at yche a sykynge þat he kaste
A þowsand sowles fro hym flowe
Out of hys mowþe into þe lowe.
The[y] were [sone] skatered wyde
Abowte hys mowþe on eche a syde,
But þat payne was not 3ette ynow3!
Whenne he a3eyn hys breth [d]row3
All þe sowles þat were kaste owte
And skatered hym all abowte,
He swolowede hem a3eyn ylke on.
Wyth þe reke & stynke of brymstone

Tho sowles þat passed owte at hys ende
Fell into þe fyr & brende.[12]

[Tundale heard and saw also
How Lucifer sighed for woe
Because he was tied up so firmly,
And at each sigh that he cast
A thousand souls flew from him
Out of his mouth and into the flame.
They were soon scattered widely
Around his mouth on each side,
But that pain was not yet enough!
When he drew in his breath again
All the souls that were cast out
And scattered all around him,
He swallowed again each one.
With the smoke and stench of brimstone
The souls that passed out at his end
Fell into the fire and burned.]

These passages, both characteristic of the *Vision of Tundale*, emphasize the horrible physicality of the punishments being inflicted. The appearance of the sinner is not an issue here, as it is in Dunbar's poem, nor do the damned act of their own volition; they are prodded, pierced, and wrenched out of shape, but would never be permitted the luxury of either dance or tournament.

Along with *Tundale*, the twelfth-century *St Patrick's Purgatory* helped define the nature of textual descriptions of the underworld that would prevail throughout the Middle Ages. In this account, Owen, an Irish knight, is shown the sights of purgatory, a place lacking the intensity of hell itself. A Middle English version of the story, with Saint John as Owen's guide, describes the punishment for the wealthy:

And I saw þe jaggys þat men were clede in turnyde all to eddyrs, dragonse, towdys, and odyre orrabyll bestes, sowkynge and byttynge and nowynge them wyth all þer myghte, streynynge and dreynynge owte of ylke gyngyll a fowle fende. Also trevly I saw fendys smyttynge rede / fyre naylles thorow þe belles and þe gyngyllys into þer flesche. Also I sawe fendys dravyng þe skyne ouer þer scholdyrs þat weyryde þe powkys on ther slevys, and threw hytt all brynnynge on þer hedeys. And I saw þe wemen wyth þe longe traynes byhynde them, fendys cut-tynge of thoys traynes and brynnynge them on þer heddys; and sum of þe fendys toke parcels of þe traylys, and all on fyre stoppyd þer mowthes, þer nose, and þer erys þerwyth. And I saue gay chappelettys of perle and odyr preciuus stones turnyd into nayllys of brasse all bryn-nynge, and wyth brynnyng [hamers] fendys smyttynge [them] into ther heddys.[13]

[And I saw the jags [i.e., ornamental points on the edges of clothing] that men were clothed in changed into adders, dragons, toads, and other horrible beasts, sucking and biting and gnawing them with all their might, squeezing and draining out of each jingling ornament a foul fiend. Also truly I saw fiends driving red fiery nails through the bells and jingles into their flesh. Also I saw fiends drawing the skin over the shoulders of those that wear the long sleeves, and they threw it all ablaze onto their heads. And I saw the women with the long trains behind them, and the fiends cutting off those trains and burning them on their heads; and some of the fiends took pieces of the trains all ablaze and with them stopped up their mouths, their noses, and their eyes. And I saw showy chaplets of pearls and other precious stones turned into burning nails of brass, and with burning (hammers) fiends nailing them into their heads.]

The extreme and unrelenting physical pain that was thought to pre-vail in the medieval underworld was often reserved for the wealthy, who were made to pay dearly for their earthly excesses. Although Dunbar's poem is satiric, his dancers are courtiers, members of the upper class, and the punishments they experience are nothing like those witnessed by the protagonists in *The Vision of Tundale* or *St Patrick's Purgatory*, or other works of this type.

In his *Ayenbite of Inwit* (c. 1340), Dan Michael explains the assault upon every one of the senses that must be endured by the damned. The atmosphere of confusion and disorder, the stench, noise, and almost tangible despair in the following account is typi-cal of this type of narrative:

Helle is wyd / wyþ-oute metinge. dyep / wyþ-oute botme. Vol of brene on- þolyinde. Vol of stenche / wy-oute comparison. Þer is zorȝe. þer is þyesternesse. þer ne is non ordre. þer is groniynge wyþ-oute ende. þer

ne is non hope of guode. non wantrokiynge of kueade. Ech þet þerinne
is : hateþ him zelue: and alle oþren. Þer ich yzeȝ alle manyere tor-
mens. þe leste of alle / is more þanne alle þe pynen þet moȝe by y-do
ine þise worlde. þer is wop. and grindinge of teþ.[14]

[Hell is wide without measure. Deep without bottom. Full of intolera-
ble burning heat. Full of stench without comparison. There is grief.
There is darkness. There is no order. There is groaning without end.
There is no hope of good. No despair of evil. Each person therein hates
himself and all others. There I saw all manner of torments. The least
of all is more than all the pain that may be done in this world. There is
weeping and grinding of teeth.]

Horror after horror tumbled from the medieval author's imagination as he attempted to shock his audience out of any sense of com-
placency in picturing the underworld. The problem these authors
faced in encouraging audiences to imagine the unimaginable is
reflected in the ongoing hyperbole of some of their accounts. Dunbar's poem clearly sidesteps this particular type of earnest, emo-
tionally charged cry, offering instead a more urbanely conceived
snicker at the expense of his noble audience.

Threats about the pains of hell appear in medieval sermons and
in various types of penitential literature in forms that are more
abbreviated than the ones cited above, but no less direct in their
promise of torments to be endured by the damned. For example, the
speaker in *Jacob's Well*, a fifteenth-century allegory that likens
man's body to a dirty well ripe for cleaning, tells the story of Ode, a
wealthy clerk who becomes ill and sends his servant to London for
a physician. On his way there, the servant takes shelter for the
night in an empty cottage. At midnight, the servant looks on in terror as devils enter the cottage and place a burning chair in the middle of the room upon which the king of the devils sits. More fiends
enter the room bringing with them the soul of Ode, his master. In
the presence of the devil-king, the soul is boiled in burning pitch
and oil, roasted on a burning grid held over fires raging underneath,
and forced to drink molten metal until it bursts out of his nose,
eyes, and ears; finally, the soul turns black all over, just like the
devil, and is cast down into hell. All the devils vanish and the servant goes home the next morning to find that his master had died
the previous night. Although along the way the devil-king explains

each torture to the soul of Ode in terms of his earthly transgressions, the author of *Jacob's Well* still follows this tale with the following warning:

þerfore, þou man & womman þat heryst þe woord of god wyth þin erys, be ware of þe peryle of þi synne & of þe articles of þe gret curs! for ȝif þou dredyst hem noȝt, ne wylt noȝt lefe hem, but dyest wythoute repentauns, þou schalt be bathyd, as Ode was, in brennyng pych & oyle! þou schalt be rostyd and fryed in þe fyir of helle! þou schalt drynken reed boylyng metal! þou schalt be lyche þe feend! ... þou schalt be drenchyd in þe pytt of helle, as þe cursyd man Ode was, ȝif þou be gylty in þe grete curs, & deye wyth-oute repentaunce![15]

[Therefore, thou man and woman who hear the word of God with thine ears, beware of the peril of thy sin and of the articles of the great curse! For if thou fear them not, and will not heed them, but die without repentance, thou shalt be bathed, as Ode was, in burning pitch and oil! Thou shalt be roasted and fried in the fire of hell! Thou shalt drink red, boiling metal! Thou shalt be like the fiend! ... Thou shalt be drenched in the pit of hell, as the cursed man Ode was, if thou be guilty in the great curse and die without repentance!]

The importance of shrift because of its impact on the relationship that exists between man's spiritual journey during his lifetime and his eventual destination in either heaven or hell is always implicit, if not explicit, in this type of account.

When Dunbar refers in the first stanza of his poem to 'schrewis that wer nevir schrevin' (7), he calls to mind a set of traditions having to do with shrift and hell and the devil that are part of the collective understanding of his audience. Having done so, however, he abandons the sombre tone that generally accompanies those traditions in favour of a satiric one in the first part of the work and one more akin to burlesque in the second part. The satire in this poem is straightforward enough. Both the dance motif and the allegorical presentation of the sins are standard fare in medieval literature. The descriptions of the dancers, although well drawn, are not startlingly original. The possibilities for satire in any medieval description of a tournament between a tailor and shoemaker are numerous, and the change in tone so noticeable today between the two halves of the piece was most probably less marked when the poems were written. Yet, as scholars have pointed out, Dunbar's setting for this demonic dance seems to be original.[16] Thus, the location is all important here because regardless of the revelry that takes place in this poem, even though sin was sometimes an element of comedy during the Middle Ages, and despite the fact that the devil was often a catalyst for action that had humorous or ironic results, hell itself was unending, unrelenting, and, most of all, unfunny. The location lends a seriousness to this poem that it would not have if the action took place in any other setting. What is singular about the events Dunbar describes here is that, considering their location, they are not really very extreme. Any number of adjectives can be applied to the events in this poem – demonic, grotesque, ridiculous. Yet a distinction ought to be made here between literal and literary tradition. Horrific and elaborate portrayals of hell, and the phenomenon of the tail-rhyme romance, represent by Dunbar's time centuries of literary baggage. Yet the dance, the tournament, Shrovetide, and shrift were all very real in Dunbar's Scotland. The unabashed display of pride, anger, envy, avarice, sloth, lechery, and gluttony is not unusual in hell; it is unusual in a dance. Scatological elements are not out of place in depictions of hell; they are out of place in a tournament. In general, all of the events in this poem that exhibit varying degrees of coarseness are unthinkable at court. Conversely, it is remarkable that a place so chaotic as the medieval underworld could host activities as refined as those of a dance that approximates a courtly pageant and a tournament that adheres to proper procedure as carefully as does this one. Because the action in this poem takes place in hell, one would expect a disordered free-for-all exacerbated by location. The tension between what is expected and what actually occurs, between action and inaction, order and disorder, nobles and craftsmen, devils and fools, engenders the tremendous swirl of energy that informs this work.

The dramatic qualities in Dunbar's dance and tournament manifest the same kind of topicality found in the various types of court and public drama popular during the Middle Ages. Dramatic performances, written with specific audiences in mind, could appeal in very particular and intimate ways to those audiences. Women watching the fortitude of the Virgin Mary in one of the Corpus Christi dramas, for example, would be encouraged to follow her example, as best they could, in coping with the deaths of their own children. The audience of a morality play, mumming or disguising in the fifteenth century, or of a court masque in the sixteenth often would have recognized the lesson implied by the allegorical figures, even without the aid of commentary. By the same token, Dunbar's audience, the court of James IV, would not have failed to understand the lesson directed toward them in this work.

Although the full scope of his audience cannot be determined with certainty, Dunbar was in the service of the king, and, as Bawcutt writes, 'many of Dunbar's most interesting poems seem to have been written for a small circle of people who knew each other well: the king and other members of the royal household.'[17] Thus Dunbar's references to things having to do with the court in most any of his poems would have been tacitly apparent to a group of courtiers familiar with one another and with the discerning eye and acerbic pen of the court poet. The nature of the dance itself that was lately come from France, the descriptions of dancers in terms of both gesture and clothing, the exactitude of detail in the tournament, and most directly of all the reference to 'courtis of noble kingis' (53) would have suggested to a courtly audience, trained to respond to literature that both delights and instructs, that they take a lesson from what is presented to them in Dunbar's dance and tournament.

The fact that the action in this poem takes place on Fasterns Eve, which is at once the time of carnival and the threshold of Lent, the most important season of fasting and repentance during the year, is essential to the irony in the poem. The opposing yet interdependent concepts of carnival and Lent, of festivity and atonement, work together in this poem to remind of the wages of sin and to entertain at the same time. Although the action takes place in hell, the most significant reference to this world in the poem lies in Mahoun's call for sinners who failed to confess. This pre-Lenten dream is meant to encourage even the most recalcitrant sinner to settle accounts while forgiveness is a possibility.

Modern discussions of the grotesque or of events having to do with carnival benefit by taking into account Mikhail Bakhtin's discussion of these themes in relation to the work of Rabelais. In *Rabelais and His World* Bakhtin describes the Renaissance as 'a direct "carnivalization" of human consciousness, philosophy, and literature' that sets out to overcome what he calls 'the official culture of the Middle Ages.'[18] He traces the ways in which medieval religious and political structures that dominated the minds and the lives of people in the Middle Ages were replaced during the Renaissance by 'the culture of folk humour which had developed throughout thousands of years' (274). Bakhtin makes the distinction between official feasts, which 'sanctioned the existing pattern of things and reinforced it,' and carnival, which 'celebrated temporary liberation from the prevailing truth and from the established order [and] ... marked the suspension of all hierarchical rank, privileges, norms, and prohibitions' (9, 10) This liberating impulse takes its strength from elements of folk culture and manifests itself in literary works in the forms of abusive, ribald, scatological, sexually explicit language and action. In images of copulation, defecation, and regurgitation, Bakhtin sees the ongoing power of regeneration:

> All the symbols of the carnival idiom are filled with this pathos of change and renewal, with the sense of the gay relativity of prevailing truths and authorities. We find here a characteristic logic, the peculiar logic of the 'inside out' (a l'envers), of the 'turnabout,' of a continual shifting from top to bottom, from front to rear, of numerous parodies and travesties, humiliations, profanations, comic crownings and uncrownings ... We must stress, however, that the carnival is far distant from the negative and formal parody of modern times. Folk humor denies, but it revives and renews at the same time. (11)

For the purpose at hand, the final element of Bakhtin that needs attention is the notion of carnival as an equalizer of social groups. The social and political hierarchy of the Middle Ages is levelled by carnival; to Bakhtin, 'in the world of carnival all hierarchies are canceled. All castes and ages are equal' (251).

Dunbar is for the most part grounded in the Middle Ages and, as a cleric, speaks for the official culture of his time. Yet as a transitional figure writing at the end of his age, he anticipates Bakhtin's Renaissance world even if he is not himself a part of it. The ways in which Dunbar's poem anticipates the Renaissance as Bakhtin describes it are of interest because the poem contains elements that characterize both eras.

Dunbar's poem certainly describes a world turned upside down, where courtiers and craftsmen perform on the same stage, bodily functions are integral parts of the action, and laughter provoked by the infusion of satire throughout informs the entire work. The oppositions, contradictions, and antinomies that invert the world of reason, oppose the official culture, and thereby provoke laughter in Rabelais also provoke laughter in Dunbar. One element that makes Dunbar a fundamentally medieval poet, rather than a Renaissance one, is the underlying didacticism in his works, in general, and in the poem under discussion here, in particular. Bakhtin states that laughter 'degrades and materializes' (20) and at the same time dissipates fear. Dunbar's laughter also criticizes; he relies on the underlying fear of hell ingrained in the minds of his audience to create the proper tension in the work. Bakhtin discusses the medieval mystery and morality plays, and describes the medieval stage in both concept and construction:

> In these plays the stage reflected the medieval idea of the world's position in space. The front of the stage presented a platform that occupies the entire first floor of the structure and symbolized the earth. The backdrop was formed by an elevated set which represented heaven or paradise. Beneath the platform representing the earth there was a large opening, indicating hell, covered by a broad curtain decorated with a huge mask of the devil (Harlequin). When the curtain was pulled back, the devils jumped out of Satan's gaping jaws, or sometimes out of his eyes, and landed on earth. (348)

Although Bakhtin's devils emerge and taunt the inhabitants of the earthly world, they remain on the playing field of humanity and become participants in the comic, sometimes cosmic, carnivalesque spectacles that transform fear into laughter. Dunbar's devils remain behind the curtain, drawing all seriously transgressing earthly inhabitants down into their unsavoury realm. Dunbar's setting negates any sense of rejuvenation or rebirth for the characters in the poem because they have no hope. Although the laughter inspired by Dunbar's satire and by the physicality in both the dance and the tournament – what Bakhtin describes as 'a transfer to the material level' (20) – mitigates the audience's fear, the work's rejuvenative power lies in the efficacy of the poem's message and the audience's compliance with the principles of the official medieval culture. Laughter for Dunbar serves as an anodyne for the status quo, while for Bakhtin it serves as a replacement.

Despite Dunbar's Bakhtinian exuberance, if such an anachronism can be allowed, each courtier confronted with this Shrovetide masterpiece must have called to mind the Dance of Death. The notion of death as the final equalizer of the estates, the grim aspect of a dance performed by those already dead, and the combination of humour and grotesquerie place Dunbar's poem in this dance tradition, the point of which Lydgate summarizes in the second stanza of his translation of the 'Dance of Death':

> In this myrrow[r]e / eueri wight mai fynde
> That hym behoueth / to go vpon this dance
> Who gothe to-forne / or who schal go be-hynde
> All dependeth / in goddes ordynaunce
> Where-fore eche man / lowely take his chaunce
> Deth spareth not / pore ne blode royal
> Eche man ther-fore / haue yn remembraunce
> Of oo matier / god hathe forged al.[19]

> [In this mirror every man may find
> That it is required of him to go on this dance.
> Who goes before or who shall go behind
> All depends on God's ordering,
> For which reason each man humbly must take whatever befalls him.
> Death spares neither poor nor royal blood.
> Each man therefore remember
> Of one material God has forged all.]

Like Lydgate's, Dunbar's poem mirrors the value and thus the vanity of earthly things. It also reflects the cultural sophistication of an audience presumed to comprehend both the message of the work and the subtlety of its interwoven traditions. Yet even though Lydgate's dance cannot be avoided, Dunbar's can.

In this poem, Dunbar is above all a satirist writing for a relatively small and familiar audience. Although satire requires a common set of values and common understanding on the part of the audience of what is being satirized in order for it to be effective, difficulties in understanding the satire arise for anyone who does not share that commonality. The familiar relationship Dunbar enjoyed with his audience allowed him latitude in his detail. Dunbar's characters in the dance are allegorical figures that are also courtiers; he has not taken aim at individuals, as he has done in other poems, because, like the author of *Volpone*, he condemns the vice rather than the individual. Although in the tournament Dunbar skewers a shoemaker and a tailor, his message has little to do with craftsmen;

these two guilds are frequent targets for medieval humour, and in this poem they represent the lowest end of a social spectrum that has the king and his court at the highest end. For example, in the *Bannatyne Manuscript*, 'The flytting betuix þe sowtar and the tailȝor' and 'The sowtar Inveyand aganis the telȝeor Sayis' both chuckle at the image of the shoemaker and tailor.[20] In the same work, 'the iusting and debait vp at the drum Betuix W[illi]am adamsone and johine sym'[21] and the tale of 'sym and his bruder'[22] describe mock tournaments after the fashion of 'The Tournament of Tottenham.' Each of these poems is humorous, an example of burlesque at its goofy best, yet none bears the striking formality of structure and in many ways of tone that characterizes Dunbar's. Dunbar has chosen ridiculous but traditional pawns to occupy positions always reserved for upper-class exploit in the Middle Ages. And although it was often a medieval crowd pleaser for an upper class audience to be able to laugh at the pretensions of the lower class, the underlying seriousness in this poem is directed primarily at the pretensions of the courtly audience rather than at those of the craftsmen; these craftsmen are puppets, not social climbers.

A major difficulty in discussing this poem lies in striking the necessary balance between its functions as both entertainment and instruction. The entertainment value is readily apparent, even to a modern audience. A clear appreciation of the poem's instructional value, however, requires a familiarity with death and its associated images, which are thankfully distant to most modern readers except in print. Necessary scholarly machinery threatens to overpower the poem's humour and to sidestep Dunbar's sophistication in interweaving moral lesson with both sardonic wit and rollicking good fun. What Dunbar gives with one hand in this poem by describing a carnival atmosphere alive with ribald intensity he takes back with the other in a veiled reminder to his audience that the things they value overmuch have no intrinsic worth. At the heart of these demonic events is Dunbar's indictment of human frailty and perhaps his caution about its ultimate effect upon the social framework of Scotland.

Notes

1 See G.R. Owst, *Literature and Pulpit in Medieval England* (New York, 1961); M.W. Bloomfield, *The Seven Deadly Sins* (East Lansing, 1952;

repr. 1967); H.R. Patch, *The Other World According to Descriptions in Medieval Literature* (Cambridge, MA, 1950; repr. New York, 1970); J. Le Goff, *The Birth of Purgatory* (London, 1984).

2 For which, see R. Hutton, *The Stations of the Sun: A History of the Ritual Year in Britain* (Oxford, 1997), 151–68.

3 E. Reiss, *William Dunbar* (Boston, 1979), 83.

4 I.S. Ross, *William Dunbar* (Leiden, 1981), 172.

5 *William Dunbar: Selected Poems*, ed. P Bawcutt (London, 1996), 178–89.

6 P. Bawcutt, *Dunbar the Makar* (Oxford, 1992), 291.

7 *The Poems of William Dunbar*, ed. J. Kinsley (Oxford, 1979), no. 52, l. 7. All further references to Dunbar's poems are to this edition and appear in the text; citations are by poem number and line number.

8 Bloomfield, *Seven Deadly Sins*, 72 ff, 237.

9 *Poems of Dunbar*, glossary, 444.

10 Compare 'The flytting betuix þe sowtar and the tailȝor,' in *The Bannatyne Manuscript*, ed. W.T. Ritchie, 4 vols, STS (Edinburgh and London, 1928–34), iii, 22–6.

11 *Vision of Tundale*, ed. R. Mearns (Heidelberg, 1985), ll. 762–73.

12 *Vision of Tundale*, ll. 1395–410.

13 *St Patrick's Purgatory*, ed. R. Easting, EETS (Oxford, 1991), 89.

14 *Ayenbite of Inwit*, ed. P. Gradon, 2 vols, EETS (Oxford, 1965–79), 264–5.

15 *Jacob's Well: An Englisht Treatise on the Cleansing of Man's Conscience*, ed. A. Brandeis, EETS (London, 1900; repr. 1973), 11.

16 See *Poems of Dunbar*, 336; Bawcutt, *Makar*, 287.

17 Bawcutt, *Makar*, 15; see 13–16 for a more complete discussion of Dunbar's audience.

18 M. Bakhtin, *Rabelais and His World*, trans. H. Iswolsky (Bloomington, 1984; first pub. Moscow, 1965), 273; all further references to Bakhtin appear in the text and are to this edition.

19 *The Dance of Death*, ed. by F. Warren, introduction and notes by B. Warren, EETS (London, 1931; repr. 1971), 49–56.

20 *Bannatyne Manuscript*, iii, 22–6, and 37.

21 *Bannatyne Manuscript*, ii, 343–8.

22 *Bannatyne Manuscript*, iii, 39.

6

'Many Injurious Words':
Defamation and Gender in
Late Medieval Scotland

ELIZABETH EWAN

In 1502 Andrew Haliburton, an Edinburgh merchant and the conservator of the Scottish merchants' privileges in the Netherlands,
found himself involved in a trading dispute with his brother-in-law
James Homyll. Haliburton had lent Homyll money to finance his
trading ventures, but was having trouble gaining reimbursement.
Finally Homyll did repay him but with extremely ill grace, or, as
Haliburton recorded it in his ledger, 'with callenzeis [challenges]
and eevil wordis and onsuferabyll.' A few months later, Homyll was
in debt again and further ill-feeling ensued, leading Haliburton to
write despairingly, 'God kep all gud men fra sic callandis [from such
customers]!' So intemperate was Homyll, that Haliburton finally
wrote off his debts because

> he mensworn me with ewyll malyssius langag, and to be quyt of hym
> in tym to cum, I gaf him a hayll quyttans [complete acquittance] and
> quhill I leif [while I live] never to deill with hym.[1]

Fortunately for Homyll, his wife, Helen Haliburton, Andrew's sister, was an equally capable merchant, and Andrew continued to
deal with her, despite his bad feelings toward her husband.

Haliburton recorded Homyll's insults in the privacy of his ledger
(although possibly with an eye to potential future legal disputes),
but other Scots were not so discreet. About the same time Haliburton was becoming so exasperated with his brother-in-law, the poet
William Dunbar delivered a stinging rebuke to the merchants of
Edinburgh over the state of their town and the poor impression it

made on visitors. One of the most disagreeable aspects of the town was the noise of vituperative quarrels found on every street:

> May nane pas throw your principall gaittis [streets]
> For stink of haddockis and scaittis [fish],
> For cryis of carlingis [old women] and debaittis,
> Or fowsum flyttingis of defame;
> Think ye not schame,
> Befoir strangeris of all estaittis,
> That sic dishonour hurt your name.

'Fowsum flyttingis of defame' is translated by the poem's most recent editor as 'foul and defamatory abusive arguments.'[2]

Ironically, Dunbar himself was as guilty of flytings of defame as the Edinburgh people he criticized. One of his best known and most popular poems, 'The Flyting of Dunbar and Kennedy,' is a vitriolic exchange of insults between two male poets; it has been described by one modern critic as 'the most repellent poem known to me in any language.'[3] The compiler of a nineteenth-century dictionary of the Scottish language was more sympathetic to such poetry, and defined the literary form of 'flyting' as 'a name given to a singular species of poetry, for which our countrymen seem to have had peculiar predilection.'[4] In other words, he seems to be saying, trust my fellow Scots to raise insult to a literary art. In fact, literary uses of invective were common to many medieval cultures and included the satire of Gaelic bards, English poets such as Skelton, and French troubadours, although it has been argued (perhaps with a measure of pride) that Scots flyting differed from these 'in their sheer intensity of effect.'[5] Flyting as a literary form remained popular in Scotland for centuries. Sixteenth-century flyting poems reflected the influence of the oral culture in which the poets lived.[6] This paper will examine the nature of that late medieval tradition of insult, invective, and defamation, looking at what insults were used, who used them, and how the authorities responded to the 'divers injurious words.'

Scottish secular authorities made no firm distinction between the offences of scolding and defamation/slander, although the surviving church court records suggest that the ecclesiastical courts heard only defamation cases. The word 'flyting' could be used for both. Two women in Stirling were convicted of being 'common flyttars' in 1520, an offence equivalent to scolding.[7] In 1545 Margaret Hay of Elgin was found guilty of the 'oppin sclandering' of Margaret Balfour and was threatened with banishment if she should ever again come 'flytand or saying such injurious words to any person.'[8] An Inverness man who was punished for a specific insult against a clergyman was warned against such 'flytand' in the future.[9]

Many of those involved in exchanges of insults found themselves called before the courts for defamation by their opponents. Post-Reformation courts are full of such cases, and some of these have been recently examined by Michael Graham and John Harrison;[10] the pre-1560 period has been less studied. Unfortunately, the records of scandal and defamation are much scantier than those after 1560.[11] Many cases appear, but the brevity of the entries means that a detailed analysis along the lines of Laura Gowing's work on the church court records of early modern London,[12] cannot be undertaken for pre-1560 Scotland. Only a minority of the records give the words used by the offenders. In some cases, this seems to reflect a certain amount of modesty or prudishness on the part of the scribe. Perhaps many medieval clerks shared the discomfort of an Inverness scribe in 1571 who reported that a husband and wife had insulted the bailie with many injurious words 'quhilk I abhor to put in wreit.'[13]

Evidence comes from burgh court cases, actions recorded by notaries public, cases in the church court of the official of Lothian, and town statutes against flyting. Strictly speaking, many such cases, especially those involving sexual morality, should have been heard in the church courts; in the fifteenth century, the Scottish church included 'common sclanderaris' among those who could be excommunicated for their offence.[14] However, the lines of authority between different courts were not clear-cut, and in practice most towns had little hesitation about claiming jurisdiction. In 1522 William Mclellan was forced to excuse himself to the town of Stirling for taking a case to the church courts; his justification was that it involved 'injurious language and slander,' over which he alleged the bailies had no jurisdiction.[15] The bailies thought otherwise. Burgh courts did keep open the option of referring difficult cases to the church courts. Canon law allowed the church courts to accept such cases in default of secular justice.[16] A Lanark inquest of 1488 decreed that a case of slander did not pertain to the bailies but to the church court, while the Stirling court, although jealous of its right to hear such cases, did allow litigants the opportunity to take their case to the church court if it could not be resolved in the town court, as long as they asked permission first.[17] For the most part, however, town authorities regarded defamation and insult as a form of 'distrublans' or public disturbance to the community,[18] and took measures to deal with it in their own courts.

What sorts of insults resulted in cases being brought before judges? In the church court of the official (the bishop's judicial representative) of Lothian in c. 1539, Jonet Brus of Edinburgh admitted calling Isabella Keringtoun 'ane common bluidy hure' and 'uther divers jniurious wordis' (not specified), and her husband Robert Litster 'ane cuckald.' This was too much for Isabella, who in return accused Jonet of 'swiffing' (swiving, fornicating) with the 'old official.'[19] Since the case was heard in the official's own court, one can imagine the intake of breath as these words were reported – and perhaps the amusement of the scribe as he for once carefully recorded the words. Unfortunately such a full record was the exception rather than the rule; in only 12 out of 138 cases coming before the Lothian court were the words recorded.

Where the words are given, most of those between women involved sexual insult, reflecting the premium placed on women's chastity as a crucial part of their reputation. Studies of slander elsewhere, as well as in post-Reformation Scotland, suggest that a similar situation prevailed throughout much of medieval and early modern Europe.[20] Although sexual insults were possibly not the most common ones used by women in daily life, they were the ones most likely to lead to a church court case for defamation, probably because of their close association with morality. Occasionally, a woman also insulted her victim's husband as a cuckold, but usually this was simply implied by the insult to the wife, as when Christian Donaldson of Dundee called James Marhone a false heretic and his wife a whore.[21]

When the women involved were married, their husbands also appeared in the court 'for their interest,' a legal requirement as husbands were responsible for any penalties incurred by their wives.[22] In these cases, 'for his interest' took on an added meaning, as a husband would be anxious to prove that his wife was not a whore and that he had what was perceived by the community as proper control over her sexuality. Indeed in 1541 when Elena Fowler and her husband, Laurence Kirkpatrick, 'for his interest' accused Cristina Ure of defamation, it was to Laurence that Cristina apologized for insulting him and calling his wife a whore. Similarly Christian Donaldson had to apologize to James Marhone alone, despite insulting his wife as well. The dangers for men whose wives lay with other men were made clear when Agnes Murray insulted Agnes Haliburton, wife of John War, with the words 'preistis hure as ye art gif [give] the barne [child] to ye preist sir James Waldy his awn fader.'[23] Jonet Bell of Stirling defamed Jonet Scharp by saying 'hir barne was David Sibbaldis, and that he lay with hir, gevand sic occasioun that the said Jonet husband hes left hir.'[24] In fact, Jonet's husband did not leave her, but men's fears about bringing up other men's children were aggravated by such insults.

There was also another concern for men who heard such accusations levelled at their wives; such behaviour by their spouses could be taken as a slur on their masculinity as defined by their sexual prowess. This fear was made explicit use of by Marion Ray of Stirling, who targeted three victims at once. She first insulted William Cunningham by saying that she had looked through a hole and seen him swive Henry Thomson's wife, Agnes Henderson, six times. The context does not make it clear whether she looked through the window six times, or only once, although her other insults seem to imply the latter, as she had an interest in emphasizing William's sexual powers and Agnes's voracious sexual appetite. She then insulted Agnes Henderson by calling her a common whore whom she knew to have swived twenty times (the implication being that this was with more than one man), and, repeating her earlier insult, that she had seen Wille Cunningham swive her six times. Finally she insulted Agnes's husband, Henry Thomson, whom she called 'Sclaverand [rumour-mongering] Henry,' saying that were he worthy to swive his wife, he would not let other men do so.[25]

Agnes Henderson, not surprisingly, responded to Marion's abuse with insults of her own, calling her a 'huir and brekair of spowsage [marriage-breaker].' In Scotland, as elsewhere, 'whore' was the most frequently recorded term of abuse used against women in both church and town courts. It was one of the most common insults recorded in post-Reformation church courts, as well.[26] The connection of the insult specifically with women was shown in Inverness when a man found guilty of calling a woman a whore was warned by the court not to say such a thing to any man's wife in the future.[27] Usually such warnings were intended to prevent future insults of anyone, woman or man, but here the court could not imagine the insult being used against anyone but a woman.

In general, whore was used as a synonym for fornicator or adulterer rather than prostitute.[28] Jonet Fulton defamed Jonet Welschort, wife of John Hucheson, in the Edinburgh market:

> Vyle preistis hure and spous braker at yow art You had John Wallace all nyt wt ye Sunday thow tuik him or [over] ye water wt ye on Sanct James day and ly wt him yare [lay with him there] and broucht him hame agayne Vyle common hure and theif at yow art.[29]

The use of 'common hure' is unusual here, as it is usually only applied to a woman accused of sleeping with more than one man, as when Elena Sutlare accused Cristina Fortoun of being a 'common hure' who swived with priests (plural).[30] 'Bloody hure,' used by William Duchol of Stirling against Marion Aikman, was probably meant to imply venereal disease. Prostitution was often associated with dirt and disease.[31] Some defamers were more specific – Megot Stuart called Ellen and Margaret Ternway 'shabbit, clangorit carlis birdis [scabby syphilitic churl's women]'; Ellen retaliated, calling Megot a 'schabit, blerit, clangorit carling [scabbed, blear-eyed, syphilitic old woman].'[32]

An interesting aspect of sexual insults was how often they involved priests, directly or indirectly. As in early sixteenth-century English church courts,[33] 'priest's hure' was one of the commonest insults used against women. 'Priest's hure' served a double purpose. First, it kept any other woman from being involved as wife of the alleged lover; and second, fornication with a man sworn to chastity may have been seen as even worse than adultery with a layman (although, given the extent to which clergy were part of the secular community and their promiscuity part of popular culture,[34] this is a debatable point). Did it also give the defamer a chance to air anti-clerical feelings indirectly? According to Muriel Caldour in Elgin in 1542, the two women who had insulted her were determined to leave no stone unturned, calling her not only 'priests' whore' but also friars' whore and monks' whore.[35] Interestingly this is one of the few cases of defamation in which the complaint was not upheld – perhaps the complainant's imagination had run wild. Both men and women also insulted priests directly, although men did so more often than women. In one case in Elgin, both husband and wife insulted a priest, although only the husband had to do public penance for it. However, both were threatened with banishment if they offended again.[36]

Insults of a non-sexual nature were often added to sexual comments when attacking women, the most common being 'thief.'[37] Jonet Blakadir insulted Jonet Bell by calling her 'notable theiff and huir' and accused her of stealing three plates which fell out from between her shift and her kirtle.[38] Women were also accused of being 'resetters,' receivers of stolen goods. Jonet Nasmit of Canongate defamed Margaret Scot by saying:

> Hure & theif at yow art thow art ane common hure and theif and res-settor of thevis thow ressettis thy nebowres gear and guds as quhit malt meall coillis [coals] fowlis wrtheris [?wedders] and collars I saw non sa ane resettear of theives and stown [stolen] geir as zow art.[39]

In this case, 'hure' seems to have been thrown in as a matter of habit. It was often used in cases which had little to do with sex – questioning a woman's sexual honesty acted as 'a shorthand for much wider grievances.'[40] Jonet's real concern was Margaret's alleged thievery. The concern about women as receivers of stolen goods had some basis in reality: it was not uncommon for women to be convicted of this offence.[41]

It does not appear to have been quite as effective for women to impugn men's chastity; as Gowing points out, there was no male equivalent to 'whore.'[42] However, while Gowing found no words to condemn male sexual misconduct in her London cases, some evidence from York church courts after 1560 does show male concern about sexual reputation. Moreover, recent work by Bernard Capp on England suggests that men cared more about their reputation for sexual honesty than some historians have assumed, and that women could use this to their advantage.[43] In Scotland, women insulted men by accusing them of adultery, as Marion Ray did William Cunningham. It was possible to strike a double blow with one insult by accusing a woman of adultery and naming her partner, as Jonet Bell did when she named the putative father of Jonet Scharp's child. Women could also question men's chastity indirectly by accusing them of suffering from venereal disease. This had the added advantage of allowing derogatory comments about the victim's appearance. Marion Murray of Elgin called Andrew Milln a 'dovr drunkyn beist and schabbit carlis get [scabby peasant's brat].'[44] In other cases, insults about physical appearance – 'crukyt carl,' 'Wolf facit carle'[45] – without sexual connotations seem to have been enough. Men also accused other men of improper sexual behaviour, sometimes in quite colourful ways. In Selkirk, Jok Mynto accused James Doungell of lying with a woman in a midden. William Malcome of Elgin contented himself with calling William Zoung 'glangorit,' infected with syphilis.[46]

For both women and men who insulted men, 'thief' was the most common epithet of choice, for the accusation tarnished men's reputation for financial honesty and thus their creditworthiness. Janet Thomson backed up her allegation with some specific details when she accosted Allan Kernot at a public well in Edinburgh with the words 'theif yow has stowen my mony and gold extending to £12 of silver.'[47] William Birneth of Elgin told James Vink that he was a 'commond theif ... and that he sud hef beine hangit four zeir syne [should have been hanged four years ago].'[48] 'Sheep stealer' and 'horse-stealer' were also favourite insults in some towns.[49]

Men were also subject to many other insults. In 1507 a cleric insulted a merchant of Glasgow by repeatedly saying of him in public: 'Johne Elphinstoun is a defamit persone perpetuall, and ane verray erratik, and a Jow.'[50] 'Heretic' may have had particular force when the accusation came from a member of the clergy, but it was also used by laypeople such as Christian Donaldson, who insulted a Dundee man with the same term.

Heresy was a crime, but it was not the only one of which people were accused by those who insulted them. An Elgin man called one of the town magistrates 'murdressar of his awin gossop [wife].'[51] Reflecting Inverness's closeness to the highlands, and the townspeoples' connections with highland politics, Molly Gotte called Finlay McConyloyr 'commond theiff and murderissar of Clan Chattan and slachterrar of tham.'[52]

Another category of insult involved the victim's family. When the poet Kennedy insulted Dunbar, one of his charges was that Dunbar's ancestors were traitors who had betrayed Scotland to the English.[53] The poets' contemporaries on the Scottish streets found their targets closer to home. Both men and women used such insults, although the victim's mother seems to have figured more often than the father. Bessie Mores of Elgin defamed Agnes Stone by claiming her mother was drowned in a well. Drowning was the most common form of execution for women. John Bayne defamed a local chaplain by claiming that 'all his motheris barnis [children] war commond thevis.'[54]

Some insults arose out of resentment at what was perceived as unfair treatment by the town authorities. Such resentment was usually expressed by men against other men, although a few women were also found guilty of insulting town officers.[55] Some of the insults were the result of disappointed plaintiffs in the town courts; David Spanky of Dundee complained at the burgh court that 'yare wes ne justice done in ye tolbouth.' For this he was ordered to apologize to the bailies.[56] Robert Lindsay of Edinburgh was found guilty of speaking irreverently to the bailies and council. In another Edinburgh case, a man expressed his contempt for the town council by insulting and threatening the provost who had come to execute their judgment on him.[57] An Inverness man publicized his feelings by following the bailies through the town, 'like a bard,' charging them that 'tha persewyt hym for malice and ewyll wyll.'[58]

The description of the Inverness man as a bard implied that he was acting as a member of a despised social group. Some insults suggest feelings of antagonism between people of different social status. Insults hurled at town officials sometimes came from those who felt they were being persecuted by the town elite. John Skinner of Inverness called the three town ale-tasters 'commone skeularis [story-tellers]' and 'glutton carles [greedy peasants]' and charged that they had no better way to earn their living than by harrying poor folk. It is interesting to note that one of his insults suggests that they are no better than poor folk or peasants themselves. Marcus Chapman, who had also been reprimanded by the town officers, seems to have felt that his social status had not been recognized by the bailies, who were no better than sheep stealers, and that they should show him respect by standing with their bonnets in their hands as he was of gentler birth than Thomas Fleming.[59] Riche Tarbat, apprentice to a wright in Dundee, was convicted of troubling his master's house with injurious words. He and his master made peace, but all must not have gone well, for two weeks later they mutually agreed to cancel their apprenticeship contract.[60]

Riche Tarbat insulted his master in his house, but this case was likely only recorded because it involved the breach of a publicly registered contract. Cases of defamation in the household were rarely brought before the court, most households apparently preferring to deal with such incidents themselves.[61] An Edinburgh court ordered Jonet Anderson that she was not to 'say na deisplesour nor iniurious language' to Thomas Wauchope or his spouse, neither openly nor privately, or else she would be banished from the town as soon as it became commonly known.[62] Here private as well as public speech is regulated, but it only became punishable when it became publicly known. However, private speech alone could also be punished if it created a public disturbance. In 1524 Jean and John Murray were fined for keeping neighbours awake by flyting all night.[63]

In most cases where the site of the defamation is recorded, it was a public place, most frequently the marketplace or the street. Partly this was because it was easier to obtain witnesses to back up a case for defamation (in some court cases, the presence of witnesses to the insult was recorded),[64] but it also reflected the importance ascribed to one's public reputation. In a society in which so many transactions were made on credit, public reputation was critically important to livelihood.[65] If one's honesty, sexual or otherwise, was publicly called into question, credit might become difficult or impossible to obtain.

The insults themselves reflected the importance of public conduct. Alleged sexual misconduct almost always took place somewhere other than the house, thus adding an extra element to the crime by breaking a convention that sexuality should be confined to the domestic space of a married couple. People were accused of having sex in the street, on middens, behind the walls, or outside the town.[66] The latter two were places at the boundary between public and private, for while they were public places, the couples might expect to find some privacy there. The marginal nature of such places emphasized the wrongful character of the activity.

The locations where insults occurred also reflect a gender difference in the use of public space. Almost all incidents involving women took place on the streets, at the well, in the marketplace, or in the doorways of their houses. However, many of the insults involving men took place in the town court, a site which was not prohibited to women but where men predominated and where their authority as town leaders was most visible. Sometimes the insults were aimed at the presiding officers. In other cases, they were hurled by competing litigants against each other.[67] Those involved had to apologize to the town officers for troubling the court, as well as to their opponents.

Punishment for defamation and insult was largely in the hands of the authorities. There is no evidence surviving for crowd-imposed popular punishments, although this may be the consequence of the lack of records; however, the tradition of rough music seems never to have been as strong in Scotland as in England and elsewhere in Europe. Punishment, when not restricted to the payment of fines, almost always took place in public places.[68] In the Lothian church courts, it appears that the type of punishment depended on who was in charge. In the period 1513 to the mid-1530s, most defamation cases resulted in fines. From the mid-1530s, the court became more insistent on rituals of public penitence. These commonly involved the guilty party appearing at the parish church, often dressed in sackcloth or a shift, at high mass, with a candle of wax to give to the church, and seeking forgiveness on their knees of the wronged person in front of the congregation. Margaret Rouch, who defamed Mariota Patersoun, had to appear at the high altar of her church and ask her forgiveness.[69]

Occasionally, the ritual of penitence imposed by the church courts was carried out in the place where the offence had occurred. One such case suggests the distinction made between public and private insult. Jonet Brus, who had insulted both Isabella Keringtoun and her husband, Robert Litster, had to appear 'in a public place before the close of Robert Bruce, burgess of Edinburgh,' and there offer a candle of wax to a chaplain in the name of God and ask forgiveness of the injured parties, each in turn. The reputations of both were to be publicly restored by her words; to Isabella she was to say, among other things, 'I knaw na thing but ye are ane honest woman and keipis gud pert to your husband,' while to Robert she was to say, 'I faillit to yow and your wiff calling you ane cukcald quhilk I confes is nocht of werite [truth] for your wiff is ane honest woman' (note that Robert's reputation was hurt by his wife's alleged misbehaviour). Isabella, who had insulted Jonet in turn, but in her own house, was allowed to do her penance in the privacy of that house.

Individual towns had their own punishments. As the civic authorities saw themselves as responsible for the general spiritual welfare of the community and regarded individual offences as a threat to this, they were concerned to achieve social reconciliation.[70] Rituals of public penitence similar to those used by the church were often imposed by town courts. Following a practice found in many towns, Besse Pilgus of Dundee was ordered to come openly to the market cross and admit her fault that she had called James Wichthand a thief. She did this, then said 'tong scho leit [tongue she lied],' asked him forgiveness, and agreed that if she insulted him in future, she would be banished from the town. In 1514 Thomas Patterson of Edinburgh was ordered to come to the market cross in his linen shirt to ask forgiveness of the bailie. William Porter of Aberdeen, who in 1488 was convicted of 'strublance' of the bailie 'maliciously in words,' was ordered to come to the tolbooth door and pass bareheaded to the common kist (chest) to do his penance.[71] In Stirling, Jonet Blakaddir was ordered to go to 'the place where she said the evil words' and there kneel and ask forgiveness of her victim.[72]

In one way, the ritual of public penance seemed designed to separate the offender from the past evil deeds, as well. As happened with Besse Pilgus, it was common for the guilty party to be required to say that his or her tongue had lied. By admonishing the part of the body which had committed the sin, the offender was asserting control over it, and promising to maintain this control in future. Thus David Stewart of Dundee, who had insulted the town magistrates with 'curious words' when they charged him with illegal trading, was ordered to ask the council's forgiveness and 'to refrane his twng fra sic sayingis in tyme cumming.'[73] Ewyn Talyeour of Inverness, who insulted and physically assaulted the town officers, was ordered to kneel at the tolbooth stair and say, 'Fals tong, yow led,' taking it in his hand.[74] For insulting Annabell Graham and her mother, Agnes Henderson of Stirling was ordered to go to church in her shift with a wax candle, and *say to her tongue*, 'You leid that said Annapill Graheme wes ane freirs get [friar's brat] and freris yawde [whore]' and other insults, then ask forgiveness of her victims.[75]

As shown by this last case, burghs also made use of the parish church for rituals of repentance. In 1503 John of Myle in Aberdeen was sentenced, not only to ask Isabel Scherar's forgiveness in court, but also to come with a candle of one pound of wax to the parish kirk of St Nicholas in time of high mass and ask her forgiveness for the words he said to her, offering the candle to the Holy Blood altar. Maggy Durtty, who had been twice convicted for the insulting and 'strublance' of Jonet Lesly, was ordered to come to St Nicholas with

a candle of two pounds of wax and kneel and ask Jonet's forgiveness, and ask the goodmen of the town to cause Jonet to forgive
her.[76] Such rituals involved the whole community in receiving back
the penitent sinner. In the case of Aberdeen, there was particular
stress laid on obtaining the town magistrates' pardon, as well.

It was important to give publicity to these rituals of penance as it
was a public reputation which had been damaged. There were also
other punishments imposed, most of which involved public humiliation. A study of sixteenth-century Selkirk has suggested that, in
deciding the type of punishment, 'the most important consideration would have been the degree to which an incident of verbal
violence posed a threat to the stability and security of burgh life.'[77]
In Aberdeen in 1405 the town passed legislation ordering that anyone who abused (maledixerit) the provost, bailies, or other officers
should kiss the cuckstool; if they repeated the offence, they would
be placed on the cuckstool and befouled with eggs, dung, mud, and
suchlike; while, for the third offence, they would be banished from
the town for a year and a day. However, this penalty only applied
to non-burgesses; burgesses would pay 8s penalty for a similar
offence.[78] There is no evidence of this punishment actually being
imposed in Aberdeen, but it is possible, as the editor of the records
suggests, that because no financial penalty was involved, it was not
regarded as worth recording. It is also possible that the mere threat
of such a punishment acted as an effective deterrent.[79]

The cuckstool, stocks, or the jougs (an iron collar often affixed to
the tolbooth) were used for men and women in many towns, with
offenders being sentenced to spend periods ranging from one hour
to two days on or in them.[80] In 1546 a Stirling woman was sentenced to punishment in an iron cage, which seems to have been
similar to the 'branks' ('scold's bridle'). There are also references to
the branks in Edinburgh and Inverness.[81] It has been suggested that
the Scots were ahead of the English in the use of such a punishment
and that the scold's bridle may have been introduced to England
from Scotland.[82]

Some towns forced the guilty party to process around the entire
community, so that everyone could witness the public humiliation.
In Peebles, women who defamed others were to bear two stones in
iron chains and be led to the four gates of the town. In Dundee, a
similar punishment was carried out in some cases: one defamer was
ordered to go through the town on her knees, bearing the 'tolbooth

beads.'[83] A couple in Inverness had to pass to the four ports of the town wearing linen clothes, before coming to the market cross to ask forgiveness.[84]

Occasionally, offenders were put in the town prison, although usually only for the most serious affronts, as when Andrew Gerves, convicted of using foul language to the Dunfermline bailie in 1487 and ordered to apologize, refused to do so.[85] All of these punishments were used selectively, as part of the authorities' means of control over public order.[86] However, in the most grievous cases, usually those in which the person was a repeat offender, he or she was banished from the town,[87] implying a limit to official willingness to forgive, or a limit to their capacity to control such rebellious elements.

A recent study of seventeenth-century Stirling has shown that in that period the branks was used exclusively for women. However, in many sixteenth-century towns, including Stirling, the branks and similar punishments were imposed on both men and women.[88] Was there a growing perception of women as more inclined than men to be quarrelsome flyters? In several studies of defamation elsewhere in this period, women have been seen as predominant among both accusers and accused,[89] although some recent studies have begun to question this.[90] In Scotland, there have not yet been enough local studies to allow historians to engage in the debate over a 'crisis in gender relations' proposed by some historians for late sixteenth- / early seventeenth-century England.[91] However, work in progress for periods from the late fifteenth to the eighteenth centuries may soon provide some evidence.[92]

In the church courts of pre-Reformation Scotland, women were in a slight minority among those accused of defamation, although they did appear as defamers more often than for any other crime.[93] From 1513 to 1551 men brought slightly more cases before the church court of Lothian than women (67:65). Of those accused of defamation, women outnumbered men over the whole period (82:52), but in the earliest years, 1513–19, male defamers outnumbered women (14:11). In the burghs, men outnumbered women in cases which included specific reference to verbal violence and insult, both as accusers and accused. It is possible that female participation increased during the later sixteenth and early seventeenth centuries, although the evidence of the town courts after 1560, apart from Stirling, has yet to be examined in detail.[94]

Unlike the court cases themselves, legislation and literary sources often portray flyting and defamation as a specifically female crime. Graham has argued for Dundee in 1580 that the authorities were concerned about both male and female violence but decided to attack neighbourly discord as a particularly female problem, perhaps because it would be more difficult to quell male violence, and 'doubtless they also found the sight of angry women particularly unseemly.'[95] However, an element of social status may also be involved. The authorities were most suspicious of unmarried and poor women, women regarded as unruly and difficult to control because they were often independent of the control of men. The Peebles legislation was directed at women who defame 'any goodman's wife or daughter' of the town, while in Edinburgh it was the women fruitsellers who were regarded as most likely to disturb the town through public quarrels.[96] Dunbar blamed the Edinburgh fishwives for the noisiness and disorder of the town market, while in David Lindsay's *Ane Satyre of the Thrie Estaits* it is the wives of a shoemaker and a tailor who are quarrelsome and likely to 'set the town on steir [astir].'[97] There appears to have been a gap between perception and reality; the authorities brought in legislation aimed at lower-status women, but those women who appeared in the courts actually accused of such offences came from across the social scale. Many of the Edinburgh women who appeared in court were the wives or widows of the town's most prominent burgesses.[98]

One source suggests another worry that the authorities might have about women's flyting; verbal quarrels gave women an opportunity to meet men on an equal playing field. An early print of the sixteenth-century 'Flyting of Montgomerie and Polwart' includes an epistle to the reader, asking for a law that would restrict flyting to poetry and forbid anyone to flyte in prose. This would have a salutary effect on public order:

How calme were then the world! perhaps this law
Might make some madding wives to stand in aw,
And not in filthy prose out-roare their men[99]

Should we accept the apparent evidence of the courts that both women and men were equally adept at using their tongues? There is some literary evidence to support this view. As mentioned earlier, one of the most vibrant forms of Scottish poetry was 'flyting.' Good vitriolic insult was a male art form in this period. Moreover, much, although not all, of the legislation dealing with flyting is gender neutral. When in 1503 Edinburgh wanted to take action against scolding and flyting, it ordered that *persons* (that is, men and women) convicted should be punished at the cross.[100] This is in contrast to some English towns, where in cases in which women and men were accused of similar offences, the term 'scold' was often applied to the women but not to the men.[101]

Historians have tended to treat verbal and physical assault as two separate offences, although the nineteenth-century Dundee historian Alexander Maxwell commented that the burgh court's jurisdiction included 'strublance' (disturbing the peace) 'whether committed by sharp tongues or otherwise.'[102] Certainly, the distinction is justified in the case of serious physical assault in which blood was shed, an offence known as 'bludewite.'[103] But did contemporaries make such a firm distinction between assaulting someone with words and some of the less serious physical attacks?

In many European courts, the charge of *iniuria*, or injury, could apply to either verbal or physical injury.[104] In Scottish courts, the charge of strublances appears to have had a similar meaning. Far more women and men appeared before the courts charged with the offence of strublance than with insult. However, many cases specifically include insults as part of this strublance, sometimes giving the words used, in other cases charging the defendant with 'strublance by words.'[105] Other charges involve strublance with specific physical aspects.[106] The question is how to read the charges of strublance which do not specify words or actions, for women appear in a very high proportion of these charges. Were Scotswomen more likely to be involved in physical brawls than their counterparts in other countries, where historians have tended to stress the low participation rate of women in violent crime,[107] or do we have here the missing domination by women of defamation? Or is the distinction made by historians between physical and verbal attack not seen as so important by contemporaries? As one historian has pointed out, 'slander is a potent assault weapon, its effects often more devastating than an outright physical thrashing. It allowed the weaker sex to strike first ... frequently with a blow so numbing as to facilitate escape from immediate counterattack.'[108]

Strubling by word and by deed often occurred together. The wife of Simon Palframan in Aberdeen in 1411 found herself before the court not only for insulting a woman but also for unjustly taking cloth from her.[109] In Elgin in 1540 Agnes Baldon was convicted of casting a stone at Katherine Falconer and shedding her blood, of menacing her with a rung (stout stick), and also for defaming her in calling her 'ane commund huir.' This may have been a case where insults led to violence; on the same day, Falconer was punished for calling Baldon a common thief and 'other injurious words.' When Cristen Varden called Margaret Froster 'vild meir [filthy mare], comond huyr and theif,' Froster responded by striking her with a pan on the head and drawing her hair 'to a great quantity' out of her head.[110] Moreover, physical assaults, like verbal assaults, could be intended to shame the victim.[111]

The punishments imposed suggest the authorities did not make a firm distinction between the types of assault. In Dundee in 1521, Janet Rynd was sentenced to bear the tolbooth beads around the town for attacking another woman so badly that she required a doctor.[112] This was the same punishment meted out to another woman who was guilty of defamation. In 1523 the Dumfries burgh court charged two men not to 'mak ony provocation be thair toungs wyth unressonable langage *or be deid*' to the other.[113] After John Nilson of Inverness attempted to slay Nicol Kar, he was made to find surety that Nicol should suffer no harm from him 'bayth of tung and hand.'[114] Verbal and physical violence can be very similar in their power to wound. As Dunbar might say, both contributed to the dishonour of the town.

Notes

This essay was awarded the Royal Historical Society's David Berry Prize in Scottish History for 2000.

1 *The Ledger of Andrew Haliburton Conservator of the Privileges of the Scotch Nation in the Netherlands, 1492–1503* (Edinburgh, 1867), 268–9.

2 William Dunbar, 'To the Merchantis of Edinburgh,' in *Selected Poems of Henryson and Dunbar*, ed. P. Bawcutt and F. Riddy (Edinburgh, 1992), 161, ll. 8–14.

3 T. Scott cited in P. Robichaud, '"To Heir Quhat I Sould Wryt": "The Flyting of Dunbar and Kennedy" and Scots Oral Culture,' *SLJ* 25/2 (Nov. 1998), 10. Some critics ascribe the whole poem to Dunbar, but Bawcutt

makes a convincing case for dual authorship. See P. Bawcutt, *Dunbar the Makar* (Oxford, 1992), 225.

4 *Jamieson's Etymological Dictionary of the Scottish Language* (Edinburgh, 1840), 412. *The Dictionary of the Older Scottish Tongue*, ed. Sir W. Craigie (London, 1974), ii, 504, defines it as 'a contest between poets in mutual abuse.'

5 G. Kratzmann, *Anglo-Scottish Literary Relations 1430–1550* (Cambridge, 1980), 153. See also Bawcutt, *Dunbar*, 235–9; and D. Gray, 'Rough Music: Some Early Invectives and Flytings,' in *English Satire and the Satiric Tradition*, ed. C. Rawson (Oxford, 1984), 21–43. For other examples of Scots flytings, see Bawcutt, *Dunbar*, 222.

6 Robichaud 'To Heir Quhat I Sould Wryt,' 9–16. See also Bawcutt, *Dunbar*, 239; P. Bawcutt, 'The Art of Flyting,' *SLJ* 10/2 (Dec. 1983), 5–9; A.J. Aitken, 'The Language of Older Scots Poetry,' in *Scotland and the Lowland Tongue*, ed. J.D. McClure (Aberdeen, 1983), 23–4, 39–44.

7 *Extracts from the Records of the Royal Burgh of Stirling*, ed. R. Renwick (Glasgow, 1887) [*Stirling Recs.*], i, 5.

8 *Records of Elgin*, ed. W. Cramond, New Spalding Club (Aberdeen, 1903) [*Elgin Recs.*], i, 84. See also Bawcutt, *Dunbar*, 222–4. For similar lack of firm definition in England, see M. Ingram, '"Scolding Women Cucked or Washed": A Crisis in Gender Relations in Early Modern England?' in *Women, Crime and the Courts in Early Modern England*, ed. J. Kermode and G. Walker (London, 1994), 51–2.

9 *Records of Inverness*, ed. W. Mackay and H. Boyd, New Spalding Club (Aberdeen, 1911) [*Inverness Recs.*], 58–9.

10 M. Graham, *The Uses of Reform: 'Godly Discipline' and Popular Behavior in Scotland and Beyond, 1560–1610* (Leiden, 1996), especially ch. 6 and 293–5; M. Graham, 'Women and the Church Courts in Reformation-Era Scotland,' in *Women in Scotland c.1100–1750*, ed. E. Ewan and M. Meikle (East Linton, 1999), 187–98; J.G. Harrison, 'Women and the Branks in Stirling, c.1600 to c.1730,' *Scottish Economic and Social History* 18/2 (1998), 114–31.

11 Ingram, 'Scolding Women,' 53, suggests that a similar problem exists for England, although some recent studies have begun to throw more light on the pre-1560 period. See M. McIntosh, *Controlling Misbehavior in England, 1370–1600* (Cambridge, 1998), especially 58–65; and K. Jones and M. Zell, 'Bad Conversation? Gender and Social Control in a Kentish Borough c.1450–c.1570,' *Continuity and Change* 13 (1998), 11–31.

12 L. Gowing, *Domestic Dangers: Women, Words and Sex in Early Modern London* (Oxford, 1996).

13 *Inverness Recs.*, 208.

14 *Statutes of the Scottish Church 1225–1559*, ed. D. Patrick, SHS (Edinburgh, 1907), 5–7.

15 Central Region Archives, Stirling Court Records, f.56v.

16 *Select Cases on Defamation to 1600*, ed. R.H. Helmholz, Selden Society (London, 1985), xviii–xix.

17 *Extracts from the Records of the Royal Burgh of Lanark*, ed. R. Renwick (Glasgow, 1893) [*Lanark Recs.*], 2; *Stirling Recs.*, 30. Similar confusion (or flexibility) existed in sixteenth-century England. See J.A. Sharpe '"Such Disagreement betwyx Neighbours": Litigation and Human Relations in Early Modern England,' in *Disputes and Settlements*, ed. J. Bossy (Cambridge, 1983), 170; J.A. Sharpe, *Crime in Early Modern England 1550–1750* (London, 1984), 87–8.

18 For a discussion of how local courts might justify claiming jurisdiction over defamation and insult, see M. McIntosh, 'Finding Language for Misconduct: Jurors in Fifteenth-century Local Courts,' in *Bodies and Disciplines*, ed B. Hanawalt and D. Wallace (Minneapolis, 1996), 90.

19 *Liber Officialis Sancti Andree*, Abbotsford Club (Edinburgh, 1845), no. 25. Also printed in *Before the Bawdy Court*, ed. P. Hair (London, 1972), 26.

20 M. Todd, 'Keeping the Peace: Parochial Arbitration of Quarrels in Early Modern Scotland,' paper delivered at Sixteenth-century Studies Conference, Toronto, October 1998. See also Graham, 'Women and the Church Courts.' The most detailed studies of such language can be found in Gowing, *Domestic Dangers*; L. Gowing, 'Language, Power, and the Law: Women's Slander Litigation in Early Modern London,' in *Women, Crime and the Courts*, 26–47; M.B. Norton, 'Gender and Defamation in Seventeenth-century Maryland,' *William and Mary Quarterly*, 3rd ser., 44/1 (Jan. 1987), 3–39; and D. Garrioch, 'Verbal Insults in Eighteenth-century Paris,' in *The Social History of Language*, ed. P. Burke and R. Porter (Cambridge, 1987), 104–19. See also D.R. Lesnick, 'Insults and Threats in Medieval Todi,' *JMH* 19 (1991), 71–89.

21 Dundee Head Court Book, ii, f.21. Transcripts have been made by *The Dictionary of the Older Scottish Tongue*. Folio numbers refer to the original court book. I would like to thank my research assistant, Dr Eila Williamson, for her work on this source.

22 J. Finlay, 'Women and Legal Representation in Early Sixteenth-century Scotland,' in *Women in Scotland*, 170.

23 National Archives of Scotland, Liber Sententiarum S Andrew Infra Laudonium (1513–51), CH5/3/1, ff 309r, 315v.

24 *Stirling Recs.*, 47–8.

25 *Stirling Recs.*, 43.

26 Dundee Book of the Church, ff 115v, 117v. For post-Reformation church courts, see Graham, 'Women and the Church Courts,' 187.

27 *Inverness Recs.*, 35.

28 This was its common meaning in post-Reformation court cases and legislation. See the discussion of the use of this term in Gowing, *Domestic Dangers*, 66, 79–102. See also M. Ingram, *Church Courts, Sex and Marriage in England 1570–1640* (Cambridge, 1987), 302.

29 CH5/3/1, f.333r.

30 CH5/3/1, f.335r.

31 *Stirling Recs.*, 48; Gowing, *Domestic Dangers*, 66–7.

32 *Elgin Recs.*, i, 72.

33 R. Houlbrooke, *Church Courts and the People during the English Reformation 1520–1570* (Oxford, 1979), 81.

34 R.N. Swanson, 'Angels Incarnate: Clergy and Masculinity from Gregorian Reform to Reformation,' in *Masculinity in Medieval Europe*, ed. D.M. Hadley (London, 1999), 171–3.

35 *Elgin Recs.*, i, 69.

36 *Elgin Recs.*, i, 74–5.

37 For example, Dumfries City Archives, Dumfries Court Book, f.6v; *Elgin Recs.*,i, 49; Bawcutt, 'Art of Flyting,' 9.

38 *Stirling Recs.*, 39.

39 CH5/3/1, f.324r.

40 Gowing, 'Language,' 35.

41 G. Walker, 'Women, Theft and the World of Stolen Goods,' in *Women, Crime and the Courts*, 91–4.

42 Gowing, *Domestic Dangers*, 62.

43 Gowing, 'Language,' 28; J.A. Sharpe, *Defamation and Sexual Slander in Early Modern England: The Church Courts at York*, Borthwick Papers (York, 1981), 16–17; B. Capp, 'The Double Standard Revisited: Plebeian Women and Male Sexual Reputation in Early Modern England,' *Past and Present* 162 (Feb. 1999), 70–100.

44 *Elgin Recs.*, i, 68.

45 CH5/3/1, f.309r; *Elgin Recs.*, i, 76–7.

46 *The Burgh Court Book of Selkirk 1503–45*, ed. J. Imrie et al., SRS (Edinburgh, 1960–9) [*Selkirk Court*], ii, 203; *Elgin Recs.*, i, 61.

47 CH5/3/1, f.332v. See also Dumfries Court Book, f.11v; *Elgin Recs.*, i, 48, 71. See Gowing's discussion of male insults, *Domestic Dangers*, 106–8.

48 *Elgin Recs.*, i, 70.

49 *Inverness Recs.*, 23; *Stirling Recs.*, 30.

50 *Liber Protocollorum M. Cuthberti Simonis Notarii Publici et Scribae Capituli Glasguensis* A.D. *1499–1513*, ed. J. Bain and C. Rogers, Grampian Club (London, 1875), no. 201.

51 *Elgin Recs.*, i, 52–3.

52 *Inverness Recs.*, 36.

53 Bawcutt, *Dunbar*, 231–3.

54 *Elgin Recs.*, i, 72, 74.

55 For example, Edinburgh City Archives, Edinburgh Town Council Records, iv, f.7v. I am grateful to Eila Williamson for her work on these records.

56 Dundee Head Court, i, f.81.

57 Edinburgh Town Council, iii, f.24r; iv, f.28r.

58 *Inverness Recs.*, 46.

59 *Inverness Recs.*, 14–15, 23.

60 Dundee Head Court, f.26B.

61 In seventeenth-century Maryland, the public nature of the defamation was also seen as important; see Norton, 'Gender and Defamation,' 12–14.

62 *Extracts from the Records of the Burgh of Edinburgh*, ed. J.D. Marwick and M. Wood, Scottish Burgh Records Society (Edinburgh, 1869) [*Edin Recs.*], ii, 27.

63 *Stirling Recs.*, 18.

64 See for example, *The Perth Guildry Book 1542–1601*, ed. M. Stavert (SRS, Edinburgh, 1993), 241.

65 C. Muldrew, 'Interpreting the Market: The Ethics of Credit and Community Relations in Early Modern England,' *Social History* 18 (1993), 163–83.

66 Aberdeen City Archives, Aberdeen Council Records, xvi, f.17; CH5/3/1, ff 338r, 333r.

67 Dundee Head Court, ff 45B, 116.

68 Such public penance showed that the defamation was a public offence; see Ingram, *Church Courts*, 294.

69 CH5/2/1 f.269r. See also f.334r.

70 A-B. Fitch, 'Civic Penitential Rituals in Late Medieval Scottish Towns,' paper delivered to NACBS, October 1995, 1. For a description of such a ritual, see 4–5.

71 Dundee Book of the Church, f.39; *Edin. Recs.*, i, 151; *Extracts from the Council Register of the Burgh of Aberdeen*, ed. J. Stuart, Spalding Club (Aberdeen, 1844) [*Aber. Council*], i, 415–6. See also Dundee Book of the Church, f.157; *Elgin Recs.*, i, 61, 74–5.

72 *Stirling Recs.*, 39.

73 Dundee Head Court, ii, f.186B.

74 *Inverness Recs.*, 43.

75 *Stirling Recs.*, 40–1.

76 *Aber. Council*, i, 429–30,198.

77 P. Symms, 'Social Control in a Sixteenth-century Burgh: A Study of the Burgh Court Book of Selkirk 1503–1545' (PhD diss., University of Edinburgh, 1986), 180.

78 *Early Records of the Burgh of Aberdeen*, ed. W.C. Dickinson, SHS (Edinburgh, 1957), cxvii, 217, 216.

79 Jones and Zell, 'Bad Conversation,' 21, 26–7.

80 The first reference to a cuckstool is in Aberdeen in 1294 (*Cartularium ecclesiae Sancti Nicholai aberdonensis*, ed. J. Cooper, Spalding Club [Aberdeen, 1888–92], ii, 313). See also *The Burgh Records of Dunfermline*, ed. E. Beveridge (Edinburgh, 1917) [*Dunf. Recs.*], 157; *Selkirk Court*, 140; *Lanark Recs.*, 13; Edinburgh City Archives, Burgh Court Book, 1507, f.31r. For stocks, see Alexander Maxwell, *Old Dundee Ecclesiastical, Burghal and Social prior to the Reformation* (Edinburgh, 1891), 208, 355. For jougs, see the 1541 reference to an iron collar in *Elgin Recs.*, i, 59. Aberdeen had jougs by 1544 (*Aber. Council*, 198).

81 *Stirling Recs.*, 43; Edinburgh Town Council, iii, 47, 51; *Inverness Recs.*, 59.

82 Ingram, 'Scolding Women,' 57–8.

83 *Charters and Documents Relating to the Burgh of Peebles*, ed. W. Chambers, Scottish Burgh Records Society (Edinburgh, 1872) [*Peebles Chrs.*], 167; Dundee Book of the Church, f.44r.

84 *Inverness Recs.*, 40.

85 *The Gild Court Book of Dunfermline 1433–1597*, ed. E.P.D. Torrie, SRS (Edinburgh, 1986), 31. See also *Elgin Recs.*, i, 68, 76–7.

86 Harrison, 'Women and the Branks,' 127–9; Ingram, 'Scolding Women,' 59–64.

87 *Elgin Recs.*, i, 71. In several cases, banishment was threatened if the offence was repeated; see i, 52, 68, 74–5, 84. For the occasional use of banishment in England, see McIntosh, *Controlling Misbehavior*, 64–5.

88 Harrison, 'Women and the Branks,' 115–16.

89 For example, Gowing, *Domestic Dangers*, and 'Language, Power and the Law,' 26; J. Sundin, 'For God, State and People: Crime and Local Justice in Preindustrial Sweden,' in *The Civilization of Crime*, ed. E.A. Johnson and E.H. Monkkonen (Urbana, 1996), 189; Norton, 'Gender and Defamation,' 3–5; K.Z. Wiener, 'Sex Roles and Crime in Late Elizabethan

Hertfordshire,' *Journal of Social History* 8 (1975), 38–60; Jones and Zell, 'Bad Conversation,' 14–15, 18. However, these patterns could change over time; see Houlbrooke, *Church Courts*, 80–1; Ingram, *Church Courts*, 189.

90 McIntosh, *Controlling Misbehavior*, 59. In Ramsey Abbey villages between 1288 and 1316, women were among the minority of slanderers, but their insults were often the most spectacular. See P. Hogan, 'The Slight of Honor: Slander and Wrongful Prosecution in Five English Medieval Villages,' *Studies in Medieval and Renaissance History*, n.s., 12 (1991), 16.

91 D. Underdown, 'The Taming of the Scold: The Enforcement of Patriarchal Authority in early modern England,' in *Order and Disorder in Early Modern England*, ed. A. Fletcher and J. Stevenson (Cambridge, 1985), 116–36. See Martin Ingram's reply in 'Scolding Women.' Other historians have posited an earlier period of concern around 1500 (Jones and Zell, 'Bad Conversation,' 11–12). Work on Irish women in the seventeenth century suggests there was no such 'crisis' there; see R. Gillespie, 'Women and Crime in Seventeenth-century Ireland,' in *Women in Early Modern Ireland*, ed. M. MacCurtain and M. O'Dowd (Edinburgh, 1990), 43–52.

92 M. Todd, 'Keeping the Peace.' See also M. Graham, *Uses of Reform*. G. DesBrisay and L. Leneman are examining the issue for the seventeenth and eighteenth centuries, respectively.

93 Similar patterns are found in other places where women do not make up the majority of those accused; for example, in Todi (27.5 per cent) (Lesnick, 'Threats and Insults,' 76).

94 Symms, 'Social Control,' 179. It was certainly common by the early seventeenth century (Graham, *Uses of Reform*, 293), although studies of kirk session and presbytery cases in several areas during 1560–1600 suggest a more varied picture (86, 100, 211, 247–8, 254–6).

95 Graham, *Uses of Reform*, 51.

96 *Peebles Chrs.*, 167; *Edin. Recs.*, ii, 141.

97 Dunbar, 'To the Merchantis of Edinburgh,' and 'This Nycht in My Sleip I Was Agast,' 81; 'The Fische Wiffis Flett and Swoir'; David Lyndsay, *Ane Satyre of the Thrie Estaits*, in *The Poetical Works of Sir David Lindsay*, ed. D. Laing (Edinburgh, 1871), ii, 168–73. English poets also associated quarrelling with fishwives from the sixteenth century (Gray, 'Rough Music,' 29).

98 For example, Alison Rouch, CH5/3/1 f.62v; Marjory Bassinden, ff 77r,111v.

99 Cited in Bawcutt, 'Art of Flyting,' 8.

100 *Edin. Recs.*, i, 97.

101 Jones and Zell, 'Bad Conversation,' 21–3.

102 Maxwell, *Old Dundee*, 206–7.

103 For example, *Stirling Recs.*, 78.

104 A. Finch, 'Women and Violence in the Later Middle Ages: The Evidence of the Officiality of Cerisy,' *Continuity and Change* 7 (1992), 36. Helmholz, *Select Cases*, xix–xx.

105 *Dunf. Recs.*, 105, 132, 133; *Aber. Council*, i, 415–16.

106 *Dunf. Recs.*, 132, 134, 188. For a post-Reformation Scottish example, see Graham, *Uses of Reform*, 217. In Todi, almost half the defamation actions also involved real or threatened physical violence (Lesnick, 'Threats and Insults,' 77–8). However, the slanders were considered to be distinct offences (Lesnick, 'Threats and Insults,' 77–8, 82n25). In Fordwich, those accused of scolding or of 'bad words' were often presented for another offence, sometimes assault, at the same time (Jones and Zell, 'Bad Conversation,' 20–3).

107 Finch stresses women's low rate of participation in violent crime ('Women and Violence,' 29). See also J.R. Dickinson and J.A. Sharpe, 'Courts, Crime and Litigation in the Isle of Man, 1580–1700,' *Bulletin of the Institute for Historical Research* 72 (June 1999), 155.

108 Hogan, 'Slight of Honor,' 17.

109 *Aber. Council*, i, 388.

110 *Elgin Recs.*, i, 48–9, 72; Finch, 'Women and Violence,' 36, 39.

111 V. Groebner, 'Losing Face, Saving Face: Noses and Honour in the Late Medieval Town,' *History Workshop Journal* 40 (Autumn 1995), 3–4.

112 Dundee Book of the Church, f37r. See L.E. Boose, 'Scolding Brides and Bridling Scolds: Taming the Woman's Unruly Member,' *Shakespeare Quarterly* 42/2 (Summer 1991), 189, for a woman punished by the cuckstool for physical violence as well as scolding.

113 Dumfries Burgh Court, f.50v.

114 *Inverness Recs.*, 21–2.

7

Tudor Family Politics in
Early Sixteenth-Century Scotland

MARGARET McINTYRE

In a book review about female rulers in early modern Europe, Pauline Stafford noted that 'the power of women is a recurring and common phenomenon.'[1] In late medieval and early modern Britain, Mary Tudor (1553–8), Elizabeth I (1558–1603), and Mary, Queen of Scots (1542–67, executed 1587), are cited habitually as examples of prominent female rulers. Far less frequently cited, if at all, are the four women who governed Scotland on behalf of their young sons during the fifteenth and sixteenth centuries. Indeed, most of the current research on medieval and early modern queenship in Britain tends to ignore the period between 1450 and 1550. This paper focuses on one of those female regents, Margaret Tudor (b. 1489 – d. 1541), in an attempt not only to put Scottish queenly power 'on the map' of late medieval British history but also to examine her access to power through a familial context.

The fact that queens exercised power is no longer under debate. What is under current investigation is the nature of that power. How, when, and to what extent did women as queens gain access to public, legitimized, and official authority?[2] While it has been argued that queens lost much of their access to official power from the twelfth century onwards as a result of increased bureaucracy and the triumph of primogeniture, this conclusion has been challenged or, at least, modified in recent studies on medieval queenship.[3] Instead, much of the current scholarship focuses on women's access to power through a familial model. As daughters, a royal woman's lineage was important and, as John Parsons concludes, her 'desirability came from her male kin's sphere of influence, but high lineage established her suitability for matrimony and maternity ...'[4]

More importantly, aside from the rare occurrences of queens regnant, a woman's access to queenly power was through marriage.

Once married, queens exercised political power as patrons, intercessors, and advisers to their husbands. Centralization in the
twelfth century did diminish a queen's role as the active political
partner of the king, and her access to direct political power was
lessened. Nonetheless, as M. Facinger argues, this loss of her earlier
status 'brought no real diminution in the queen's potential for exercising power [but] [i]t did ... reformulate the mode in which she
would have to act ...'[5] Queens retained power in the domestic
sphere, and they preserved a share in rulership as intercessors,
regents, and, perhaps most significantly, as mothers. Medieval
women's (supposed) incapabilities were transcended by their maternity, and many of the more positive images of medieval queens
grew from their maternal role.[6] For medieval queens, Parsons notes,
'women's exclusion from the succession guaranteed the disinter-
ested exercise of power by mothers already naturally devoted to
their children's welfare.'[7] A royal mother's right to act as guardian
of her son was usually the basis of a widowed queen's right to act as
regent. Thus, Margaret Tudor's access to formal power as regent
was based on her status as the young king's mother rather than the
dead king's wife.

Queens, therefore, had varying degrees of power based upon the
adoption of several roles and identities during particular phases of
their life cycles. As queen of Scotland, Margaret Tudor embodied all
of these expected roles. She also had an additional identity, however, as the sister of Henry viii (1509–47). Sibling relations and
queenship have not been addressed to any great extent in the current scholarship on queenship. This paper partially fills that lacuna
by examining the sometimes friendly, sometimes estranged, relationship between Margaret and Henry Tudor during the high-profile
period of her career – the minority of her son, James v, from 1513 to
1528. Based on the voluminous correspondence between Margaret
and Henry as well as additional official documents, it underlines
the difficulties of a woman who, as sister to one of the most powerful monarchs in sixteenth-century Europe, confronted the contradictory expectations and demands of her natal and marital families
with varying degrees of success. Since 'sovereignty ... does not exist
apart from gender,'[8] as a regent exercising formal legal rule and as
mother of the young king, Margaret Tudor's exercise of authority

depended upon the manifestation of both 'masculine' and 'feminine' constructs of gender. In addition, the complex configuration of powers that Margaret Tudor exhibited existed within a culture which held to the belief that women as a sex were naturally unfit for political rule. The extent to which this 'crossover' and 'fluidity' of gender challenged early sixteenth-century notions of female power will also be addressed.

Margaret Tudor's actions during the minority of James v can be outlined in brief. She began her life as queen of Scotland when she married James iv (1488–1513) in 1503. This marriage was the final seal on a treaty of perpetual peace signed the year before by her father, Henry vii (1485–1509), and the Scottish king. During her marriage to James iv, she bore six children, only one of whom survived: the future James v was born on 10 April 1512. A year and a half later, James iv was dead. Having declared war against Henry viii in support of France, Scotland's long-standing and traditional political ally, he was killed at the battle of Flodden on 9 September 1513. The results of that conflict led to serious rethinking by the Scots of the advantages and, more importantly, the disadvantages and dangers of supporting French policy. France, by contrast, because of its preoccupation with the Holy Roman Empire, sought association with whoever would support it, even to the point of treating with its old enemy, England, in 1514. Previous obligations to Scotland were forgotten or conveniently ignored.[9]

The growth after 1513 of a group of nobles favourable to closer ties with England also considerably altered Anglo-Scottish relations. This enabled Henry viii to pursue a policy within Scotland of supporting those lords who wished the 'Auld Alliance' with France to be discarded and of making whatever trouble or nuisance he could whenever French interests were ascendant. Thus, during James v's minority, Scotland was tied to, and was dependent upon, the flow of Continental affairs and the untidy course of Tudor diplomacy.

By the terms of James iv's will, Margaret Tudor was appointed regent and guardian for her eighteen-month-old son. Unfortunately, her first regency was short-lived and factious. Rifts in the governing council soon became evident,[10] and Margaret's marriage to Archibald Douglas, sixth earl of Angus, on 6 August 1514 brought her regency to an abrupt end.[11] According to Scots law, a mother could remain tutor to her children as long as she remained a widow. Upon remarriage, she forfeited the office, which would then pass to the nearest agnate.[12] Accordingly, the Scottish lords sent for John Stewart, duke of Albany, who had been born and raised in France and was next in line of succession to James v.[13] He arrived in Scotland in May 1515 and, although Margaret attempted to reconcile herself to the situation, her husband and several of his supporters refused to accept Albany's authority. By August, she was compelled to give up custody of her children and, seeing her cause was lost, fled to England with Angus in September.

Margaret spent the next twenty-one months in England. She gave birth to a daughter, Margaret Douglas, on 7 October 1515, and it took her the next two and a half months to recover. During her sojourn in England, negotiations for a truce with Scotland were ongoing, and Albany made repeated attempts at a reconciliation. She eventually returned to Scotland in May 1517 on the condition that she would behave like a 'good Scots woman.'[14] Albany left Scotland for France in May 1517 and did not return again until 1521. Without a central head, the government in Scotland during those four years was factious and unruly. Rifts in Margaret's marriage to Angus also became apparent, and by 1519 she refused to live with him. Between 1521 and 1524, Albany left Scotland twice in order to raise men and munitions for two ultimately abortive invasions into England. Angus, whose loyalty was never consistent, was banished to France in March 1522. Although Margaret supported Albany upon his return in 1521, by 1523 she was actively campaigning for his removal from the government.

In May 1524 Albany left Scotland for the last time, and on 26 July 1524 James v was formally invested with the symbols of sovereignty. In November 1524 the Scottish parliament declared that Albany had lost his tutory and that power was now in the king's hands with 'advice of his dearest mother and her council.'[15] The queen was given custody of the king and was named head of the governing council.

The factious politics of James v's minority, however, did not allow for any long-lasting stability. Angus returned from France and was in Scotland by the end of October 1524. Plans were soon afoot to curb the queen's authority, and in February 1525 she was forced to agree to a new ruling council that not only included Angus but significantly diminished her authority. A parliament held in July declared that Margaret would lose her authority in twenty days if she did not cooperate with the lords.[16] In addition, it had been decided that James V would remain in the custody of each of the leading nobles, who would keep him for three months in rotation. Having now lost custody of the king, Margaret's fate was sealed.

Although she no longer held a central position on council, the queen continued to be involved in Scottish politics by becoming a member of the faction which formed against Angus when he refused to give up custody of the young king in November 1525. Two unsuccessful attempts were made to free the king from the earl, who kept him virtually as a prisoner. In May 1528, however, and with his mother's help, James escaped from the Douglases and began his personal rule. Angus and the Douglases were forfeited in parliament and lived in exile in England until the death of James V in 1542. Margaret's place on the Scottish political agenda diminished, and she now took on the more peaceful role of dowager queen mother.

Taking another cue from Stafford's review, however common women's power has been, 'historiography has either ignored, dramatised or sentimentalized it ...'[17] More seriously, women who have exercised power have often been 'maligned and trivialized.'[18] This is nowhere more evident than in the historiography of Margaret Tudor, who has been harshly criticized by Scottish historians. From the sixteenth to the twentieth centuries, historical accounts of Margaret's political career have ranged from indifference to outright hostility. John Major, for example, barely mentions Margaret in his *A History of Greater Britain* of 1521, except to note the date of her marriage to James IV. Her role in dynastic politics, rather than any exercise of authority, is clearly what Major deems important. Indeed, throughout the work he argues that the long-standing enmity between Scotland and England can be resolved through the marriage of Scottish kings with English women. Citing the example of Saint Margaret (d. 1093), Major concludes that 'the Scots never had more excellent kings than those born of Englishwomen ...'[19] Nevertheless, those same Englishwomen, Major argues, must be willing to adapt completely to their new country by relinquishing their identity as *English* women: 'When a king has taken to wife a woman of another kingdom, he should assign to her attendants belonging to his own kingdom, and lead her by the exercise of kindness *to change her old skin and put on a new one*' (my emphasis).[20]

George Buchanan's *History of Scotland* (1582), while according more importance to Margaret's political role, is far less charitable. He argues that Margaret's first regency was tolerated only because there was a 'scarcity of noblemen.'[21] Blatantly ignoring the precedents set by Joan Beaufort and Mary of Gueldres, both of whom acted as regents for their sons,[22] he concludes that Margaret Tudor's regency was 'the first example of female government among the Scots.'[23] When she was forced to give up control of the government after her marriage to Angus in August 1514, Buchanan argues that there 'could be no indignity in substituting another to fill the situation she had deserted, and which, indeed, the ancient laws refused her; for they did not suffer women to administer the government, even in times of tranquillity, much less in such turbulent times as these ...'[24] Of her later regencies, Buchanan remains equivocal. Although he promotes her to head of the pro-English faction in Scotland, he implies that her 'private ambition' was to divorce Angus and gain control of the government with ample help from Henry VIII.

John Leslie's narrative (1579) of her regencies is more temperate and provides a different motivation for Margaret's estrangement from Angus; namely, that he had been betrothed to another woman before their marriage.[25] His *Historie of Scotland* provides less comment regarding her actual governance than on her marital woes.[26] Nevertheless, Leslie notes that Margaret continued to advocate for peace with England and was always concerned for the safety and protection of her son.[27]

William Drummond's seventeenth-century commentary on James V's minority in *The History of the Lives and Reigns of the Five James's* is relatively charitable toward Margaret, although he concludes that her governance was never entirely accepted by the Scots because of her relationship with the English king. Moreover, her desire for a divorce from Angus, Drummond concludes, was a flaw particular to the Tudors: 'it was fatal to her, as to her Brother King Henry, to delight in Change of Wedlock, and be jealous of her Matches.'[28]

By the nineteenth century, narrative sources were securely rooted in Victorian attitudes toward sexuality and gender roles. Agnes Strickland's biography in her massive *Lives of the Queens of Scotland and English Princesses* (1850) is perhaps the most hostile and bigoted account of Margaret Tudor to date. Strickland does not hesitate to characterize Margaret's many faults and provides numerous epithets to this effect. The Scottish queen was, among other things, 'wilful ... capricious [and] petulant'; 'sullen, spoiled'; 'avaricious' and 'despotic.'[29] Not willing to allow Margaret's flaws to remain within the time frame of her own lifetime, Strickland ascribes to Margaret the death of James V, the assassination of Darnley, and the execution of Mary, Queen of Scots:

> Some of Margaret Tudor's mistakes in government ... may be attributed to the fact that she is the first instance that occurs, since Christianity was established in the island, of regnant power being confided to the hands of a woman who was expected to reign as *femme seule* [*sic*]. She had no education, scarcely any religion, and was guided entirely by her instincts, which were not of an elevated character. Her misdeeds, and the misfortunes attributable to her personal conduct, gave rise to most of the terrible calamities which befell her descendants ... A succession of tragedies, for three generations, was the consequence of Margaret Tudor's indulgence of her selfish passions.[30]

By contrast, M.A.E. Green's discussion in *Lives of the Princesses of England from the Norman Conquest* (1852), although also written during the Victorian period, remains the most balanced account of Margaret's life to date. Well-researched and thoroughly grounded in historical sources, Green admits that Margaret made mistakes but concludes that it would have been difficult for any woman to exercise authority in such an environment because 'her position gave prominence to her faults whilst it left little scope for the display of her virtues.'[31]

Patrick Tytler's narrative in his *History of Scotland* (1864) echoes many of Strickland's criticisms and presents Margaret in an unfavourable light. Tytler censures Margaret, more than anyone else involved in Scottish politics at that time, for changing allegiances. In addition, 'the licentious manners of the times, and the well-known gallantries of that princess,'[32] suggest that Margaret may have been intimate with Albany. While ascribing many of Margaret's actions to her personality, Tytler implies that such behaviour was not uncommon as the governance of Scotland remained under the dark shadow of 'feudalism.'

Only one major twentieth-century biography of Margaret Tudor has been written: Patricia Buchanan's *Margaret Tudor, Queen of Scots*, published in 1985. Unfortunately, this work, which is not scholarly, does not advance any new conclusions regarding Margaret's role in the politics of early sixteenth-century Scotland. More seriously, Buchanan's biography has not yet been superceded by a balanced and informed approach. Instead, even reputable Scottish historians have chosen to repeat the same outdated and gender-biased opinions that have been prevalent in studies of Margaret's career since the sixteenth century.

Margaret Tudor's access to power and the fact that she married not once, but three times,[33] has engendered much of the criticism aimed at her. Gordon Donaldson, for example, described her in his study, *Scottish Kings*, as 'capricious' and as 'conspicuously unstable in her affections.' He continues: 'Indeed, her matrimonial adventures came near to rivalling those of her brother, Henry VIII ... This was the woman who, in terms of James IV's will, was tutrix to her son as long as she remained a widow, and therefore head of the government.'[34] E.J. Cowan, in a review of Buchanan's biography, asserts that Margaret was 'every bit as vain, fickle and treacherous as her younger brother Henry VIII ... [and that her] main historical significance is that of dynastic linchpin.'[35] Michael Lynch, although not as flamboyant in language, concludes that Margaret Tudor had 'a bewildering succession of liaisons.'[36] This particular criticism is, in many ways, puzzling. Margaret Tudor, like most other women, did not choose to become a widow, but became one involuntarily. After the death of her first husband, she remarried twice – this was neither a 'bewildering' nor an unusual experience for women in the sixteenth century. While Margaret Tudor was, as Donaldson claims, the woman who was appointed by James IV (a much-beloved king by his contemporaries and by Scottish historians alike) to act as regent for her son, what these historians fail to recognize, or perhaps choose to ignore, is that the king's nomination suggests that he had confidence in her abilities to govern. As Suzanne Dixon notes, criticisms of women who exercised formal power reflect an enduring tradition of 'a conscious attempt to control and diminish ... [female] power by defining it as illegitimate and unnatural and by making it sound ridiculous or offensive.'[37]

Two recent works have included brief analyses of Margaret Tudor's political career. Unfortunately, only one of them provides a meaningful contribution to the historiography. A recent essay by Andrea Thomas on the role of women at the court of James V, published in the volume *Women in Scotland* (1999), discusses Margaret's role briefly but adds little relevant material. Thomas's work is not informed by recent studies on medieval queenship; nor does it recognize the gendered nature of late medieval family politics. Consequently, Thomas concludes that women's position at James v's court 'reflected many of the experiences of women in the wider society of the sixteenth century,' thus relegating them to the 'limited spheres of family [and] household.'[38] Margaret Tudor, therefore, is promptly dismissed as a political failure not only as regent but as queen dowager as well.[39]

By contrast, Louise Fradenburg's analysis of historians' accounts of Margaret Tudor's regencies provides perhaps one of the most in-depth and edifying portraits of Margaret's political role to date. Since her essay is framed within a postmodern methodology (an approach, it must be noted, too frequently dismissed by late medieval Scottish historians), Fradenburg questions recent Scottish historians' somewhat contradictory approach to documentary sources and, consequently, their conclusions about Margaret Tudor's role in James v's minority.[40] By examining Margaret's regencies within the context of the struggle between national and regional identities, Fradenburg concludes that Margaret's role 'should be evaluated from a standpoint that recognizes the extent to which calculation may be impelled by desire. Passion is embedded in the structures and practices of power that both obstruct and instantiate historical change.'[41] Thus, the supposed dichotomy between public and private interests, and women's concomitant lack of political agency, is not as static as many Scottish historians have concluded.

It is readily apparent, however, that with few exceptions, most accounts of Margaret Tudor's political career have cooperated in Dixon's 'enduring tradition' of belittling or ignoring women's exercise of power. The remainder of this paper, therefore, attempts to present a more balanced perspective by evaluating Margaret Tudor's ability to manage the complex issues of gender, family, and authority in early sixteenth-century Scotland.

Margaret Tudor's access to political power was closely tied to her relationship with her brother Henry VIII. Three themes have been chosen to illustrate this: Margaret's financial situation; her dual identities as the Scottish king's mother and the English king's sister; and how popular attitudes toward women and power influenced her political career.

Throughout James v's minority, Margaret was besieged by financial difficulties. While she has been criticized both by contemporaries and later historians for shifting her political allegiances, these criticisms fail to recognize that not only were *all* political allegiances precarious and flexible during Scotland's royal minorities, but Margaret's financial situation influenced where and with whom she chose to place her political support. Her financial difficulties were inseparable from her political motivations. J.T. Rosenthal has noted that economic support for dowager queens 'depended on the good will and whims of others. What was given was frequently taken away.'[42] Similarly, the influence and power wielded by queens was 'often dependent on their family and financial circumstances.'[43] Margaret Tudor was no exception.

Throughout her son's minority, Margaret continually complained to both Henry VIII and the governing lords in Scotland that she had not been 'answered of her living.'[44] Not only did her second husband plunder the revenues from her dower lands, but several Scottish lords took advantage of the unruly political situation and refused to forward the rentals to her.[45] Fortunately, during her self-imposed exile in England, Henry VIII supported her financially.[46] More significantly, Henry attempted to alleviate her financial difficulties by sending commissioners to Scotland to deal with her affairs. In February 1516 Margaret formally requested the return of her clothing and jewellery that had been confiscated the year before, although no agreement was finalized until seven months later in September.[47] For over a year, her English commissioners endeavoured to settle the problems of her rents and revenues. In October 1516, for example, it was noted that of over £14,000 due to the queen, only £114 had been paid.[48] The excuses the Scottish lords presented attempted to place the blame for her financial situation squarely upon her own shoulders. Some of her goods, they stated, belonged to the late king, and if she required them as executrix, she would have to return to Scotland and pay the king's debts. As for her rents, the lords argued that they could not be collected because the officers she appointed were either 'simple poor men, not responsible nor able to pay the things with which they have interfered' or they were great lords living away from court.[49] In addition, they pointed out that many of her forest lands had been wasted by war. The lordship of Dunbar, for example, had been burnt and ravaged, the lords concluding pointedly, 'her grace knows by whom, though they have no good cause.'[50]

When Margaret Tudor returned to Scotland in 1517, her financial troubles were far from over. By March 1518, she had still not received either her jewels or her rents and was forced to pawn the plate that Henry had given her.[51] Although the lords had agreed that redress of her finances be written into the terms of truce with England in December 1518, Angus registered a protest in council that, as her husband, he should have full access to any of her rents, dowry, or duties.[52] By October 1519, she was borrowing money from the comptroller, Robert Barton.[53] Once her marriage to Angus fell apart, his 'interference' with her dower lands increased. Realizing that her options for retaining any kind of financial and political security were narrowing, she began to campaign actively for Albany's return. When the duke did return to Scotland in 1521, Margaret supported him, not only because he allowed her custody of her son, but because he gave her rent money from the young king's lands. By 1523, when she was just as actively working for Albany's removal, her reasons were, again, closely tied to her financial situation. After appealing to the Scottish lords through numerous unsuccessful supplications for access to, and revenue from, her dower lands,[54] she sought and received financial aid from Henry VIII.[55] Although she received criticism from the Scottish lords for this action, she protested in May 1524 that

> since she had guided her[self] as a good Scots woman and for the weal of this realm, that suppose for very necessity she sought in other parts where she might be furnished, what inconvenience happened to this realm therethrough or trouble afterwards no reproach nor blame should be imputed to her ...[56]

Both Margaret's political allegiances and her loyalty to Henry VIII were closely tied to her financial situation. Unfortunately, they were also intertwined with her relationship to Angus.

From June 1524 Margaret made continual requests to Henry VIII to keep her estranged husband out of Scotland. These were based not only on political and personal reasons, but financial ones as well. The continual remonstrances to Angus, from both the Scottish council and Henry VIII, forbidding his 'intromission' with her dower lands, confirms that her complaints were justified. Once the decision was made to return Angus to Scotland, attempts were made to protect Margaret's financial interests. In August 1524 Wol-

sey and Angus drew up several articles which included a promise
that Angus would not meddle with Margaret's lands.[57] But, because
her continued political support depended upon financial aid from
her brother, Henry VIII was able to use Margaret's precarious financial situation as leverage. Although his largesse was sporadic,
Henry often threatened to withdraw the payments he made to Margaret and her supporters if she refused to follow his directions.[58]
Similarly, Angus made several requests to Henry for permission to
revoke his promise not to interfere with her lands once it became
clear that she would neither reconcile with him nor grant him a
position on the governing council.[59] Margaret, however, used similar tactics and countered Henry's threats with those of her own. In
August 1524 she informed Henry that if he did not honour his
promise to keep Angus out of Scotland, she and her supporters 'may
and can, when they will, undo that [which] is done, and make their
friends in other places.'[60] Similarly, a year later she threatened to
abandon Henry when Louise of Savoy promised her a French duchy
and a pension of 4,000 livres.[61]

As mother of the Scottish king and sister of the English king,
Margaret Tudor's ability to exercise political authority was contingent upon the successful integration of those dual identities. Since
most women 'were the daughters [or sisters] of one family ... [and]
the wives and mothers of another ... they understood themselves,
and were understood by their society, within the context of a dual
kinship relationship.'[62] As noted above, the Scottish historian John
Major advised that queens from foreign countries should revoke
their natal identities. Yet, for many women, this kind of transformation remained impossible. Margaret Tudor was the mother of the
king of Scotland; yet not only was she a foreigner, she was also the
sister of the English king, Scotland's oldest enemy. Although she
often referred to herself as a Scotswoman in her correspondence,
the majority of the Scottish political community never entirely
accepted her as one of their own. Her relationship to Henry VIII was
often used by the Scots to prevent her from gaining custody of the
king and, concomitantly, access to sovereign powers. In 1517 when
she returned to Scotland, for example, the lords restricted her
access to James V by not allowing her to lodge with him over-
night.[63] Similarly, in December 1523, when she asked the Scottish
lords why they would not allow her to have custody of her son, the
reason they gave was that she was Henry VIII's sister.[64]

Suspicions of her became more prevalent, of course, during those periods when she had more direct access to formal authority. In one of their first attempts to oust Margaret from power after she became the head of the government in November 1524, the lords claimed that they 'desired no authority but that of barons of the realm like their ancestors.'[65] When they approached the queen in person, they were accompanied by the two English ambassadors, Thomas Magnus and Roger Radcliffe. According to Magnus and Radcliffe, the lords had specifically requested their presence 'because we were Englishmen, and supposed therefore to be better heard than Scotsmen.'[66] Margaret, however, rejected this implication and ordered the ambassadors 'right roundly' to go home and not meddle with Scottish affairs.[67]

The suspicion that she was her brother's agent was not lost on the queen. Throughout the tortuous minority of James v, attempts at a peace settlement with England were complicated, and most often thwarted, by Anglo-French relations. Margaret, as the sister of the English king, had to tread carefully whenever the issue of peace arose. As she herself noted in a letter to Henry viii, if she attempted to 'make a final peace with England excluding all other realms, it will be thought that she cared more for her brother than for her son.'[68]

Margaret's management of these divided loyalties worked both for and against her. She often cited her 'honour' as Henry's sister when asking him for money, and rarely failed to mention that any diminution of her honour and status could only reflect poorly on him. During her exile in England, for example, the Scottish queen wrote to Wolsey in December 1516 asking for money for New Year's Day gifts, noting that 'I must give part of rewards and other needful things both for the king my brother's honour and mine.'[69]

Nevertheless, Margaret's honour as the sister of Henry viii was also used by his agents to obtain her compliance with Henry's Scottish policy and, in particular, her reconciliation with Angus. In March 1522 Thomas, Lord Dacre, Warden of the English Marches, sent the queen a number of articles indicating Henry's displeasure at her support for Albany's government. Henry criticized Margaret for neglecting her role as peacemaker between Scotland and England. She had been married by her father to the king of Scotland, he claimed, in order to promote peace between the two kingdoms and 'it was not for her wisdom to side with those who were enemies to the same [i.e., Albany].'[70] She was also advised that since 'few Scotsmen will give her good counsel ... she should lean to such as be naturally born.'[71] Margaret, however, found the articles 'right sharp' and defended her actions in a detailed reply to Dacre:

> And where you say that I am ruled by the counsel that will never do me good nor honour, – my lord, I did never dishonour to myself nor to them that I am come of; nor methinks you should not give credence to that of me, both for the king's grace my brother's sake and the king my father's, (whose soul God pardon), and I have made you better cause ... [than] my lord of Angus hath done or any of his.[72]

Margaret Tudor's difficulties in maintaining consistent access to power were closely tied to her sexual reputation. The medieval 'preoccupation with queenly sexuality'[73] was no less prevalent in early sixteenth-century Scotland than elsewhere, and one of the most common methods of removing a queen from power was to accuse her of adultery.[74] After her marriage to Angus broke down, Margaret's reputation was impugned through slanderous accusations that she was sexually involved with Albany. Henry viii accused Albany of advising Margaret to divorce Angus,[75] while Angus's uncle, the bishop of Dunkeld, claimed that Margaret was 'much inclined to the Duke's pleasure' and that they were 'always together.'[76] Lord Dacre, not surprisingly, seconded the bishop's slander by exclaiming that there was 'marvellous great intelligence' between the queen and Albany both by day and night.[77] Margaret maintained that her support for Albany was based on his good governance and financial help, and, as for the bishop of Dunkeld, her anger was apparent: 'Since I helped him to get the benefice of Dunkeld, I shall help him as well free the same.'[78]

The Scottish bishop was not the only cleric who slandered Margaret publicly. In a meeting of the English council, Wolsey reproached Albany's secretary of having dishonourable intentions toward the queen. When she learned of this, Margaret was especially upset that Henry had allowed her name to be slandered in such a public forum and made her reactions clear in a letter to him:

> I think it will not be to your honour to suffer such false and untrue report made upon me, your sister. It had been your part, dearest

brother, to have been my defender in all evil reports, and not to have alleged wrongously to dishonour me ... But your grace may do to me, your sister, as ye please, but I shall make no evil cause, but it does me great displeasure in my heart of your unkindness.[79]

Sexual gossip was not only more damaging for women than men, but, as Suzanne Dixon notes, the paradox of sexual gossip is that 'women become particularly prone to such attacks once they are taken seriously ... [and] the aim of the attack is ... to ridicule and thereby ensure that nobody will take them seriously again.'[80]

Margaret Tudor's usefulness to Henry VIII was primarily as an English agent. Her reliability, however, was always considered within a gendered context. In a letter to the duke of Norfolk dated 1 August 1524, Wolsey noted:

I think good that the Queen of Scots is to be used, as most proper and convenient instrument in this matter ... pretending that nothing shall be wrought but only by her means; nevertheless so to be used, that all shall depend upon her proceeding and doing, it were perilous and dangerous ... For it is no folly for a good archer to have two strings to his bow, specially whereas one is made of threads wrought by women's fingers ...[81]

Recognizing that her authority was regarded in gendered terms, Margaret complained to Henry that Dacre was undermining her authority by revealing to the Scots 'that he marvels that they will let any woman have authority, and specially me ...'[82] This popular suspicion and derision of women's authority made her attempts to exercise formal power even more difficult.

More seriously, Henry's VIII's continued political and financial support was contingent upon Margaret's obedience. When she deviated from her brother's directives, his wrath was barely containable and was couched in familial and gendered language. Her 'unreasonable desires,' 'arrogant and dishonourable requests,' and 'insolent behaviours' caused the 'blemishing of the royal house whereof she is descended.'[83] In a letter from Wolsey to Norfolk, the cardinal described Henry's anger, concluding that

she is not only the most ingrate and unkind sister that ever was ... but also that she, digressing from all good qualities and virtues, doth in

manner alter, vary, and decline from the loving affections and direct
operations and course of nature towards her self, her blood, and the
house that she came of; showing thereby that she is to be accounted
rather like an *unnatural* or *transformed* person, than like a noble
Princess, or a woman of wisdom, regard, honour or kindness ...[84]
(My emphasis)

Margaret Tudor's deviance from the role of dutiful and obedient
sister, as well as her access to the sphere of male power, challenged
sixteenth-century notions of gender. Once her femininity became
both suspect and blurred, she was labelled 'unnatural' and 'dangerous.' These labels were not uncommon for those women who tra-
versed gender barriers. As Stafford concludes, in the realm of formal
power, 'male virtues become female vices; reward and generosity,
vengeance and protection are strengths and virtues when exercised
by kings, but become partiality, intrigue, and personal vindictiveness when practised by queens.'[85] Margaret Tudor's attempts to
remain faithful to her natal and marital families have been unfairly
and unjustly criticized in precisely those terms. Faced with an
unruly, unpredictable, and hostile Scottish political environment,
as well as a domineering and interfering brother, she utilized her
dual identities as English sister and Scottish queen mother to her
advantage – sometimes with success, sometimes without. Like all
late medieval and early modern queens, Margaret Tudor worked
within a familial context, and, as such, she was subject to, and
capable of subverting, the restrictions placed upon her access to formal power. The criticisms of her, from both contemporaries and
later historians alike, merely confirm her ability to transcend and
challenge the stereotypes of women in power.

Notes

1 P. Stafford, 'More than a Man, or Less than a Woman? Women Rulers in
   Early Modern Europe,' *Gender and History* 7/3 (Nov. 1995), 487.
2 Two kinds of power, only one of which was normally available to medieval women, have been identified. Women could exercise public power,
   possessing 'the ability to act effectively, to influence people or deci-
   sions, and to achieve goals' (M. Erler and M. Kowaleski, 'Introduction,'

in *Women and Power in the Middle Ages,* ed. M. Erler and M. Kowaleski [London, 1988], 2). By contrast, formal power or public authority, defined as recognized and legitimized power 'encompass[ing] the worlds of politics, legal rights and obligations, and the market' (Erler and Kowaleski, 3) was not usually available to women. Medieval queens, however, as regents and/or queens regnant, had access to both kinds of power.

3 For example: *Medieval Queenship,* ed. J.C. Parsons (New York, 1993); *Women and Sovereignty,* ed. L.O. Fradenburg (Edinburgh, 1992); and *Queens and Queenship in Medieval Europe,* ed. A.J. Duggan (Woodbridge, 1997).

4 J.C. Parsons, 'Introduction: Family, Sex, and Power: The Rhythms of Medieval Queenship,' in *Medieval Queenship,* ed. Parsons, 3.

5 M. Facinger, 'A Study of Medieval Queenship: Capetian France, 987–1237,' *Studies in Medieval and Renaissance History* 5 (1968), 40.

6 See the essays by J.C. Parsons, L. Huneycutt, and E. McCartney in *Power of the Weak: Studies on Medieval Women,* ed. J. Carpenter and S. MacLean (Chicago, 1995); as well as those by J.C. Parsons, M. Chibnall, L. Huneycutt, and M. Shadis in *Medieval Mothering,* ed. J.C. Parsons and B. Wheeler (New York, 1996).

7 Parsons, 'Introduction,' in *Medieval Queenship,* ed. Parsons, 7.

8 L. Fradenburg, 'Introduction: Rethinking Queenship,' in *Women and Sovereignty,* ed. Fradenburg, 1.

9 For background on the reigns of James iv and v, see N. Macdougall, *James iv* (Edinburgh, 1989; repr. East Linton, 1997); and J. Cameron, *James v: The Personal Rule 1528–1542* (East Linton, 1998). Both works are very much studies of kings.

10 *Acts of the Lords of Council in Public Affairs 1501–1554: Selections from the Acta Dominorum Concilii,* ed. R.K. Hannay (Edinburgh, 1932) [*ADC*], 17–18.

11 Although historians have appeared baffled at Margaret's decision to remarry, a close look at the evidence provides several clues. Flodden placed Scotland under yet another minority government, this time headed by a woman who was the sister of the enemy. Henry viii's continued belligerent actions toward Scotland placed Margaret in a vulnerable position. Not only was she pregnant with James iv's child (her son Alexander was born on 30 April 1514), but what remained of the Scottish nobility was neither trustworthy nor supportive. In addition, within hours of James iv's death, both Henry and Wolsey were considering sev-

eral candidates for Margaret's remarriage (*Calendar of State Papers and Manuscripts Existing in the Archives and Collections of Venice, vol II, 1509–1519*, ed. R. Brown [London, 1867], nos. 340, 371, 367, 369, 383, 415). Historians' 'surprise' at her second marriage is more a reflection of their own particular biases than of an examination of the available evidence. Ultimately, Margaret must have felt the need for a male protector in what can only be described as an unstable, unpredictable, and hostile environment.

12 *ADC*, 22.

13 Albany was the son of Alexander Stewart, the exiled brother of James III.

14 *ADC*, 57.

15 *Acts of the Parliaments of Scotland*, ed. T. Thomson and C. Innes, 12 vols (Edinburgh, 1814–75) [*APS*], ii, 286.

16 *APS*, ii, 298.

17 Stafford, 'More than a Man, or Less than a Woman?' 487.

18 S. Dixon, 'The Enduring Theme: Domineering Dowagers and Scheming Concubines,' in B. Garlick et al., *Stereotypes of Women in Power: Historical Perspectives and Revisionist Views* (London, 1992), 210.

19 John Major, *A History of Greater Britain* (1521), ed. A. Constable and A.J.G. MacKay (Edinburgh, 1892), 42 [Bk I, Ch VIII].

20 Major, *History of Greater Britain*, 306 [Bk V, Ch XXIV].

21 George Buchanan, *History of Scotland*, trans. J. Aikman, 4 vols (Glasgow and Edinburgh, 1830), ii, 262–3.

22 Joan Beaufort was a member of the triumvirate government which was formed after the death of James I in 1437. She remained head of the regency council until 1439. Similarly, Mary of Gueldres had the support of the majority of Scottish magnates when she took up the reins of government in August 1460 after James II was killed at Roxburgh. Although Bishop James Kennedy was her only real rival for the position of regent, he did not obtain a central role in Scottish politics until after Mary's death in December 1463. For background on the reigns of James I, II, and III, see M. Brown, *James I* (Edinburgh, 1994); C. McGladdery, *James II* (Edinburgh, 1990); and N. Macdougall, *James III: A Political Study* (Edinburgh, 1982).

23 Buchanan, *History of Scotland*, ii, 262–3.

24 Buchanan, *History of Scotland*, ii, 265.

25 John Leslie, *Historie of Scotland*, ed. E.G. Cody and W. Murison (Edinburgh, 1888–95), ii, 173–4, 206.

26 The historical context in which Buchanan and Leslie wrote their accounts should be taken into consideration when reviewing their

assessments of Margaret's regencies. Both men wrote their histories during the reign, deposition, and political exile of Mary, Queen of Scots, and both held equally divided opinions not only about Mary's personal conduct (particularly her choices of marriage partners) but also about her effectiveness as a ruler.

27 Leslie, *Historie*, ii, 190, 198–9, 205.

28 William Drummond, *The History of the Lives and Reigns of the Five James's, Kings of Scotland, from the Year 1423 to the Year 1542* (Edinburgh, 1711). Reprinted in William Drummond, *The Works* (New York, 1970), 95.

29 A. Strickland, *Lives of the Queens of Scotland and English Princesses*, 8 vols (Edinburgh, 1850), i, 6, 67, 100, 103.

30 Strickland, *Lives of the Queens of Scotland*, i, 268.

31 M.A.E. Green, *Lives of the Princesses of England from the Norman Conquest*, 6 vols (London, 1852), i, 50.

32 P.F. Tytler, *The History of Scotland*, 4 vols (Edinburgh, 1864), ii, 318.

33 Margaret married Henry Stewart, Lord Methven, sometime in December 1527 shortly after receiving a sentence of divorce from Angus. News of the marriage was not made public, however, until March 1528.

34 G. Donaldson, *Scottish Kings* (London, 1967), 148. See also his *Scotland: James v–James vii* (Edinburgh, 1965).

35 E.J. Cowan, review of *Margaret Tudor: Queen of Scots*, by Patricia Hill Buchanan, *Scottish Tradition* 14 (1986–7), 60.

36 M. Lynch, *Scotland: A New History*, rev. ed. (London, 1992), 162.

37 Dixon, 'The Enduring Theme,' 211.

38 A. Thomas, '"Dragonis baith and dowis ay in double forme": Women at the Court of James v, 1513–1542,' in *Women in Scotland c. 1100–c. 1750*, ed. E. Ewan and M. Meikle (East Linton, 1999), 91.

39 Thomas's analysis is primarily based upon Strickland's hostile account and Buchanan's weak biography, which may account for its somewhat outdated and simplistic approach.

40 L. Fradenburg, 'Troubled Times: Margaret Tudor and the Historians,' in *The Rose and the Thistle: Essays on the Culture of Late Medieval and Renaissance Scotland*, ed. S. Mapstone and J. Wood (East Linton, 1998); see page 46 for an important discussion of Norman Macdougall's analysis of historical sources.

41 Fradenburg, 'Troubled Times,' 53

42 J.T. Rosenthal, *Patriarchy and Families of Privilege in Fifteenth-century England* (Philadelphia, 1991), 182.

43 J. Carpenter and S. MacLean, 'Introduction,' in *Power of the Weak*, ed. Carpenter and MacLean, xvi.

44 *Letters and Papers, Foreign and Domestic, of the Reign of Henry VIII 1509–47*, ed. J.S. Brewer, J. Gairdner, and R.H. Brodie, 21 vols (London, 1862–1920) [*L&P*], ii, nos. 50, 1672; iii, no. 396; *ADC*, 27.

45 *ADC*, 34, 38, 71–2, 77–8.

46 She made a point of emphasizing Henry's generosity to the Scottish lords when several of them visited her shortly after the birth of her daughter in October 1515: 'So, my Lords, here you may see that the King my brother hath not forgotten me, and that he would not I should die for lack of clothes' (*L&P*, ii, no. 1350).

47 *L&P*, ii, no. 1598; *ADC*, 69–71; *Letters of James V*, collected and calendared by R.K. Hannay, ed. D. Hay (Edinburgh, 1954), 37.

48 *L&P*, ii, no. 2481.

49 *L&P*, ii, no. 2398.

50 *L&P*, ii, no. 2398.

51 *L&P*, ii, no. 3986; see also ii, p. 1475.

52 *ADC*, 137.

53 *L&P*, iii, no. 396; *ADC*, 148.

54 *ADC*, 156, 158–60.

55 *State Papers of the Reign of King Henry VIII*, 11 vols (London, 1830–52) [*St.P.*], iv, nos. 23, 33, 49, 59, 61.

56 *ADC*, 200

57 *St.P.*, iv, no. 68.

58 *St.P.*, iv, nos. 73, 78, 84, 95.

59 *St.P.*, iv, nos. 99, 106.

60 *St.P.*, iv, no. 52; *L&P*, iv, no. 573.

61 *L&P*, iv, no. 1462; *Letters of James V*, 123.

62 C. Wood, 'The First Two Queens Elizabeth, 1464–1503,' in *Women and Sovereignty*, ed. Fradenburg, 127.

63 *ADC*, 91

64 *L&P*, iii, no. 3643.

65 *L&P*, iv, no. 854.

66 *L&P*, iv, no. 854.

67 *L&P*, iv, no. 854.

68 *L&P*, iii, no. 3643.

69 H. Ellis, *Original Letters Illustrative of English History*, 3 vols (London, 1824), i, 130; *L&P*, ii, nos. 2701, 2729.

70 *L&P*, iii, no. 2084.

71 *L&P*, iii, no. 2084.

72 *Letters of Royal and Illustrious Ladies of Great Britain from the Commencement of the Twelfth Century to the Close of the Reign of Queen Mary*, ed. M.A.E. Green, 3 vols (London, 1846), i, 250.

73 Parsons, 'Introduction,' in *Medieval Queenship*, ed. Parsons, 6.

74 P. Stafford, *Queens, Concubines and Dowagers: The King's Wife in the Early Middle Ages* (Athens, GA, 1983), 94.

75 *Letters of James v*, 86.

76 *L&P*, iii, no. 1897.

77 *L&P*, iii, no. 1897.

78 *L&P*, iii, no. 1938.

79 Letter from Margaret to Henry, 11 February 1522, in Green, *Lives of the Princesses of England*, i, 310.

80 Dixon, 'Enduring Theme,' 218.

81 *St.P.*, iv, no. 49.

82 Letter from Margaret to Henry, 31 August 1524, *St.P.*, iv, no. 56.

83 *St.P*, iv, no. 84.

84 5 November 1524, *St.P.*, iv, no. 84.

85 Stafford, *Queens, Concubines and Dowagers*, 24.

8

Commeationis et affinitatis gratia: Medieval Musical Relations between Scotland and Ireland

ANDREA BUDGEY

In his *Topographia Hibernica* (c. 1188), Giraldus Cambrensis, or Gerald of Wales, described the instrumental music of Ireland in terms which suggest a high degree of complexity and sophistication, although their precise technical interpretation remains a matter of debate.[1] The passage concludes with a further observation:

> It is to be remarked that Scotland and Wales, the latter by grafting, the former by intercourse and kinship, strive to emulate Ireland in the practice of music. Ireland uses and delights in two instruments: the *cithara* [?harp] and the *tympanum* [Irish *timpán*]; Scotland three: the *cithara*, *tympanum*, and *chorus* [not conclusively identified; see discussion below]; Wales the *cithara*, *tibiae* [pipes], and *chorus*.
>   They also use strings of brass, not made of leather/gut. In the opinion of many, Scotland today not only equals its teacher, Ireland, but indeed greatly outdoes and excels her in musical skill. Therefore people now look there as though to the fount of the art.[2]

These remarks provide a useful vantage point from which to examine the question of Scottish-Irish musical relations in the Middle Ages, and the various problems associated with the nature of the evidence. Gerald's comments have, naturally enough, attracted the attention of many writers on Scottish musical history. In his 1927 lecture to the Royal Philosophical Society of Glasgow, subsequently published as *Music in Medieval Scotland*, Henry George Farmer enthused, 'Thus we see that at the very outset of our enquiry, Scotland was leading the musical culture of these "Tight Little Islands."'[3] Twenty years later, in his much more comprehen-

sive *History of Music in Scotland,* Farmer examined Gerald's identification of the instruments used by the three nations, conjecturing
that *cithara* might have referred to 'both the rote and the harp,'
remarking that the *timpán* was 'forgotten by the poets,' and suggesting that the *chorus* might have been 'the early type of bagpipe.'[4]
He also asked the significant question, 'in which domain of this
Orphean delight was it that Scotland excelled? Perhaps it was only
on the practical instrumental side that Giraldus speaks, but even
this implies practical theory ...'[5] Farmer came to no conclusions on
this subject, but the question is one to which we shall return.

Francis Collinson, in *The Bagpipe,* echoed Farmer's identification
of the *chorus;* he also attempted to account for the complexities of
pìobaireachd, the much later genre of elaborate variations for the
highland pipes, as a development originating in the Irish (and Scottish) style of harping which Gerald described.[6] John Bannerman, on
the other hand, in an article entitled 'The Clàrsach and the Clàrsair,' suggested that *chorus* refers to the *crwth* or 'crowd,' a lyre-
shaped instrument which features in later medieval Scots poetry
and English minstrel lists,[7] and which survived in Welsh folk tradition (played with a bow); he argues that the Gaelic Scots might have
acquired this instrument from Strathclyde in the tenth or eleventh
century. His more important contention, however, concerns the
superiority in musical skill which Gerald attributed to the Scots:
should it be seen 'in part at least, as due to the recent introduction
from Scotland to Ireland of a new type of harp, the triangular frame
harp or *clàrsach?'*[8]

In his wide-ranging and picturesque account of Scottish music
from prehistory to the present, John Purser used Gerald's remarks
to support several suppositions. Gerald's description of an elaborate
pan-Gaelic instrumental style is evidence, he claims, for a tradition
of '*organum* and other techniques implying more elaborate music.'
Like Collinson, he endeavours to connect this elaborate music with
later *pìobaireachd;* on the matter of the *chorus,* he prefers the identification advanced by Bannerman.[9]

Tree of Strings / Crann nan teud, the study of the Scottish harp
by Keith Sanger and Alison Kinnaird, summarizes many of the earlier discussions of Gerald's comments and raises a number of other
points. They point out that, although Gerald refers to the *tympanum* (Irish *timpán*) as one of the instruments used in Scotland, references to the instrument by that name in Scottish sources are

rare.[10] They observe that Gerald's account of music was still regarded as relevant by Walter Bower in the fifteenth century, but remind the reader, on the other hand, that Gerald is not known to have visited Scotland.[11]

The foregoing synopsis is not, of course, a comprehensive account of the scholarship dealing with the mention of Scottish music in the *Topographia Hibernica*, but it should serve to convey an impression of the various ways in which these few sentences have been turned to use by writers with particular interests. Before examining the substance of Gerald's comments further, we might pause to consider a few very basic questions. First, how much did Gerald know about music? Second, how much did Gerald know about Scotland? And third, where did he get his information on this particular subject and how reliably did he interpret his source?

That Gerald was interested in music, and regarded himself as competent to discuss it, we are left in no doubt. The description of instrumental music in the *Topographia Hibernica* (most of which – minus the comments on Scotland – appears again in Gerald's *Descriptio Kambriae* of c. 1193)[12] is enthusiastic and detailed, employs technical terms from the theoretical vocabulary of the day, and includes the smug observation that 'the very things that afford unspeakable delight to the minds of those who have a fine perception and can penetrate carefully to the secrets of the art, bore, rather than delight, those who have no such perception ...'[13] Elsewhere in the *Descriptio Kambriae*, Gerald describes the Welsh practice of singing in parts and remarks on a similar custom which, he has heard, prevails in the parts of England north of the Humber. He also reports that there are harps in every Welsh household, and young women ready to play them for visitors.[14] In the *Itinerarium Kambriae* he mentions the playing of 'trumpeters and buglers,' noting that in Welsh they are called *cornhiriez*;[15] he also recounts a marvellous anecdote to do with the horn of Saint Patrick.[16]

Later recensions of the *Topographia* allude to the *cithara*-playing, in former days, of Irish abbots and bishops, the reverence in which the *cithara* of Saint Kevin of Glendalough was still held, and the chants of funeral lamentation characteristic of Ireland and Spain. A lengthy digression on the powers and properties of music is profusely ornamented with classical and scriptural references.[17] Gerald's own confidence in his account of music is revealed in a letter to William of Hereford which appears in some manuscripts of the

Topographia; he describes the section on music and musical instruments as praiseworthy above all the other sections of the work, not only for its style but for its content.[18]

No less striking than Gerald's fascination with music in his early, primarily ethnographic works is his abandonment of the subject in his later writing; it may well be that he saw the discussion of non-liturgical music as inappropriate in any other context. His one later reference to harp-playing appears in the *Speculum Duorum*, where he mentions his nephew's use of *citharae Walensicae* (plural) in terms of the strongest disapprobation, as a time-wasting frivolity.[19] Of the developments taking place in the music of Paris during the time he lived and studied there, and of musical life in England, he appears not to have written at all.

The extent to which we can rely on Gerald's competence in musical subjects has been discussed in detail by Shai Burstyn and Paul Nixon. Both conclude that the question is still open: Gerald's use of musical terminology suggests acquaintance with theoretical treatises or the discourse of theoreticians. What he intended to convey remains to be satisfactorily deciphered, but the effort may yet yield results; Nixon, in particular, calls for an interdisciplinary approach to the problem.[20]

How much Gerald knew about Scotland (particularly at the time when the *Topographia Hibernica* was written) may be easier to determine. He never, so far as we know, travelled there. He announced his intention to write ethnographic works about both Wales and Scotland and a 'Topography of Britain,'[21] but only the Welsh project ever came to fruition, and the information which he provides about Scotland in his early works, apart from those comments on music which interest us here, is limited in scope to geographical position, the political presence of the Northmen in the islands, the distribution of beaver and one-eyed mullet, the Scottish antecedents of the legendary Welsh prophetic figure Merlinus Silvester (or Merlinus Celidonius), and the role of the threat from the Picts and the Scots ('people about whom there is nothing good to say') in the Germanic invasions of Britain.[22] By *Scotia* he appears to mean the entire kingdom of Scotland, understanding its culture to be uniformly Gaelic: 'The northern part of Britain is also called Scotia, because it is known to be inhabited by a people which was originally propagated by Gaidelus and Scotia. The affinity in language and culture, as well as in weapons and customs, to this day bears out this fact.'[23] In the *Itinerarium Kambriae* (c. 1191) and the *Topographia*, he alludes to the reverence in which the Irish, Scots, and Welsh held the relics of saints; when he describes ecclesiastical organization and the apparent vindictiveness of native saints in the *Itinerarium*, however, he omits reference to Scotland.[24] In the *Expugnatio Hibernica* (c. 1188), the most narrowly 'historical' of his early works, the only references to Scottish affairs are a brief mention of the capture of William the Lion (1165–1214) at Alnwick in 1174, and the circumstance of the papal legate's trip from Scotland to Ireland in 1177.[25] Taken together, Gerald's remarks on Scotland give an impression of haphazard knowledge, compounded of casually acquired information and some imperfectly understood written source such as the Irish *Lebor Gabala*, or 'Book of Invasions,' a collection of origin legends which also informed Scottish historical works of the later Middle Ages.[26] Perhaps, had he not become preoccupied in later life with the struggle for the bishopric of St David's, he might have had the intellectual leisure to research and write a *Topographia Scotiae*. Whether he made any attempt to become better acquainted with Scottish culture or politics is rendered questionable by his bland assertion, in *De iure et statu menevensis Ecclesiae*, that the Scottish Church historically owed submission only to Rome, and not to Canterbury.[27] Although this was technically true as of 1192, the twelfth century had seen a lengthy struggle involving the bishops of St Andrews, the kings of Scotland, and the papacy, over the question of whether the Scottish Church ought to acknowledge the metropolitan authority of the archbishop of York.[28] Unless he was being extremely disingenuous, using this simplification in support of metropolitan authority for St David's, Gerald must have been oblivious of recent Scottish history; it might, in fact, be argued that an account of Scotland's 'escape' from the domination of York would have strengthened Gerald's case.

Gerald's web of family, court, and ecclesiastical connections was extensive, and it is impossible to pinpoint the likeliest source for his information on Scottish music. Since it is described in terms of a comparison with Irish music, however, it seems probable that his informant was acquainted with both. Either a native Irishman who had travelled to Scotland (speaking through an interpreter or competent in Latin or French) or an Anglo-Norman who had visited both places (in the retinue of the papal legate in 1177, for example, to suggest only one of numerous possibilities) might have remarked to Gerald on the two countries' similarity of musical style, and the superiority of Scottish musicians. The perspectives of two such hypothetical informants would, however, have been entirely different, and they might have intended such a comment in completely different ways. We must also entertain the possibility, of course, that Gerald gave undue weight to some casual utterance, or applied to the playing of stringed instruments a remark originally about some other genre.

This lengthy dissection of a brief passage in a single twelfth-century literary source may seem a trifle laboured, but it serves as an admonitory example of the problems associated with most of the evidence for medieval music in the Celtic-language areas. Descriptions more deliberately 'factual' than Gerald's remain to be discovered. Such information as we have is to be found in fragmentary references in narrative, poetry, and chronicle, depictions of instruments and musicians (primarily on well-weathered stone monuments), and judicious 'back-breeding' of the more fecund clues of the early modern period. These scraps of evidence behave less like the pieces of a jigsaw puzzle than the shards of a kaleidoscope, creating fascinatingly varied shapes depending on their angle to one another and to the viewer. Bearing all these reservations in mind, it will nevertheless be profitable to outline what can be known about our subject with reference to the questions raised by Gerald's comments.

What instruments were in use in Ireland and Scotland in the Middle Ages, and how did the *instrumentaria* of the two countries differ? This issue was addressed, at least in part, as early as 1862 by Eugene O'Curry in his *On the Manners and Customs of the Ancient Irish*,[29] and his pioneering investigations have been lavishly amplified by the detailed research of more recent scholars.[30] An impressive gleaning of instrument names and other musical terms from a large corpus of manuscript sources provides evidence that, while the *cruit* and *timpán* were the most highly regarded instruments in the musical culture of medieval Ireland,[31] there were also numerous wind instruments in use: *corn, stoc, adarc, buinne, fedán, cuiseach, cuisle.* Some of these were probably lip-blown aerophones, others reed instruments or duct flutes, but it is difficult, if not impossible, to match individual Irish words with exact English (or Latin) equivalents; precise understanding of the

terms *cruit* and *timpán* is also elusive. The loan-words *pipai* and
fidli in a poem on the assembly at Carman (Wexford), from the
twelfth-century *Book of Leinster*,[32] tempt one to think of 'pipes'
and 'fiddles' in the modern sense, but these names (and their Latin
equivalents *pipa* and *vidula*) are nearly as ambiguous as the others
under discussion here. Perhaps the most fruitful organological
investigation of late has been in the area of monumental depictions.
Ann Buckley's 'Musical Instruments in Ireland from the Ninth to
the Fourteenth Centuries,'[33] for example, dealt with visual representations and with the few surviving examples and fragments, and
has been followed by 'Music-related Imagery on Early Christian
Insular Sculpture: Identification, Context, Function,'[34] which expanded the field to include western Scotland, eastern Scotland, and
England, making reference as well to Continental examples. A survey of the Irish monumental record reveals (from the ninth and
tenth centuries) eleven quadrangular, asymmetrical, and round-
topped chordophones (harps and lyres, none with bows);[35] (from the
early tenth century) three single pipes, horns, and/or trumpets, and
two sets of triple pipes (divergent, with one pipe longer than the
other two); and (from the late eleventh century) a triangular harp.
The general consensus among scholars is that the variety of harps
and lyres depicted on the earlier of these monuments were desig-
nated by the name *cruit*, but that some time after the introduction
of the triangular harp, the name came to be applied to that instrument, and *timpán* to be reserved for the more archaic form.[36]

The cultural connections between Ireland and (particularly the
west of) Scotland in the Middle Ages require no demonstration
here,[37] and such evidence as we have for musical instruments is in
keeping with this affinity. Our first Scottish literary reference to
the playing of *cithara* and *tympanum*, from the Latin *Vita* of Saint
Kentigern by Gerald of Wales's near-contemporary Joceline of Furness, places them in the hands of an Irish entertainer.[38] In the early
thirteenth century, we find mentions of the *cruit* in works by the
Irish/Scottish poet Gille-Brígde Albanach or Mac Conmidhe. One of
these appears to lament the loss of the instrument belonging to
Donnchadh Cairbreach O'Brien, and addresses it in a sequence of
descriptive epithets; one of these is *an clar tana taoib-leabar*, 'the
thin, slender-sided board (or plank).'[39] By the fifteenth century, the
word *cláirseach/clàrsach*, meaning, apparently, 'the planked one,'
came to refer in Scottish Gaelic specifically to the harp, while the

older term *cruit* became a generic name for stringed instruments of all sorts. The *Book of the Dean of Lismore*, for example, gives two poems by Gille-Críst Brúilingeach concerning the request for, and receipt of, a harp from Tomaltach MacDiarmata, king of Magh Luirg, Connacht, in which the word *cláirseach* is used.[40] The new word found its way into Irish usage, particularly in the north, and into Lowland Scots,[41] while *timpán* seems to have fallen out of use in Scottish Gaelic.[42]

The survey of the depictions of instruments in Scotland given by Buckley[43] is divided into two groups, western and eastern. The small western group, comprising examples from Iona, Ardchattan, and the Isle of Man, show (from the eighth and tenth centuries) two quadrilateral and asymmetrical chordophones, two sets of triple pipes, perhaps a horn, and what appears to be a triangular harp (from the tenth century). The relevant eastern, or 'Pictish,' group of monuments are both more numerous and richer in instrumental depictions: six triangular harps; two, or perhaps three, horns, trumpets, or single pipes (from the eighth to the tenth century); and one set of triple pipes (tenth century). The distribution of the instrument types, with non-triangular chordophones predominating in the west (as in Ireland) and triangular harps confined, before the eleventh century, almost exclusively to eastern Scotland, has led writers to conclude that the triangular harp (with rigid forepillar) was an eastern Scottish, Pictish, or perhaps 'Picto-Scottish' invention, which then spread to western Scotland, Ireland, and England,[44] although Northumbria has also had its supporters as the *fons et origo* of the instrument.[45] More recently, Isabel Henderson suggested that the triangular harps of the eastern monuments, which appear primarily in the context of David iconography, are in fact based on an English or Continental iconographic model, and do not reflect the distribution of an actual instrument type.[46] It must be pointed out at this juncture, however pedantic it may seem to do so, that stone monuments were probably intended to be 'read' and understood by a larger audience than might have been the case with manuscript depictions; triangular harps must, at some stage, have been recognized by that audience as real instruments. The distribution of the images suggests that this 'recognition' came earlier in Scotland than in Ireland. The most exhaustive discussion of stringed-instrument types in Scotland was published in 1998 by Alasdair Ross, who brought to light two new depictions, analysed six different morphologies, mapped their occurrences, traced the historical and ecclesiastical connections among the sites, evaluated the importance of David-cycle iconography, and concluded that while more than one of the hypotheses of earlier writers on the subject might reflect historical reality, none is susceptible of proof.[47] The study of the origins of the triangular frame-harp, so potent a cultural symbol in many minds, is one which must be undertaken without nationalistic predispositions, and with a proper regard for the fluid taxonomy of musical instruments all over medieval Europe. The systematic study of wind-instrument depictions in both Scotland and Ireland has been well launched with articles by Peter Downey, and Collinson's work on the bagpipe presents a number of useful references and photographs, albeit in a somewhat haphazard way.[48]

Having sketched a brief account of the (invisible) instruments named in medieval manuscript sources and the (unnamed) instruments depicted in Irish and Scottish monuments, let us revisit briefly the remarks of Gerald of Wales. If by *cithara* he intended to indicate the triangular harp – and this is by far the likeliest meaning – then his observation that the Irish 'used and delighted in' the *cithara* and the *timpán* is accurate but incomplete. By *delectatur*, however, he may have meant to imply that these were the instruments especially prized – an idea borne out by medieval Irish legal and literary sources[49] – allowing that others existed but were outside the scope of the complex 'art-music' which he had just described. Certainly the iconographic evidence suggests that there was a great proliferation of instruments in the ninth and tenth centuries, and the literary record maintains the impression of rich and varied instrumental possibilities through Gerald's lifetime and beyond. Since he himself makes mention of a miraculous Irish horn-relic, it is clear that he was not ignorant of the existence of other instruments, and the interpretation of *delectatur* advanced above seems plausible. What makes this possibility particularly interesting is that he apparently dignified three of the instruments of Scotland in the same way, adding the *chorus* to the list of those competent to be used in elaborate and learned music. As mentioned near the outset of this paper, opinion has been divided as to whether the *chorus* was a wind instrument or a stringed instrument, but its appearance among the instruments of Wales, with whose *crwth* Gerald could hardly have avoided being familiar, tips the balance gently in favour of the latter. With his amply demonstrated interest in philology, he could not have missed the connection between Irish *cruit* and Welsh *crwth*, but he opted to use *cithara* for the harp, suggesting that the semantic shift from '*cruit* as lyre' to '*cruit* as triangular harp' had already occurred (at least in the strictly delimited part of Ireland which he came to know). Even keeping in mind the chronological discontinuity between the extant depictions and the time of Gerald's writing, the number of chordophone morphologies identified by Ross makes a list of three separate names for Scottish stringed instruments very reasonable; it is also possible that *chorus* and *timpán/tympanum* covered a very similar semantic range.

A comparison of the instruments of Scotland and Ireland is, of course, the straightforward part of this investigation: names and depictions, although not cross-referenced for our convenience, are at least extant. The instrumental music of the medieval Gaelic world survives only in allusions and depictions. The first notated sources of Scottish and Irish harp music date from the seventeenth and eighteenth centuries, beginning with lute-books and tune-books, and finding a conscientiously antiquarian form in the collections published by Edward Bunting in the wake of the 1792 Belfast Harpers' Festival,[50] but even the most archaic pieces in these sources cannot be proven to date back even to the late Middle Ages.[51] Optimists may point hopefully to the conscious conservatism of the native learned orders, but the centuries and the geographical distance between the *Topographia Hibernica* and the Straloch Lute-Book of 1627, for example, can be bridged by nothing securer than speculation.

That the music which Gerald heard was disciplined and sophisticated seems clear. Whatever his use of theoretical terms may eventually be shown to mean,[52] his genuine enthusiasm for the aesthetic effect of the music is striking, particularly because he found so little about Irish culture to praise. He introduces the subject by remarking, 'It is only in the case of musical instruments that I find any commendable diligence among these people.'[53] The one other Irish artistic product which seems to have impressed him similarly was an illuminated manuscript shown him at Kildare. His observations on the need for a connoisseur's appreciation to penetrate the subtleties of this art echo the corresponding passage in the section on music, but he recounts a story of angelic instruction and saintly intercession to account for the scribe's execution of the illumination – no such aid is ascribed to the musicians.[54] Of them he says also, '... they are incomparably more skilled than any people we have seen,'[55] suggesting that the style may have been unlike anything he had heard in his previous travels, but the assertion that Wales (and Scotland) 'strive to emulate Ireland in the practice of music' might lead one to conclude that, at least in Wales, he had witnessed performances which were comparable in kind, if less brilliant in their execution.

That the performance which Gerald describes was richly virtu-osic has led some writers to infer that the triangular frame-harp must have been long established in Ireland for such a tradition to have developed: 'Nor would ... this quotation from Giraldus Cam-brensis make much sense if the harpists of Scotland and Ireland had not been long practised in the use of instruments with many more strings than eight.'[56] Purser's reference here is to the *ocht-tedach* or 'eight-stringed one' mentioned as the instrument of Irish clerics in a tale set in the ninth century;[57] Patrick, bishop of Dublin (conse-crated in 1074), referred to both a *cithara* of six strings and a *cytara nova* (perhaps a more recent introduction).[58] It may indeed be the case that the introduction of the triangular harp into Ireland pre-ceded its depiction on the late eleventh-century 'Breac Maedóic'[59] by some considerable time, but any attempt to use Gerald's descrip-tion as supporting evidence is wilfully subjective – the performance of a virtuoso on the Ethiopian *krar*, a lyre of six strings, might easily be praised in terms similar to those used by Gerald, and other musi-cal cultures undoubtedly offer parallel examples. Furthermore, the first depictions of triangular harps show only six to ten strings; this range may reflect the exigencies of working in stone, but these monuments may also be faithful reflections of at least some of the instruments in use at the time of carving. A development in the shape and construction of the available stringed instruments need not automatically have been accompanied by an immediate expan-sion of the available range of the instruments.

The musical relationship between Scotland and Ireland can, to some extent, be illuminated by such information as we have con-cerning the movements of musicians. Bannerman has argued for the existence of Scottish musical dynasties, notably the MacBhreat-naichs and the MacGille-Sheanaichs, relatively untouched by Irish influence:

... the origins of many of the important Scottish professional and craft families of the late medieval period can be traced to Ireland in the relatively recent past, ... [but] it is not possible to trace any direct Irish influence of this kind in the musical profession. Not only were these surnames unrecorded in Ireland at an early stage but they have a Scottish rather than an Irish flavour. So *MacBhreatnaich* means literally 'son of the Briton' and the family must have been in existence at least as early as the twelfth century, for their eponymous ancestor cannot have been so identified later than this ...

Bannerman also connects the name *MacGille-Sheanaich* with the church name Kilmachanach in Kintyre.[60] Harpers of the MacBhreatnaich family appear in Scottish court records in the latter part of the fifteenth century, and Bannerman suggests that the designation 'Ersche clareschaw' in these accounts refers only to the Gaelic spoken by the harpers and not to any real or perceived Irish origins.[61]

The assumption that an absence of Irish surnames among the Scottish Gaelic musicians of the late Middle Ages reflects a musical tradition more-or-less free of Irish influence is, however, a simplistic one, even if we accept (as is by no means certain) that the appearance of the names traces a completely orderly pattern of family succession and inheritance. Musical training and influence are not, after all, determined entirely by genetics. Derick Thomson's study of the Gaelic learned orders suggests close relations between the musical families and those of the hereditary bards, whose ties with Ireland can be traced from at least the early thirteenth century.[62] In fact, one of the poets whose work is recorded in the *Book of the Dean of Lismore* (c. 1512), Giolla Críost Brúilingeach, appears, on the evidence, to have been one of the MacBhreatnaichs of Leim in Gigha;[63] one of his poems in the book requests the gift of a harp from the Irish lord Tomaltach MacDiarmada of Magh Luirg (d. 1458), and a second gives thanks for the receipt of the instrument, comparing Tomaltach to Thomas Maguire of Ulster, to the latter's considerable disadvantage.[64] The example of Giolla Críost provides us with evidence of the interpenetration of the poetic and musical orders, and of a continuing cultural connection (and patronage relationship) between western Scotland and Ireland. Colm O Baoill pointed out that, of the few harpers whose names

have come down to us, even from the seventeenth and eighteenth
centuries, An Clàrsair Dall (c. 1656–1714) and Murchadh Clàrsair
(d. 1738) are known to have studied and travelled in Ireland, while
the Irish harpers Ruarí Dall O Catháin (d. c. 1650), Thomas O Con-
nellan (d. after 1717), Echlin O Catháin (d. c. 1790), and Denis
Hempson (c. 1695–1807) spent much of their respective careers in
Scotland.[65] There is no reason to suppose that the pattern of training, travel, and patronage suggested by the lives of these men[66] was
an innovation of the seventeenth century. On the contrary: the
Scots Treasury Accounts for 1512 record a payment to the harper of
the chief of Donegal;[67] Walter Bower, abbot of Inchcolm, in his continuation of the *Scotichronicon* (for the year 1437), praised the
musical abilities of James I (1406–37) as 'surpassing wonderfully
even the Irish themselves in performances on the harp.'[68] It seems
likely that the surviving evidence represents traces of a long-estab-
lished cultural habit, precisely the sort of *commeatio* and *affinitas*
to which Gerald alluded in the late twelfth century. It is tempting
to suppose that the handful of tunes attributed to the harpers
named above may preserve elements of a tradition reaching back
into the Middle Ages, but they survive, for the most part, as single-
line melodies or in settings for lute or keyboard, and their recon-
struction as 'archaic' harp pieces is destined to remain a speculative
enterprise, unless fresh manuscript evidence should appear. A note
of caution: in such exercises in experimental musical archaeology,
such considerations as melodic construction, hypothetical 'harmo-
nization,' playing techniques, and possible external influences
must be combed apart and dealt with separately. Echlin O Catháin,
for example, favoured the older technique of playing with the fin-
gernails, but was known for his performance of the works of such
popular European composers as Corelli.[69] Folklorists have shown us
that innovations and evolutions in performative genres may not be
perceived as such by the practitioners;[70] even a consciously conservative art may alter considerably over the centuries, but whether
gradually or in short bursts is, on the currently available evidence,
impossible to trace.

    In the realm of instrumental music, then, a great deal of evidence
supports the existence of a close relationship between Scotland and
Ireland. The only concrete suggestion to account for Gerald's assertion of Scottish musical superiority, however, is Bannerman's view
that the introduction of the triangular frame-harp from Scotland to

Ireland in the late tenth/eleventh century would have constituted an innovation important enough to warrant such a remark. Future discoveries in literature or iconography may bear out Bannerman's contention, but it would be as well to turn our attention briefly to other musical forms which might have occasioned the remarks of Gerald's informant(s).

The passage in question does not appear to deal with liturgical music, but, given the uncertainty of the transmission of Gerald's information (discussed above), we ought to consider what can be known of music in the liturgies of the Scottish and Irish churches. In the section of his survey of medieval music which deals with geographically marginal liturgical traditions, Richard Hoppin stated baldly, 'The Celtic liturgy need not detain us long,'[71] and, so far as the early medieval period is concerned, this is musicologically indisputable – we have no notated sources from anywhere in western Europe before the ninth century, and the earliest examples come from the Continent. The extent to which the musical traditions in such centres as St Gall may have been affected by their Irish foundation, and by continued contact with Irish monasticism, is a question which seems destined to provide scope for scholarly examination and re-examination, for future as for past generations.[72] From the fourteenth and fifteenth centuries, we have rhymed chant offices of Irish provenance for Saint Patrick and Saint Brigid, which conform in their general outlines to Sarum models,[73] and even isolated examples of two- and three-part polyphony.[74] The matter of the chant usage which prevailed in Scotland in the later Middle Ages was examined in a 1987 article by Isobel Woods:[75] Sarum use (with occasional modifications) was adopted in Glasgow, St Andrews, Elgin, Dunkeld, Aberdeen, Dunblane, Brechin, Fortrose, and Dornoch; the use which preceded it, in at least some of these establishments, was presumably that of the archdiocese of York.[76] In 1507, James IV (1488–1513) licensed the production of liturgical books following 'our awin Scottis use,' and the Aberdeen Breviary of 1509 reveals that this 'Scottis use' consisted of a Sarum core with substantial additions to the Sanctorale, mostly of offices for Scottish saints. The music of these offices must have preserved much that was distinctive about Scottish chant, but unfortunately most of it has not survived. A rhymed office for Saint Kentigern, dated c. 1300, is contained in the Sprouston Breviary (Edinburgh NLS Adv. 18.2.13B), but the manuscript follows the Sarum use;[77]

this circumstance, and the metrical structure of the office, suggest that the Kentigern office represents a later product of the cult of the saint, influenced by fashions of the European mainstream rather than any earlier 'native' chant tradition. Part of an office for Saint Columba, or Colum Cille, is preserved in a fourteenth-century manuscript fragment known as the Inchcolm Antiphoner (Edinburgh University Library MS 211.iv), which has been convincingly shown to have come from the Augustinian abbey (earlier a priory) of Inchcolm in the Firth of Forth. Woods's analysis of the chants of this office[78] revealed that four of the items have analogues in Roman use, six correspond to Sarum examples, five are related to Sarum chants only in their openings, or *incipits*, and a further five appear to be unique: these last may offer the best clues we have about the style and structure of 'Scottish' chant. They would not strike a casual listener as dramatically different from either Sarum or 'Gregorian' chant, but closer examination permits a few tentative observations. These chants are tightly constructed, making use of the repetition of small melodic units, or 'cells'; the two *Magnificat* antiphons for the Octave are extraordinarily long, and *Sanctorum piissime Columba* in particular has the unusually wide melodic range of a twelfth (or an octave and a fifth). The building of melodies out of small cells has been adduced as a characteristic of 'Celtic' – or at least Continental Irish – chant,[79] but, as usual, the surviving evidence is too scattered to permit firm conclusions to be drawn from any comparison. For the moment, it seems reasonable to describe the unique Inchcolm pieces as idiosyncratic, pending the discovery of similar material in other Scottish sources.[80]

The house at Inchcolm ('Columba's island') in the Firth of Forth was founded as an Augustinian priory in 1123.[81] Many Scottish Augustinian foundations were created by taking over communities of the Céli Dé, or Culdees, adherents of what had begun as an Irish ascetic reform movement in the eighth century,[82] and while there is no direct evidence for an antecedent Céli Dé community on Inchcolm, it was certainly within the Augustinian tradition that any elements of Irish musical and liturgical practice would have been maintained.[83] Inchcolm's dedication to Saint Columba may also reflect a connection with the saint's original foundation in Scotland, on the island of Iona. It is particularly interesting that Inchcolm, like Dunkeld and St Andrews (a Céli Dé foundation), is known to have kept abreast of liturgical developments on the Continent, and that such innovations as the observance of Trinity Sunday and the censing of the Host at the elevation are recorded in Scotland even before they took hold in Rome.[84] In these particular Scottish religious communities, then, at least in the thirteenth century, we have reason to believe that liturgical elements of considerable antiquity (and possible Irish origin) coexisted with a spirit of ecclesiastical modernity. If the same could be said of the music of these houses, we might have another possible explanation for Gerald's remark about Scottish musical superiority, especially if we assume that his information was at least second-hand. Unfortunately, relevant sources for the twelfth century are not known to be extant, but we do have a remarkable piece of evidence for the musical life at St Andrews in the thirteenth century: the manuscript of polyphony in the 'Notre-Dame' style now in the Herzog August Bibliothek at Wolfenbüttel (Cod. Guelf. 628 Helmst., *olim* 677).[85] This contains *organum* and *discantus* also found in Continental sources, as well as works in a similar style thought to be local products – examples of 'cutting-edge' composition in the early thirteenth century. The most recent study of the manuscript[86] suggests that the Parisian repertoire was brought to St Andrews during the episcopate (1202–38) of Guillaume Mauvoisin, the last in a line of French bishops of the see. Perhaps, we may conjecture, musical connections between St Andrews and Paris already existed during the tenure of some of Mauvoisin's French predecessors – maybe even at the time of Gerald's writing. A thirteenth-century theorist and composer named Simon Tailler is said to have studied in Paris and returned to Scotland to 'reform' its church music, but the treatises attributed to him have been lost, and no further details of his life are known.[87] Precisely when the musical connection between Scotland and the Continent may have been established, then, is something which cannot be determined on the basis of the evidence currently available, but it is certainly not improbable that the state of Scottish liturgical music in the late twelfth century – insofar as it is possible to generalize about a subject so complex – combined an ancient, at least partially Irish, stratum with newer elements, some of them sufficiently technically innovative to provoke admiring comment.

The interpretation of Gerald's remarks offered in these last paragraphs is not intended to replace those theories based more closely on what we know of instrumental music of the period, but to complement them; the rigid boundaries between vocal and instrumental music, and between sacred and secular genres, have been maintained, if not in large measure created, by modern musicology, and efforts to overcome the separation must continue if the music of the period is to be properly understood in its variety and complexity – not only with respect to Scotland, but to all of Europe.

The question raised by an emphasis on the musical intimacy between Scotland and the medieval European mainstream is one of identity: could Gerald possibly have meant to imply, on the one hand, that Scotland's musicians were *au courant* with the music of the Continent, while, on the other, affirming the country's abiding connection with Ireland ('The affinity in language and culture, as well as in weapons and customs, to this day bears out this fact')[88]? Are we faced here with the results of Gerald's lack of knowledge about Scotland, and about the 'Anglicization' of the south-east begun under Malcolm Canmore (1058–93) and his Anglo-Saxon wife, Margaret, and intensified under David I (1124–53)? Or can an emphasis on Scotland's Irish heritage and identity be sustained in the face of the political and ecclesiastical developments of the twelfth century? As has been amply demonstrated here, we cannot answer these questions definitively so far as Gerald is concerned. From a century later, however, at a point when the Anglo-Norman role in Scotland was considerably larger than in Gerald's day, we have a letter from Robert I (1306–29) to the kings, clerics, and people of Ireland, appealing for their aid in restoring him to his throne. He referred to the 'common language and custom' of the Scots and the Irish, 'sprung from one seed of a nation,' and looked forward to 'permanently strengthening and maintaining inviolate the special friendship between us and you so that with God's will our nation may be able to recover her ancient liberty.'[89] Even allowing for the elements of flattery and desperation, the emphasis of the Norman Bruce on the Gaelic culture and origins of his country is striking, and Dauvit Broun has shown, in his study of Scottish origin legends, how long it took for the importance of Ireland in these legends to be downplayed by Scottish writers.[90]

What, finally, are the implications of these questions of cultural identity in the study of music? Musicologists must avoid the temptation to treat the music of medieval Scotland as a series of barely related pockets – 'Celtic,' 'Gaelic,' 'Scottish,' liturgical, secular, vocal, instrumental – and undertake instead the much more difficult task of an integrated study. Evidence of Continental influence in one part of the country ought not to be taken as a sign of its musical 'de-Gaelicization,' nor should chant scholars search for fossils of the Celtic rite as though for 'fifth column' survivors in later liturgies; those who examine the earliest surviving instrumental music need to take into account the possibility of influence from other European musical cultures. This breadth of outlook can only enrich the study of medieval Scottish Gaelic music, not 'exclusively' but 'inclusively Gaelic,' welcoming any developments which might enrich and vary (and eventually, over the course of centuries, alter) a powerful and coherent musical culture, integral to the complex society which it served to entertain.[91]

Notes

1 *Giraldi Cambrensis opera*, ed. J.S. Brewer and J.F. Dimock, RS (London, 1861–91), vol. 5 (*Topographia Hibernica*; hereafter *TH*), III/xi, pp. 153–4. P.J. Nixon, in 'Giraldus Cambrensis on Music: How Reliable Are His Historiographers?' *Proceedings of the First British–Swedish Conference on Musicology: Medieval Studies* (Stockholm, 1992), 264–89, gives the following translation:

> It is only in the case of musical instruments that I find any commendable diligence among these people ... The manner of playing is not as on British instruments to which we are accustomed, slow and solemn, but truly quick and joyous, while the sound is sweet and pleasant. It is remarkable how, with such rapid fingerwork, the rhythm of the music is maintained; and with unimpaired art throughout, against the ornate measures [variations? extemporizations?] and the extremely intricate organa [counterpoint? linear interplay?], with such smooth rapidity, such sharing of the material between the parts, such concord achieved through [rapidly shifting] discord, melodic line is preserved and complete.
>
> Whether the strings strike together the intervals of a fourth or a fifth [the players] always begin on a B flat and return to the same, so that everything is concluded with the sweetness of joyous sounds.
>
> So subtly do they approach and leave their rhythmic patterns; they freely play the tinkling sounds [on the thinner strings] above the more sustained tone of the thicker strings, they take such delight and caress [the strings] so sensuously that the most important element in their art appears to be in veiling it ...

2 'Notandum vero quod Scotia et Wallia, hæc propagationis, illa commeationis et affinitatis gratia, Hiberniam in modulis æmula imitari
nituntur disciplina. Hibernia quidem tantum duobus utitur et delectatur instrumentis; cithara scilicet, et tympano. Scotia tribus: cithara,
tympano, et choro. Wallia vero cithara, tibiis, et choro.

Æneis quoque utuntur chordis, non de corio factis. Multorum
autem opinione, hodie Scotia non tantum magistram æquiparavit
Hiberniam, verum etiam in musica peritia longe prævalet et præcel-
lit. Unde et ibi quasi fontem artis requirunt' (TH, III/xi, pp. 154-5; my
translation).

3 H.G. Farmer, *Music in Medieval Scotland* (London, 1927), 10.

4 H.G. Farmer, *A History of Music in Scotland* (London, 1947; repr. New
York, 1970), 49-50. It is clear from the description that Farmer is referring not to a bagpipe, but to a bladder-pipe.

5 Farmer, *History of Music in Scotland*, 57.

6 F. Collinson, *The Bagpipe* (London, 1975), 82.

7 Farmer, *History of Music in Scotland*, 39, 43, 49-50; C. Bullock-Davies,
Menestrellorum Multitudo: Minstrels at a Royal Feast (Cardiff, 1978),
31-2; idem, *A Register of Royal and Baronial Domestic Minstrels 1272-
1327* (Woodbridge, 1986), 35-6.

8 J. Bannerman, 'The Clàrsach and the Clàrsair,' *SS* 30 (1991), 1-17.

9 J. Purser, *Scotland's Music* (Edinburgh and London, 1992), 50, 75, 78.

10 K. Sanger and A. Kinnaird, *Tree of Strings / Crann nan teud: A History
of the Harp in Scotland* (Temple, 1992), 31-3.

11 Sanger and Kinnaird, *Tree of Strings*, 32, 81.

12 *Giraldi Cambrensis opera*, ed. J.S. Brewer and J.F. Dimock, RS (London,
1861-91), vol. 6 (*Descriptio Kambriae*; hereafter *DK*), I/xii, pp. 186-7.

13 *TH*, III/xi, p. 154; translation from J.J. O'Meara, *The History and Topography of Ireland* (Harmondsworth, 1982), 104.

14 *DK*, I/xiii, pp. 189-90; I/x, p. 183.

15 *Giraldi Cambrensis opera*, ed. J.S. Brewer and J.F. Dimock, RS (London,
1861-91), vol. 6 (*Itinerarium Kambriae*; hereafter *IK*), I/ii, p. 62.

16 *IK*, I/ii, pp. 26-7; *TH*, III/xxxiv, pp. 180-1. In the description of this incident in some manuscripts of *TH*, Gerald refers to the instrument as the
horn of Saint Brendan.

17 *TH*, III/xii, pp. 155-7. If Gerald had ever come in contact with the formu-
lation of three musical modes (or 'moods') – gentraige ('laugh- or smile-
strain'), goltraige ('weeping- or wail-strain'), and súantraige ('sleep-
strain') – found in many Irish literary works, as, for example, *Táin Bó*

Fraích, ed. W. Meid (Dublin, 1967), 4–5, there is no indication of it in this passage on the effects of music.

18 'Prae omnibus autem titulis, meo judicio, de musicis instrumentis et arte musica tractatus pro sui capta laudabilior; quanto ibidem et materia inusitatior et stilus elegantior invenitur' [In my judgment, the treatise on musical instruments and the art of music is more praiseworthy than all the (other) sections, for in it are to be found rather uncommon information and elegant style] (*TH*, 204; my translation).

19 *Speculum Duorum: A Mirror of Two Men*, ed. Y. Lefèvre, R.B.C. Huygens, and M. Richter (Cardiff, 1974), 138.

20 S. Burstyn, 'Is Gerald of Wales a Credible Musical Witness?' *Musical Quarterly* 72 (1986), 155–69; Nixon, 'Giraldus Cambrensis on Music.'

21 *TH*, I/xxvi, p. 59; *DK* first preface, p. 158.

22 *TH*, I/i, p. 22; *TH*, I/xx, p. 59 and *IK*, II/iii, pp. 114–15; *IK*, II/ix, p. 136, and *DK*, I/v, p. 171; *IK*, II/viii, p. 133; *DK*, II/ii, p. 208.

23 *TH*, III/vii, p. 174; translation from O'Meara, *The History and Topography of Ireland*, 99.

24 *IK*, I/ii, p. 27; *TH*, III/xxxiii, p. 179; *IK*, II/vii, p. 130.

25 *Expugnatio Hibernica: The Conquest of Ireland*, ed. and trans. A.B. Scott and F.X. Martin (Dublin, 1978), 123, 175, 221.

26 O'Meara, *The History and Topography of Ireland*, 126n5. For a detailed account of medieval Scottish origin legends, see D. Broun, *The Irish Identity of the Kingdom of the Scots* (Woodbridge, 1999).

27 *Giraldi Cambrensis opera*, ed. J.S. Brewer and J.F. Dimock, RS (London, 1861–91), vol. 3 (*De iure et statu meneuensis Ecclesiae*), 169ff; translated in H.E. Butler, *The Autobiography of Gerald of Wales* (London, 1937), 185, 187.

28 W.C. Dickinson, *Scotland from the Earliest Times to 1603*, 3rd ed., revised and edited by A.A.M. Duncan (Oxford, 1977), 126–39.

29 E. O'Curry, 'Of Music and Musical Instruments in Ancient Erinn,' in *On the Manners and Customs of the Ancient Irish*, vol. 3, ed. W.K. Sullivan (London, 1873), *passim*.

30 J. Rimmer, *The Irish Harp* (Cork, 1969); A. Buckley, 'What Was the Tiompán? A Study in Ethnohistorical Organology: Evidence in Irish Literature,' *Jahrbuch für musikalische Volks- und Völkerkunde* 9 (1977), 53–88; 'Musical Instruments in Ireland from the Ninth to the Fourteenth Centuries: A Review of the Organological Evidence,' *Irish Musical Studies* vol. 1, ed. G. Gillen and H. White (Blackrock, 1990), 13–57; 'Music-related Imagery on Early Christian Insular Sculpture: Identifica-

tion, Context, Function,' *Imago Musicae / International Yearbook of Musical Iconography* 8 (1991), 135–99; P. Downey, 'Lip-blown Instruments of Ireland before the Norman Invasion,' *Historic Brass Society Journal* 5 (1993), 75–91; '"If music comes from many horns, then the sound is sweeter": Trumpets and Horns in Early Medieval Ireland,' *Historic Brass Society Journal* 9 (1997), 130–74.

31 The special status of stringed instruments and their players, resulting, perhaps, from their compatibility with the singing or recitation of poetry, is borne out in numerous Irish prose, poetic, and legal texts, as, for example, the *Uraicecht Becc*, in *Corpus Iuris Hibernici*, ed. D.A. Binchy (Dublin 1978), vol. 5, 1616, and *Crith Gablach*, ed. D.A. Binchy (Dublin 1941), 23; the issue is also discussed in Bannerman, 'The Clàrsach and the Clàrsair.' *Timpán* might occasionally be used to refer to a drum, but this usage is the exception rather than the rule; see Buckley, 'What Was the Tiompán?'

32 R.I. Best and M.A. O'Brien, *The Book of Leinster, Formerly Lebar na Núachongbála* (Dublin, 1965), vol. 4, 850; discussed in B. Breathnach, *Ceol agus Rince na hÉireann* (Dublin, 1989), 29, and O'Curry, 'Of Music and Musical Instruments in Ancient Erinn,' 329, 335.

33 Cited in note 30, above.

34 Cited in note 30, above.

35 A harp is defined here as an instrument whose strings run perpendicular or nearly so (in at least one plane) to the sounding board; a lyre has strings which run across the sounding board, sometimes supported by a bridge. In stone carvings, it is not always possible to be sure which type is intended.

36 Bannerman, 'The Clàrsach and the Clàrsair'; Sanger and Kinnaird, *Tree of Strings*, 33–5. This supposition is partially borne out by the Welsh names for these instruments: a *crwth* has apparently always been a lyre-shaped instrument, while the name *telyn*, unrelated to any instrument name in Irish, was applied to the triangular harp. See A.O.H. Jarman, 'Telyn a Chrwth,' *Llen Cymru* 6 (1961), 154–75.

37 D.S. Thomson, 'The MacMhuirich Bardic Family,' *TGSI* 43 (1960–3), 276–304; 'Gaelic Learned Orders and Literati in Medieval Scotland,' *SS* 12 (1968), 57–78; Broun, *The Irish Identity*; M.B. O Mainnín, '"The Same in Origin and in Blood": Bardic Windows on the Relationship between Irish and Scottish Gaels, c. 1200–1650,' *Cambrian Medieval Celtic Studies* 38 (Winter 1999), 1–51.

38 Joceline of Furness, *Vita S. Kentigerni*, in *Lives of S. Ninian and S. Kentigern*, ed. A.P. Forbes (Edinburgh, 1874), 226.

39 O'Curry, 'Of Music and Musical Instruments,' 272–3.

40 See p. 219 below.

41 Bannerman, 'The Clàrsach and the Clàrsair.'

42 Sanger and Kinnaird, *Tree of Strings*, 31–3.

43 Buckley, 'Music-related Imagery.'

44 Rimmer, *The Irish Harp*, 16–24; J. Porter, 'Harps, Pipes and Silent Stones: The Problem of Pictish Music,' *Selected Reports in Ethnomusicology* 4 (1983), 243–61; Bannerman, 'The Clàrsach and the Clàrsair'; Sanger and Kinnaird, *Tree of Strings*, 29–30.

45 R. Bruce-Mitford and M. Bruce-Mitford, 'The Sutton-Hoo Lyre, *Beowulf*, and the Origins of the Frame-Harp,' *Antiquity* 44 (1970), 7–13.

46 I. Henderson, 'The David Cycle in Pictish Art,' in *Early Medieval Sculpture in Britain and Ireland*, ed. J. Higgitt, British Archaeological Reports, British Series, 152 (Oxford 1986), 87–123.

47 A. Ross, '"Harps of Their Owne Sorte"? A Reassessment of Pictish Chordophone Depictions,' *Cambrian Medieval Celtic Studies* 36 (Winter 1998), 37–60.

48 Downey, 'Lip-blown Instruments of Ireland'; "If music comes from many horns"'; Collinson, *The Bagpipe*. R.D. Cannon's more recent and very solid *The Highland Bagpipe and Its Music* (Edinburgh, 1988) devotes a concise and unspeculative introductory chapter to the instrument's medieval background.

49 See note 31.

50 See Purser, *Scotland's Music*, 66, 72, 74, 106–11, for references to early tune-sources. E. Bunting, *The Ancient Music of Ireland* (Dublin, 1840), contains several pieces collected from Denis Hempson, the oldest and most conservative of the harpers at the Belfast Festival.

51 Some of the pieces in the Welsh 'Ap Huw' manuscript (B.L. Add. 14905) may go back to the fourteenth century; see W. Thomas, 'Bardic Traditions and Transcriptions' (review of *Welsh Music History 3: Robert ap Huw Studies*, ed. S. Harper [Cardiff, 1999]) in *Early Music* 27/4 (Nov. 1999), 659–60. The same chronological depth of repertoire cannot, unfortunately, be demonstrated for the surviving Scottish repertoire.

52 Concerning Gerald's use of musical terminology, particularly with respect to modes, the structure of polyphony, and instrumental technique, see: L. Hibberd: 'Giraldus Cambrensis and English "Organ" Music,' *Journal of the American Musicological Society* 8 (1955), 208–12; 'Giraldus Cambrensis on Welsh Popular Singing,' in *Essays on Music in Honor of Archibald Thompson Davison*, ed. R. Thompson et al. (Cambridge, MA, 1957), 17–23; S. Burstyn: 'Gerald of Wales and the Sumer

Canon,' *Journal of Musicology* 2 (1983), 135–55; 'Is Gerald of Wales a Credible Musical Witness?'; Nixon, 'Giraldus Cambrensis on Music'; P. Weller, 'Gerald of Wales's View of Music,' *Hanes Cerddoriaeth Cymru / Welsh Music History* 2 (1997), 1–32. Much work remains to be done before we can claim to understand what Gerald meant.

53 *TH*, iii/xi, p. 153.

54 *TH*, ii/xl, p. 124.

55 *TH*, iii/xi, p. 153; translation as in note 1.

56 Purser, *Scotland's Music*, 50.

57 A. Fleischmann, 'Celtic Rite, Music of the,' *New Grove Dictionary of Music and Musicians*, ed. S. Sadie (London and Washington, 1980), iv, 52–4. The *ocht-tedach* appears in the hands of an abbot of the Uí Cormaic, in a tale set in the days of Feidlimid mac Crimthain (d. 845) in the *Book of Lecan*, quoted by O'Curry, 'Of Music and Musical Instruments,' 262.

58 *The Writings of Bishop Patrick*, ed. A. Gwynn (Dublin, 1955); quoted in Rimmer, *The Irish Harp*, 25.

59 Shown in Buckley, 'Music-related Imagery.'

60 Bannerman, 'The Clàrsach and the Clàrsair,' 6.

61 Bannerman, 'The Clàrsach and the Clàrsair.' Bannerman's attempt to separate the use of the Gaelic language from participation in an Irish-Scottish Gaelic culture appears forced; certainly Bower's continuation of the *Scotichronicon* refers quite clearly to *Hibernienses* as a standard of comparison for harping in the mid-fifteenth century (*Scotichronichon*, viii, 304–5).

62 Thomson, 'The MacMhuirich Bardic Family'; 'Gaelic Learned Orders and Literati in Medieval Scotland.'

63 Thomson, 'Gaelic Learned Orders and Literati in Medieval Scotland'; Bannerman, 'The Clàrsach and the Clàrsair.'

64 *Scottish Verse from the Book of the Dean of Lismore*, ed. W.J. Watson, STS (Edinburgh, 1937), 32–45 and 46–59.

65 C. O Baoill, 'Some Irish Harpers in Scotland,' *TGSI* 47 (1971–2), 143–71.

66 Women were not excluded from influential positions in the harping profession – Denis Hempson learned to play from Brighid Ní Chatháin (of the same family as Ruarí Dall and Echlin), for example – but the evidence does not indicate that they travelled extensively; see O Baoill, 'Some Irish Harpers in Scotland.'

67 O Baoill, 'Some Irish Harpers in Scotland.'

68 Sanger and Kinnaird, *Tree of Strings*, 81; Bower, *Scotichronicon*, viii, 304–5.

69 O Baoill, 'Some Irish Harpers in Scotland.'

70 R. Davis, 'Traditional Arab Music Ensembles in Tunis: Modernizing Al-Turath in the Shadow of Egypt,' *Asian Music* 28/2 (Spring/Summer 1997), 73–108.

71 R. Hoppin, *Medieval Music* (New York, 1978), 37.

72 For example, A. Fleischmann, 'Die Iren in der Neumen- und Choralforschung,' *Zeitschrift für Musikwissenschaft* 16 (1934), 352–5; B. Münxelhaus, 'Der Beitrag Irlands zur Musik des frühen Mittelalters,' in *Die Iren in Europa im frühen Mittelalter*, ed. H. Löwe (Stuttgart, 1982), II, 630–8.

73 A. Hughes, 'British Rhymed Offices: A Catalogue and Commentary,' in *Music in the Medieval English Liturgy*, ed. S. Rankin and D. Hiley (Oxford, 1993), 239–84. Irish liturgical use was subject to energetic reform in the twelfth century: the Synod of Kells (1152) attempted to enforce Roman usage, and the Synod of Cashel (1172) imposed the English Sarum use (S. Bodley, 'Ireland: Art Music,' *New Grove Dictionary of Music and Musicians*, ix, 315–16).

74 A three-part colophon in a psalter (London, B.L. Add. 36929, f. 59) and a two-part verse *Dicant nunc* for the Easter responsory *Christus resurgens* (Oxford, Bodleian Library, Rawlinson C. 892); see the discussion in Bodley, 'Ireland: Art Music,' and F.L. Harrison, 'Polyphony in Medieval Ireland,' in *Festschrift Bruno Stäblein*, ed. M. Ruhnke (Erlangen, 1967), 74–8.

75 I. Woods, '"Our Awin Scottis Use": Chant Usage in Medieval Scotland,' *Journal of the Royal Musical Association* 112 (1987), 21–37.

76 Woods, '"Our Awin Scottis Use."'

77 G.M. Hair, CD booklet notes, *The Miracles of St. Kentigern* (ASV Gaudeamus CD GAU 169), 1997; Purser, *Scotland's Music*, 48.

78 Woods, '"Our Awin Scottis Use."'

79 B. Stäblein, 'Zwei Melodien der Altirischen Liturgie,' in *Musica Scientiae Collectanea: Festschrift Karl Gustav Fellerer zum 70. Geburtstag*, ed. H. Hüschen (Cologne, 1973), 590–7.

80 New manuscripts of Scottish liturgical music are still occasionally being discovered; see S.N. Atkins, 'A Fragment of Medieval Church Music in Stranraer Museum,' *Transactions of the Dumfriesshire and Galloway Natural History and Antiquarian Society* 74 (2000), 69–75.

81 Bower, *Scotichronicon*, iii, 110–11.

82 Dickinson and Duncan, *Scotland*, 115–16; on the Céli Dé, see also T. Clancy, 'Iona, Scotland and the Céli Dé,' in *Scotland in Dark Age Britain*, ed. B. Crawford (Aberdeen, 1996), 111–30, with further references.

83 Woods, '"Our Awin Scottis Use."'

84 Woods, '"Our Awin Scottis Use."'
85 The most recent published facsimile of this manuscript, known to musicologists as 'W$_1$,' is *Die mittelalterliche Musik-Handschrift W$_1$*, introd. M. Staehelin, trans. B. Haggh (Wiesbaden, 1995).
86 M. Everist, 'From Paris to St. Andrews: The Origins of W$_1$,' *Journal of the American Musicological Society* 43 (1990), 1–42.
87 K. Elliott and F. Rimmer, *A History of Scottish Music* (London, 1973), 8–9; Farmer, *A History of Music in Scotland*, 58–9.
88 *TH*, III/vii, 174; translation from O'Meara, *The History and Topography of Ireland*, 99.
89 Broun, *The Irish Identity*, 1; translation from G.W.S. Barrow, *Robert Bruce and the Community of the Realm of Scotland*, 3rd ed. (Edinburgh, 1988), 314.
90 Broun, *The Irish Identity*, passim.
91 I would like to thank my colleague Randall Rosenfeld for his advice and assistance with several bibliographic citations and Latin translations, for discussing many of the points addressed in the paper, and for his support and encouragement throughout its preparation. I must also express my thanks to Andrew McDonald for his unexampled editorial forbearance.

Notes on Contributors

GEORGE M. BRUNSDEN is a Lecturer in the School of Arts and Letters at the University College of Cape Breton in Sydney, Nova Scotia. He has presented many conference papers, and contributed a chapter on the Wallace and Bruce traditions to *The Polar Twins* (1999).

ANDREA BUDGEY is a scholar and performer of early music. She is a founding member of the Sine Nomine Ensemble for Medieval Music, and has presented many conference papers on medieval music and culture. Her research concentrates on musical life in medieval Ireland and Wales.

ELIZABETH EWAN is Associate Professor of History / Scottish Studies at the University of Guelph in Guelph, Ontario. She is the author of *Townlife in Fourteenth-century Scotland* (1990) and co-editor, with Maureen Meikle, of *Women in Scotland c. 1100– c. 1750* (1999).

BENJAMIN T. HUDSON is Associate Professor of History and Medieval Studies at Pennsylvania State University. He is the author of *Kings of Celtic Scotland* (1994) and *The Prophecy of Berchán* (1996).

R. ANDREW MCDONALD is Assistant Professor of History at the University College of Cape Breton in Sydney, Nova Scotia. He is author of *The Kingdom of the Isles: Scotland's Western Seaboard c. 1100–c. 1336* (1997) and is co-editor, with E.J. Cowan, of *Alba: Celtic Scotland in the Medieval Era* (2000).

MARGARET MCINTYRE is an Archivist at the National Archives of Canada. She has taught European women's history at Trent University in Peterborough, Ontario, and has presented several conference papers on women and power in medieval Scotland.

RICHARD J. MOLL is Visiting Assistant Professor in English Literature at Suffolk University. His work examines the relationships between romance and historiography in late medieval England and Scotland, and he is preparing a book on English readers of Arthurian literature.

MARY E. ROBBINS is the Director of the Office of Graduate Studies for the College of Arts and Sciences at Georgia State University in Atlanta, Georgia. She has contributed to *Animals in the Middle Ages: A Book of Essays* (1996) and is preparing a book on the relationship between spiritual and physical health in the Middle Ages.